Eco-activism and Social Work

Social workers are called upon to shift from a human-centric bias to an ecological ethical sensibility by embracing love as integral to their justice mission and by extending the idea of social justice to include environmental and species justice. This book presents the love ethic model as a way to do eco-justice work using public campaigns, research, community arts practice and other nonviolent, direct action strategies.

The model is premised on an active and ongoing commitment to the eco-values of love, eco-justice and nonviolence for the purpose of upholding the public interest. The love ethic model is informed by the stories of eco-activists who used nonviolent actions to address ecological issues such as: pollution; degradation of the environment; exploitation of farm animals; mining industry overriding First Nation Peoples' land rights; and human health and social costs related to the natural resource industries, private land developments and government infrastructure projects.

Informed by practice insights by activists from a range of eco-justice concerns, this innovative book provides new directions in social work and environmental studies involving transformational change leadership and dialogical group work between interest groups. It should be considered essential reading for social work students, researchers and practitioners as well as eco-activists more generally.

Dyann Ross is a senior lecturer in social work in the School of Social Science at the University of the Sunshine Coast in Queensland. Dyann is a social worker with over forty years of practice in the areas of mental health, training and development in the human services and mining sectors and community and tertiary education.

Martin Brueckner is the co-founder and co-director of the Centre for Responsible Citizenship and Sustainability (CRCS) and senior lecturer at the School of Business and Governance at Murdoch University. Martin is a social ecologist whose work focuses on the politics and political economy of sustainable development, sustainable communities and regional sustainability using a transdisciplinary approach.

Marilyn Palmer teaches eco-social work theory and practice at Edith Cowan University through the curriculum in community development, gender, and social policy. She uses participatory research methodologies to better understand how post-structural ecofeminism can inform social work practice in the areas of domestic violence, community building and disaster recovery.

Wallea Eaglehawk is a sociologist, freelance writer and works in the community arts sector in roles such as arts producer, place making and events coordination. Wallea's interests include the areas of veganism, self-care and critical reflection, health, well-being and cultural phenomena.

Indigenous and Environmental Social Work Series
Series Editor: Hilary Weaver
University at Buffalo, USA

Sustainability is the social justice issue of the century. This series adopts a global and interdisciplinary approach to explore the impact of the harmful relationship between humans and the environment in relation to social work practice and theory. It offers cutting-edge analysis, pioneering case studies and current theoretical perspectives concerning the examination and treatment of social justice issues created by a disregard for non-Western cultures and environmental detachment. These books will be invaluable to students, researchers and practitioners in a world where environmental exploitation and an ignorance of indigenous peoples is violating the principles of social justice.

Titles:

Decolonised and Developmental Social Work
A Model from Nepal
Raj Kumar Yadav

Eco-activism and Social Work
New Directions in Leadership and Group Work
Edited by Dyann Ross, Martin Brueckner, Marilyn Palmer and Wallea Eaglehawk

For a full list of titles in this series, please visit: www.routledge.com/Indigenous-and-Environmental-Social-Work/book-series/IESW

Eco-activism and Social Work

New Directions in Leadership and Group Work

Edited by Dyann Ross, Martin Brueckner, Marilyn Palmer and Wallea Eaglehawk

LONDON AND NEW YORK

First published 2020
by Routledge
2 Park Square, Milton Park, Abingdon, Oxon OX14 4RN

and by Routledge
52 Vanderbilt Avenue, New York, NY 10017

Routledge is an imprint of the Taylor & Francis Group, an informa business

First issued in paperback 2021

© 2020 selection and editorial matter, Dyann Ross, Martin Brueckner, Marilyn Palmer and Wallea Eaglehawk individual chapters, the contributors

The right of Dyann Ross, Martin Brueckner, Marilyn Palmer and Wallea Eaglehawk to be identified as the authors of the editorial material, and of the authors for their individual chapters, has been asserted in accordance with sections 77 and 78 of the Copyright, Designs and Patents Act 1988.

All rights reserved. No part of this book may be reprinted or reproduced or utilised in any form or by any electronic, mechanical, or other means, now known or hereafter invented, including photocopying and recording, or in any information storage or retrieval system, without permission in writing from the publishers.

Trademark notice: Product or corporate names may be trademarks or registered trademarks, and are used only for identification and explanation without intent to infringe.

British Library Cataloguing-in-Publication Data
A catalogue record for this book is available from the British Library

Library of Congress Cataloging-in-Publication Data
A catalog record for this book has been requested

ISBN: 978-0-367-25004-1 (hbk)
ISBN: 978-1-03-208456-5 (pbk)
ISBN: 978-0-429-28547-9 (ebk)

Typeset in Bembo
by Apex CoVantage, LLC

Contents

List of figures vii
Foreword viii
List of contributors xiii

PART I
What love looks like in public   1

1 Eco-activism and social work: in the public interest   3
  MARTIN BRUECKNER & DYANN ROSS

2 Home-grown community activism in Yarloop   26
  DYANN ROSS & VINCE PUCCIO

3 Researching disaster recovery: the case for an activist participatory design   39
  MARILYN PALMER

4 Just(ice) arts in practice: processes and collaborations   49
  HELEN SEIVER

5 The wrong side of native title, the right side of mining   61
  MICHAEL WOODLEY

6 Saying no to Roe 8   74
  DANIELLE BRADY

7 Hands off Point Peron   89
  DAWN JECKS

8	Species justice is for every body WALLEA EAGLEHAWK	100
9	International experiences with social licence contestations MARTIN BRUECKNER & LIAN SINCLAIR	111

PART 2
Clarion call for social work 123

10	The love ethic model DYANN ROSS	125
11	Transformational change leadership and dialogue between groups DYANN ROSS & MARILYN PALMER	143
12	Conclusion: new directions in leadership and group work DYANN ROSS, MARILYN PALMER, WALLEA EAGLEHAWK & MARTIN BRUECKNER	163

Resources for practice 171
Index 180

Figures

1.1	Eco-values and responsibilities	5
1.2	The social actuarial (legal) political (SAP) analysis method	12
6.1	Save Beeliar Wetlands supporters gather outside the Federal Court in Perth in 2016	77
6.2	Save Beeliar Wetlands Fremantle Festival parade in 2015	78
6.3	Mass protest at the road reserve boundary during the Roe 8 campaign	80
6.4	Women gathered at the Beeliar Wetlands in February 2017	84
6.5	Roe 8 protestors posing with the WA Premier at the Rottnest Swim 2017	85
10.1	Overview of components of the love ethic model	130
10.2	Love ethic practice method	133
10.3	Eco-activism process 8 step schema	137
12.1	The leaf art installation, Yarloop	168

Foreword

First law is the natural law of the land

The world in which we live and act is all about stories. This book of powerful stories shares the lived experience of development within the state of Western Australia. The foreword provides an opportunity to share my lived experience, hopes, dreams and actions that are informed by the collective wisdom and actions of human and nonhuman beings. I've referred to the first people of Australia as Aboriginal, traditional owner, Indigenous First Australian, First People and First Nations throughout this foreword to encompass the many synonyms for Australia's original peoples. For First Australians land, water, people and the environment are intrinsically entwined. It is interesting to note that in November 2015, the Western Australian Constitution was amended to recognise the existence of the First People of Western Australia (Western Australian Government, 2016). The amendment was a gesture of support for Aboriginal People; however, Western Australian governments have not sufficiently recognised Aboriginal rights or interests to create meaningful or sustainable First Law-centred development. As an Indigenous leader at the forefront of invasive and exploitative development, I've had to shift my focus beyond responding to the colonial paradigm towards creating freedom and justice by establishing local Aboriginal community-driven forever industries.

Ngajanoo Yimardoowarra marnil in my language means "a woman who belongs to the Mardoowarra'" (Fitzroy River). The Mardoowarra is globally unique. It is home to the oldest living culture in the world. Traditional owners continue to live on our country and guard fragile and rich biodiversity. My ideology, practice and fiduciary duty is as a guardian and custodian of Warloongarriy First Law; Nyikina customary law determines that in regard to my relationship to the river, the Mardoowarra owns me. I am duty bound to protect the river's right to life because it is the river of life. Importantly, I cannot break Nyikina First Law. I must stand and be accountable for holding the law of the land. First Law is ancient, from the beginning of time. These natural laws continue to exist. First Law teaches us that the law is in the land and not in the human.

Indigenous people are generous in sharing our rich lived experiences which come from our deep intergenerational relationship with nature. When we are born, we are given a *jarriny* (totem) to give us a place in the universe from where we learn the ethics of care. We learn to have empathy for all other living things: people, animals, plants, rivers and landscapes. Importantly, we learn to co-exist with nature and not to own, dominate or exploit it. Notwithstanding traditional owners receiving recognition of the continuation of their governance of country from the High Court of Australia, the Native Title Act 1993 (Australian Government, 1993) does not allow traditional owners the right to veto invasive destructive development on their ancestral lands. Ethical sustainable development can bridge the divide between the need to generate income and the need to maintain culture and nature. Through sharing our knowledge of country Indigenous people explain how and why management and protection of landscapes and ecosystems are integral elements of human heritage and culture.

It is vital to consider the cumulative impacts of development on sustainable life on country. Traditional ecological knowledge is Indigenous science. The evidence suggests that culture – the beliefs, practices and ethics of law and custom – is the mechanism that Indigenous people use to participate in the world around us as guardians. A more extensive understanding of environmental justice requires linking the rights of human beings with nature's natural rights. Indigenous communities' traditions and practices protect the essential relationship between Indigenous peoples' human rights and our ancestral lands and living waters. Indigenous people are key to reimagining sustainable development and sustainable life on country around the globe.

The Mardoowarra is one of the few remaining wilderness rivers in Australia which is relatively unregulated and unmodified by human development. Most of the 7,000 people who live in the Mardoowarra catchment are Indigenous from one of the nine First Nations. The catchment encompasses the traditional lands and living waters of the Ngarinyin, Nyikina, Warrwa, Mangala, Walmajarri, Bunuba, Gooniyandi, Jaru and Gija peoples. A general word for country throughout First Nations within the catchment is *Booroo*. Booroo includes the deep connection traditional owners feel from millennia of their family engaging the unique spirit of each site. Booroo is more than land; it is more than just a place to Aboriginal People; it is the spirit of family, culture and identity. Booroo is made up of human and nonhuman beings formed by the same substance, by the same ancestors who continue to live in the land, water and sky. First Law maintains the balance between human and nonhuman relations by respecting each other.

First Nation People from within the Mardoowarra catchment have collectively cared for the river since the beginning of time. As traditional owners we view country as alive, vibrant and all encompassing. Country and all it encompasses is thus an active participant in the world and fully connected in a vast web of dynamic, interdependent relationships. These relationships are strong and resilient when they are maintained. Healthy relationships are maintained by a proactive philosophy of ethics, empathy, equity and love. Conversely, traditional owners know that these relationships can unravel if they are not respected and actively maintained.

Indigenous communities in this area have maintained their significant cultural and traditional economy relationships to the natural resources of the river and the riparian and savanna ecosystems. Customary fishing, hunting and harvesting contribute substantially to local food security as well as medicinal remedies and cultural practices.

This globally important social-ecological system, like many others throughout the world, is facing growing threats from intensive irrigated agriculture, altered hydrology, inappropriate fire regimes, mining, fracking, unmanaged tourism and invasive species. The state and federal governments are promoting the catchment as a focus for tropical northern Australian development. The Mardoowarra is one of two rivers most likely to face increased water extraction from mining, fracking and agricultural development. Grazing is the most extensive land use in the catchment, whereas mining interest and activity continue to be promoted with investment and policy reforms that diminish environmental values. The conflict I have with these colonial approaches to policy is in the values that we, Indigenous Australians, have for our country and our relationship to family, culture and lifestyle. The contemporary invasive destruction of our lands, living water systems, diverse people and cultures is a direct result of continuing colonisation.

The characteristics of colonisation need to be understood through the frame of invasion, divide and conquer, manipulation and conquest. Australia is a white settler country shaped by colonialism grounded in a white supremacy values system where capitalism promotes business profits before people and place. Laws, policies and practices have been developed to provide the illusion of probity. Undoing colonisation requires substantive changes to the relationship between Indigenous Australians and other Australians, particularly regarding law and policy as well as social and economic structures that generate material outcomes. The process of decolonisation requires change in the political relationship between the state and Indigenous peoples, including constitutional, legal, policy and institutional reforms. In this instance I refer to decolonisation as a process that requires diversity in dialogue to build action and transformational change based on mutual respect and critical reflection.

There is much Indigenous people can share with fellow global citizens about adverting the impact of colonial expansion that is spearheaded by the international epidemic of greed and destruction. The Intergovernmental Science-Policy Platform on Biodiversity and Ecosystem Services (IPBES, 2019) is the preeminent international scientific body advising the United Nations on biodiversity loss. Recently the IPBES pointed out that the rate of species extinction is accelerating, and this is in large part due to the rapidly deteriorating health of our ecosystems globally. According to IPBES (2019), 63% of vegetal species on Earth are threatened by biodiversity erosion. Part of this ongoing disaster is due to global warming itself related to our past and current use of fossil fuels. Furthermore, the systematic destruction of biosystems is directly induced by current economic pathways to destruction through urbanisation, artificialisation of soils, intensive agriculture, plastic and chemical wastes and other impacts of the Anthropocene.

The future survival of our human species is at risk whether in my home state of Western Australia, throughout Australia or around the globe. Governments continue to promote destructive invasive development despite it being in contrast to traditional owner values and interests. Business as usual is no longer acceptable; enough is enough! Transformational change is needed to deal with our extinction record. The remote north-western Kimberley region where I live is at a crossroad. Despite platitudes of not repeating the development mistakes of southern Australia, the Kimberley has become the new frontier where state and federal governments promote international business collaboration in new colonial expansion efforts that grievously exploit the natural resources of the catchment.

Traditional owners in the Kimberley have spent considerable time analysing, discussing and researching economic alternatives that look to develop the region's natural competitive advantage in the people, landscape, culture, botany and proximity to Asia. Sustainable economic development opportunities include building a flexible seasonal workforce for example in cultural tourism, bushwalking and trail riding, geo tours, archaeological tours, birdwatching, carbon farming and health and education services. The Kimberley Aboriginal caring for country plan (Griffith & Kinnane, 2011) has a vision for healthy country and healthy people. The plan identifies priorities such as creating jobs that respect cultural protocol and promote traditional owners' access to country. A salient example is the Indigenous ranger program in which environmental and cultural monitoring is aligned with the local Indigenous vision. Most Indigenous ranger land and sea management programs undertake commercial activities that create jobs and generate revenue in the knowledge economies such as land management research and education. Furthermore, these programs are thought to indirectly stimulate other Indigenous business activities in the same region.

The many stories told in the book show what can be achieved when people engage in well-organised, nonviolent direct action. In this way the book is part of the broader social movements of our time. I am pleased to see the language of love being made explicit in justice struggles as it has been strangely absent from Indigenous peoples' contact with government, the mining industry and human services, including social work as a profession.

The book records examples of the havoc wreaked in the name of the dominant ways of being and relating. For ecological justice to be experienced, powerful non-Indigenous peoples and entities need to take up the responsibility that comes with their privilege. It cannot be tolerated that a small number of people and multinational corporations control and exploit the world's natural resources for their own wealth and power. There are no signs in the eco-activists' stories of dominant groups readily giving up their privilege and power.

There are few signs of loving regard for the places, people and animals adversely affected by wealth seeking and domination.

Collective wisdom incorporating multiple disciplines inclusive of Indigenous knowledge and practices is required to prevent climate change spiralling into climate chaos. We need to reimagine ourselves if we are to give our planetary home a climate chance. The storytellers in this book point towards an eco-activist agenda which needs to include an ongoing commitment to decolonising ideas, practices and relationships. The book champions the need for collective efforts through collaboration as a means of transforming hope into action for ecosystem recovery.

Australia's laws have failed to avert an extinction crisis. For those of us working to protect, conserve and promote biodiversity, we now look to new legal approaches for answers. To this end we need to consider combining Indigenous First Laws with ecological jurisprudence to rebalance the Earth towards a sustainable future. For this reason, the second part of the book is likely to be of considerable value in encouraging eco-activists to persist in the most challenging of unjust power dynamics. The love ethic model articulates ways of thinking, being and doing that places faith in the power of love to shift us from colonialism and capitalism as the basis for our society.

I commend this book to you as it gives a clarion call to social workers and asks you as reader and actor to take the ideas and lessons from our stories into your professional practice and lives as citizens. I wish to extend this call to all people, with the ideology that we as human beings are all Indigenous to Mother Earth. As an original Australian, Nyikina person, I call on my fellow human beings to join me and other First Nation People from around the world in the loving and sustainable stewardship of our precious homelands, rivers and oceans, all that is on this Earth home of ours.

Kalia maboo (Goodbye – finish),

Dr Anne Poelina
www.majala.com.au

References

Australian Government. (1993). *Native Title Act 1993*. Retrieved from www.legislation.gov.au/Details/C2012C00273

Griffith, S. & Kinnane, S. (2011). *Kimberley Aboriginal caring for country plan*. Retrieved from http://webadmin.communitycreative.com.au/uploads/rangelands/publications/KimberleyAboriginalCfoCPlan_Report.pdf

Intergovernmental Science-Policy Platform on Biodiversity and Ecosystem Services. (2019). *UN report: Nature's dangerous decline 'unprecedented': Species extinction rates 'accelerating'*. Retrieved from www.un.org/sustainabledevelopment/blog/2019/05/nature-decline-unprecedented-report/

Western Australian Government. (2016). *Aboriginal constitution recognition (W.A.) constitutional amendment*. Retrieved from www.parliament.wa.gov.au/Parliament/Bills.nsf/08CEDFB61948DAEB48257E67000A0DA4/$File/EM138-1.pdf

Contributors

Editors

Dr Dyann Ross is a senior lecturer in social work in the School of Social Science at the University of the Sunshine Coast in Queensland. Dyann is a social worker with more than 40 years of practice in the areas of mental health, training and development in the human services and mining sectors and community and tertiary education. Dr Ross is currently researching and writing in the areas of corporate social responsibility; systemic trauma and violence, including seclusion and restraint in mental health systems of care; social work education; and the ethic of love in social work. Her first book with Dr Brueckner – *Under corporate skies*, was shortlisted by the Blake Dawson (Ashurst) Business Literary Award 2010.

Dr Martin Brueckner is the co-founder and co-director of the Centre for Responsible Citizenship and Sustainability (CRCS) and senior lecturer at the School of Business and Governance at Murdoch University. Martin is a social ecologist whose work focuses on the politics and political economy of sustainable development, sustainable communities and regional sustainability using a transdisciplinary approach. His research also focuses on the areas of environmental politics, CSR and corporate governance. In recent years, Dr Brueckner's research has focused on industry-community relations in Western Australia's mining industry and the contribution of mining to sustainable development in the state. Currently, his research targets Indigenous social enterprise in East Arnhem Land and renewable energy transitions in Germany and Australia. His work is published nationally and internationally.

Dr Marilyn Palmer teaches eco-social work theory and practice at Edith Cowan University through the curriculum in community development, gender and social policy. She uses participative research methodologies to better understand how post-structural ecofeminism can inform social work practice in the areas of domestic violence, community building and disaster recovery. Marilyn is a well-known and highly regarded social worker who is active in the environment movement in the south-west area of Western

Australia. Dr Palmer has provided support and her expertise to the research work undertaken by Edith Cowan University with Alcoa and Yarloop in the early 2000s and most recently undertook research to ascertain local peoples' views of leadership relating to the disaster management response to the major bush fire which almost destroyed Yarloop.

Ms Wallea Eaglehawk is a sociologist and freelance writer and works in the community arts sector in roles such as arts producer, place-making and events coordination. Wallea's interests include the areas of veganism, self-care and critical reflection, health, well-being and cultural phenomenon. These interests pivot on an exploration of the intersectionalities between the personal and the political. Thus, Wallea produces her own writing and publication space for cutting-edge opinions and revolutionary practices as part of her passion for being part of contemporary social change movements. Ms Eaglehawk grew up in Bunbury seeing and hearing the struggles occurring in Yarloop and has continued to lend her support to the town, including in her editing work for this volume.

Contributors (alphabetical by first name)

Dr Anne Poelina is Managing Director of Madjulla Inc, Chair Martuwarra Fitzroy River Council and Deputy Chair Walalakoo (Nyikina and Mangala PBC). Poelina is Nyikina Traditional Custodian and Chair of the Martuwarra Fitzroy River Council. Anne is a Peter Cullen fellow (2011) awarded Laureate Women's World Summit Foundation (Geneva) in 2017, was a recent board member and councillor with the Australian Conservation Foundation (ACF) and holds an adjunct senior research fellow with Notre Dame University in Broome. Her work champions the "New Economy" opportunities for Indigenous people in relation to green-collar jobs in diverse science, culture, heritage and conservation economies. A vital ingredient is to include Indigenous science – traditional ecological knowledge, First Law and the rights of nature to the solutions for planetary health and well-being.

Dr Danielle Brady is Coordinator of Higher Degrees for Arts, Design, Communication and Media in the School of Arts and Humanities at Edith Cowan University. She has postgraduate qualifications in both the arts and science and over the last decade has worked on collaborative research projects with the Department of Education WA, the ARC Centre of Excellence for Creative Industries and Innovation, Landgate, the City of Perth, the Cancer Council WA and the Department of Health WA. She is particularly interested in research which benefits communities. Dr Brady was a chief investigator on an ARC Industry linkage project investigating communication aspects of a satellite-based fire mapping system for regional communities, which resulted in a new service being provided to the public. Her research interests also concern community and cultural values attached to the environment, and she is a member of the multidisciplinary environmental advocacy organisation: The Beeliar Group.

Ms Dawn Jecks has worked in the civil engineering construction sector in laboratory operations for more than 30 years. Her most recent position has been as a vocational trainer/assessor working for a registered training organisation delivering the Laboratory Operations Training Package to adults in the workplace. Dawn founded the Hands Off Point Peron campaign in 2007 and was the driving force behind the successful campaign which ultimately stopped the privatisation of public land for a proposed canal and marina housing estate at Mangles Bay, Cape Peron, near Rockingham in Western Australia, Dawn's hometown.

Ms Helen Seiver, since graduation in 2000, with a bachelor of arts (honours) visual arts, has been a studio artist developing a practice which embraces painting, mixed media, and sculpture. Her work functions as a review of social, political and cultural values. It also attempts to find processes which investigate and explore these issues from a female perspective. Helen has a fundamental belief in the strength and power of arts processes to give individual expression and voice. Ms Seiver was a member of the Edith Cowan University research team who worked with the people of Yarloop and surrounding towns, the state government of Western Australia and Alcoa World Alumina at Wagerup to seek constructive and sustainable solutions to issues of Alcoa's operations in the areas of pollution, community and environmental impact. Helen has undertaken a number of community arts projects in the town of Yarloop since this time in the early 2000s.

Ms Lian Sinclair is a PhD candidate at the Asia Research Centre, Murdoch University in Western Australia. Her research focuses on social conflict and participation between affected communities and multinational mining corporations in Indonesia, corporate power and global governance. Currently, Ms Sinclair is conducting research about Australian mining companies operating in Indonesia. Lian is interested in how CSR and community development programs can be used to minimise or change particular forms of conflict. She also researches global resources politics with a focus on the politics of resource nationalism. Lian's research in Indonesia was made possible by a 2017 Endeavour Postgraduate Scholarship for long-term fieldwork.

Mr Michael Woodley is a Yindjibarndi elder from the Roebourne area of north-west Western Australia. In 2007 he was appointed as chief executive officer of the Yindjibarndi Aboriginal Corporation, and he continues in the key leadership role to the present time. The responsibilities of this position encompass every aspect of the management of Yindjibarndi Native Title business in providing secretariat, policy and research services that inform Yindjibarndi's: forward strategy; heritage management; coordination of negotiations with developers/disturbance proponents; and retaining professional legal and anthropological services as required. Mr Woodley, in partnership with many other individuals and organisations, developed the Juluwarlu Group Aboriginal Corporation from a small-scale, subsistence-funded, cultural recording organisation into a thriving archiving, publishing, digital media, television broadcasting, media training, cultural consultancy and advocacy enterprise.

Mr Vince Puccio is Chairperson of Community Alliance for Positive Solutions Inc. (CAPS) and a long-term resident of Yarloop. Vince worked for Alcoa at its mine site for many years until retiring recently. He has been a key leader in Yarloop's struggle for social and environmental justice for more than 20 years. Vince is also a guest lecturer and advisor in the social work program at the University of the Sunshine Coast in relation to his work for Yarloop. Vince is respected in the higher echelons of government due to his diplomatic manner and his well-researched and substantial appeals against Alcoa and has worked tirelessly for many people at the grassroots level of his town. He is the initiator of the local activist group that has offered positive solutions to the government to protect people from impacts from the Alcoa Wagerup refinery operations.

Part 1

What love looks like in public

Part 1 provides an introduction to the book by outlining the ethical premises and an analytical method for eco-activism in a pro-development political and economic context. This is followed by stories of eco-activism which give a rich account of the opportunities for nonviolent, direct action to challenge the injustice and harm caused by developmentalism. Eco-activism is what love looks like in public as citizens seek eco-justice and thereby endeavour to uphold the public interest.

Chapter 1

Eco-activism and social work

In the public interest

Martin Brueckner & Dyann Ross

Eco-activism: a new agenda for social work

The book describes the experiences and insights of eco-activists to establish some of the key eco-justice issues and to explore what is being done about them. The aim is to provide a set of context- and power-sensitive leadership strategies and resources to address ecological threats. The threats arise from the adverse impact of mining operations, animal farming, state infrastructure projects and private property developments. The book fills a gap in social work regarding how to think about and practice community activism for justice causes in a strongly pro-development political context. Social work's dictum of "person-in-environment" refers to people in their social, cultural and political milieu or context. An ecological orientation to social work includes the natural environment alongside this context-sensitive concern for people (Jones, 2013, p. 214). Significantly, to address the human-centric bias of social work, an ecological turn in social work includes the rights and interests of nonhuman life (Hanrahan, 2011; Boetto, 2019). The book takes up Boetto's (2019) call for action by placing eco-activism at the centre of social work's social justice mission. Eco-activism involves a critical understanding of the relationship, power and context dimensions of justice concerns linked to nonviolent social action premised on a love ethic.

Eco-activism has much to offer social work, which is finding its activist imperative languishing in neo-liberal contexts (Greenslade, McAuliffe & Chenoweth, 2015). Eco-activism dovetails for social workers into the developing area of research and practice variously referred to as eco-social work (Molyneux, 2010; Bailey, Hendrick & Palmer, 2017; Tischler, 2011; Boetto, 2019), deep-ecological social work (Besthorn, 2000), eco-social practice (Peeters, 2011; Norton, 2011), green social work (Dominelli, 2012, 2018) and environmental social work (Gray, Coates & Hetherington, 2013). Boetto (2019, p. 143) summarises the range of characteristics linked to eco-social work as: anti-oppressive and community development skills and processes; sustainability and degrowth; change approaches which span the micro and macro levels of practice; working across differences; embracing the interconnectedness of humans and the natural world and, related to this interconnectedness, learning from First Nation Peoples' knowledge and ways; relational and collective approaches to well-being; and critical awareness and analysis. Walter, Taylor and Habibis argue that consistent with whiteness theory, colonialist countries such as Australia reflect the majority status of "Euro-Australians" (2013, p. 232). Walter et al. write that social work in fact is "very white", and because it is constructed on the laws, knowledge and privilege of Euro-Australians, this "allows it to mask its privilege" (2013, p. 232). Therefore, the book's editors wish to acknowledge the importance of First Nation knowledge that already is located within a lived tradition over thousands of years of ecological sustainability, stewardship and care for Planet Earth (Poelina, 2019; Green, 2018; Woodley, see Chapter 5). First Nation writers and activists are contributing to ideas and ways of being that are consistent with eco-social work as there is no separation between humans, nonhuman animals and country (Bennett, Green, Gilbert & Bessarab, 2013). Their work implies that an eco-activist agenda needs to include an ongoing commitment to decolonising ideas, practices and relationships (Yellow Bird, Coates & Gray, 2013).

The book articulates an ecological justice (eco-justice) approach to eco-social work which places issues of power and inequality at the centre of eco-activist practice. This brings to the foreground values, skills and strategies which can challenge the power elites of society (Mills, 1953) who gain disproportionately from the exploitation of people, animals and natural resources. Eco-activist approaches respond to conflict, and possibly violence, by fostering long-term multi-stakeholder relationships and multifaceted struggles for just and sustainable outcomes. Figure 1.1 shows the values and responsibilities to be exercised for ecological justice.

The diagram shows the ideas at the heart of a love ethic model (see Part 2), which provides an integrated method of ethics, analysis and strategies for addressing issues of ecological injustice. The love ethic model's goal of safeguarding the public interest and its eco-values are now discussed to extend the human-centric idea of social justice to be responsive to the interconnectedness of all beings, ecosystems and Planet Earth. Wheeler explains that whereas the idea of public interest is difficult to define in terms of citizens' and public officials' responsibilities, the Australian government describe it as "a convenient concept for aggregating any number of interests that may bear upon a disputed question that is of general – as opposed to merely private – concern . . . [and it] . . . provides a balancing test by which any number of relevant interests may be weighed one against another" (2006, p. 14). For present purposes, the public interest ideally refers to the highest expression of collective wisdom and dialogue based on love of humanity equally with love of animals and love of Planet Earth. To be useful in contested situations, the concept needs an overt definition such as the one given by Wheeler (2006) with the overarching ideal of public interest guiding the ethical orientation of eco-activism. What constitutes the public interest cannot be left to political pronouncements from the

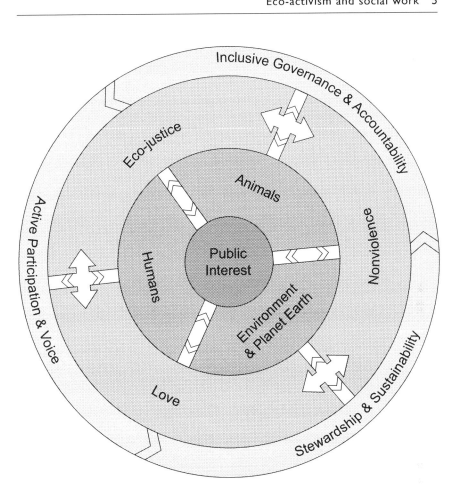

Figure 1.1 Eco-values and responsibilities

government of the day or multinational companies seeking mining approvals (see Chapter 5). Further, the public interest understood in this ideal way cannot be upheld through violence of any type or by any decisions which threaten the sustainability of people, animals, places and ecosystems. At the same time, there is no outside of the political context, and eco-activists must necessarily work in possibly ethically unwelcome and compromised situations. As such, the public interest that can be achieved in any specific justice struggle will be borne of the societal context, the collective capacity of the activism and the backlash from dominant interest groups to this activism (Conde, 2017).

Justice goals are achieved by the citizens of civil society upholding their appropriate responsibility in alignment with the eco-values of love, nonviolence and justice. The responsibilities comprise: stewardship and sustainability of Planet Earth and all life; inclusive governance and accountability; and active participation and voice of impacted interest groups in the justice concern. The responsibilities are recognised in: the international declaration of human rights (United Nations, 1948) and by animal rights groups (World Animal Protection, 2019; Our Planet. Theirs Too, 2011); nation-state's constitutions and treaties with First Nation People (e.g., New Zealand Government, 1840); key environmental and climate change reports (Intergovernmental Panel on Climate Change, 2018); and United Nations governance mechanisms (e.g., United Nations Global Compact, 2019). Chapter 10 discusses how the love ethic model can enable the responsibilities which underpin these key commitments of civil societies. The term *civil society* is not to be read as implying there are uncivil societies; rather, it is used in the manner suggested by Jaysawal (2013) to refer to the capacity of citizens who collectivise in the public sphere to promote the public interest independently of the government and business sectors.

Social work as a profession does not explicitly include love alongside social justice as one of its key values. This is reflected in the almost total absence internationally of the word *love* in social work codes of ethics (see the exception, Swedish Union for Social Sciences Professionals, 2015). Love, although a contested term, can be understood as a necessary capacity for social justice struggles (Nussbaum, 2013). For leaders such as Gandhi, love is related to empathy and compassion and needs to be linked to nonviolent activism (Gandhi, 2013). Nonviolence refers to a collection of ideas and strategies that range from appeals to the moral integrity of a dominating group to direct actions such as peaceful protests and campaigns (Sharp, 2005). International research shows that mass movements for justice and peace based on nonviolence are more successful than violent uprisings (Chenoweth & Stephan, 2011). hooks (2001) describes love as a political capacity that brings people to an awareness of domination and violence in all its forms and a commitment to struggle for equality, peace and justice. She explains that love "is exemplified by the combined forces of care, respect, knowledge and responsibility" (hooks, 2001, pp. 4–5). Freire writes that "a profound love for the world and for people" is needed to engage in dialogue to achieve nonviolent justice. Dialogue is a "horizontal relationship of which mutual trust between the dialoguers is the logical consequence" (Freire, 1970, pp. 70–72) made possible by the absence of violence and exploitation. Where there is love and willingness to dialogue as equals about justice concerns, there is no violence. West (2011) explains that justice is what love looks like in public.

Eco-social work incorporates love as feelings of compassion and care as well as the political idea of love as a nonviolent, dialogical method involving the capacities of critical understanding and working with power differentials among interest groups. A defining feature of eco-activism is the adoption of a loving, nonviolent and just ethics to guide practice. According to hooks's love ethic (2000, 2001), the high order capacity implied by this approach is to engage dominant interest groups in dialogue to address their part in creating injustice. To this end, the book adapts Godden's interpretation of hooks's love ethic when she describes it as a "model of relationship-based activism" (2017, p. 405). Broadly, this requires transformational, anti-oppressive leadership in ongoing nonviolent direct action and inter-interest group dialogues. The book outlines these main approaches to eco-activism with an explicit ethical focus to foster justice premised in a love of humanity, a love of animals, including all sentient beings, and a love of Planet Earth.

According to the International Federation of Social Workers (IFSW, 2018), social justice is the distinctive feature of social work's mission. Social justice refers to the responsibility: to challenge negative discrimination and institutional oppression; respect diversity; enable access to equitable resources; challenge unjust policies and practices; and work in solidarity to enable social inclusion (IFSW, 2018). Social justice can be understood as a value, as well as the method, for achieving human well-being. In light of the imperatives of eco-social work, the idea of social justice is revised further to include environmental justice and species justice. There is an intersectionality of issues of injustice (Besthorn & McMillen, 2002) such that social justice cannot exist without environmental and species justice (Gaard, 2011; Hollo, 2018). Social justice with this ecological sensibility is in turn linked with sustainability considerations and the enactment of social responsibility by key entities. Sustainability refers to ecological, social and economic factors being in a dynamic balance across generations so that life is maintained and flourishes (Ross, 2015). For example, interpersonal violence such as sexual assault and domestic violence cause harm, reinforce the condoning of violence as a mechanism of power over people (hooks, 2000) and create unsustainable relationships. Another example is environmental pollution and degradation from large-scale mining operations (Munro, 2012; Cleary, 2012) which threaten the lives and livelihoods of communities and nature's ability to rebalance as evidenced by climate change (Alston, 2015).

Environmental justice is defined by adapting White's idea of ecocentrism, which "requires [that] all social practices incorporate ecological sensitivities and heightened awareness of the intrinsic value of flora, fauna, eco-systems and non-living entities such as rivers and mountains" (2018, p. 342). The point of difference is this book conceptually separates fauna with the term *inter-species justice* to ensure it remains an explicit consideration of eco-activism. Additionally, the holistic perspectives of many First Nation People believe that: rivers and mountains are living beings; humans are inseparable from the environment; and all sentient beings are of equal worth (Poelina, 2019; Green, 2018; Creative Spirits, 2019). White suggests that there can be "nonhuman victims" (2018, p. 342) in situations of "environmental insecurity" (White, 2017, p. 58), where environmental degradation and unsustainability by natural resource businesses may constitute state crime if the state fails to adequately protect the environment.

The main sectors that affect environmental security are natural resource-intensive developments such as: large-scale public infrastructure initiatives; real estate development projects; animal farming; and mining businesses (e.g., in the mining sector, Sandlos & Keeling, 2016; Mazzeo, 2018; Pedersen, 2014). All these activities directly affect the natural environment, including animals, which can intersect with, and compound, pre-existing social and economic inequalities. Martinez-Alier (2002) describes how ecological conflicts are inevitable due to the increased use of the environment for economic gain. Humans' insistence on exploiting the natural environment beyond its capacity to regenerate, coupled with the failure of humans to proactively and responsively care for the natural environment, has been one of the main causes of slow-onset disasters such as habitat loss, desertification and species extinction (Suzuki, 1997). Therefore, environmental justice involves the enactment of social responsibility by the power elites such as governments and natural resource-based businesses to address the harm and loss they cause (Brueckner & Ross, 2010; White, 2017, 2018).

Finally, social justice is refined to include inter-species justice to address the anthropocentrism of social work (Ryan, 2011). Boetto suggests that this human-centric bias in social work needs shifting towards a recognition of the "holism and interdependence with the natural world" (2019, p. 139). Inter-species or trans-species justice refers to the need to recognise all animals as co-equals with an intrinsic value that is not dependent on their use value to human animals (Matsuoka & Sorenson, 2014). A purist ethical position states that nonhuman animals should not be used or killed for human consumption or otherwise used for sport, entertainment and research (Francione & Charlton, 2013). According to Bigould (2014), Canada's first animal rights lawyer, nonhuman animals should have legal rights and not be regarded as the property of humans. The United Nations Biodiversity Report (Intergovernmental Science-Policy Platform on Biodiversity and Ecosystem Services, 2019a) makes direct and irrefutable links between climate change, environmental degradation and unprecedented rates of species extinction. Natural resource-based business practices, farming of animals, real estate development and government infrastructure projects directly add to this concerning state of affairs. The term *animals* is used to refer to the diversity of species and nonhuman sentient beings including the native species of avian (e.g., kookaburras); marine (e.g., whales); aquatic (e.g., river fish); and terrestrial (e.g., kangaroos) (White, 2018, p. 246). The book focuses on domestic animals who have an economic value such as sheep who are farmed and shipped overseas for human consumption (see Chapter 8).

The book challenges the limited human-centric idea of social justice and extends it to include environmental justice and inter-species justice as the mission for social work. Hereafter, the term *eco-justice* is used to be inclusive of these dimensions and also accented are the ideas of love and nonviolence as interlinked, co-existing values with eco-justice. The next part of the chapter provides an analytical method for understanding how eco-justice concerns can be conceptualised to avoid simplistic and politically naïve activism. The context of the eco-activists' practice presented in this volume is also established by explaining the dominant politico-economic forces in Western Australia (WA), which are strongly pro-development. An overview of the rich tradition of eco-activism against the development agendas in WA shows the contested political context of eco-activists' justice work.

Eco-activism, social licence and the public interest

Eco-activism safeguards the public interest by advocating for the protection of environmental goods and services on behalf of nature and on behalf of society. Human and animal health and well-being are critically dependent on functioning ecosystems (Intergovernmental Science-Policy Platform on Biodiversity and Ecosystem Services, 2019b). Further, it is through eco-activism that the environment is given a voice politically (Stead & Stead, 1992; Starik, 1995). Just as social work is an effort to enhance social functioning and overall societal well-being (Payne, 2014), eco-activism is an assertion of standards that need to be upheld and maintained to ensure the protection of social and environmental systems (Walters, 2017). In this sense, both social work and eco-activism seek a transformation towards sustainability with justice and well-being at their core.

An analytical method using the social licence to operate (SLO) concept is presented to guide eco-activism and social work practice. SLO is commonly understood in terms community approval or acceptance of industry and/or its activities (Moffat & Zhang, 2014). It can also refer to the meeting of expectations of local communities or those of wider society (Gunningham, Kagan & Thornton, 2004), and in this sense SLO can be regarded as an expression of the public interest. As such, SLO can serve as a measure of what is deemed socially and environmentally just and acceptable, representing a shared goal of eco-activism and social work.

Social and environmental acceptability are also legal concerns, reflected in countries' lawmaking pertaining to environmental protection and public health and well-being. Legal or so-called actuarial licences (Haines, 2009, 2011; Morrison, 2014), understood here as permits, approvals and rules of conduct, can take the form of occupational health and safety standards, product safety requirements or pollution caps. These legal measures serve the purpose of protecting society from harm and ensuring that environmental impacts are minimised or avoided. Ideally, by way of providing legal standing to the public interest in areas such as health and safety, legal licences are reflective of social licences, helping address market failures (Bomsel, Börkey, Glachant & Lévêque, 1996) and ameliorate conflict between economic and social interests (Bridge & McManus, 2000). Legal licences are often being targeted by eco-activists with a view to enhance the legal protection of the environment, for example, the case of climate change with environmental action groups and grassroots organisations calling for dramatic reductions in anthropogenic greenhouse gas emissions (see Greenpeace, World Wildlife Fund, Extinction Rebellion and Strike4Climate).

Another type of licence that interacts with social and legal licences and is often also the target of eco-activism is the political licence. Political licences can be seen on the one hand as elected leaders' "licence to govern" (Morrison, 2014, p. 21) and as a marker of their political legitimacy. On the other hand, they can also be read as support provided by government to a particular organisation (for-profit or otherwise) and/or a particular activity (see Brueckner, Durey, Pforr & Mayes, 2014, p. 315). Analogous to social and legal licences, politically licences are ideally aligned with the public interest in that elected governments are expected to further, and to act in, the public interest. However, as will be shown in the following chapters, governments can be found to be supportive of particular industries (Chapter 2) or infrastructure projects (Chapter 6) despite considerable community opposition. Political licences are therefore also often the target of eco-activists seeking to challenge the legitimacy of, and enhance political risks for, governments that are deemed to be out of step with community views. Climate denialism as perpetuated for many years by conservative parties in countries like Australia, and the United States has become increasingly toxic politically, owing – at least in part – to the work of eco-activists who indefatigably have been drawing attention to the emerging climate emergency (Intergovernmental Panel on Climate Change, 2018) and social justice issues a warming planet entails (Levy & Patz, 2015; Klinsky et al., 2017). Ongoing political inaction on climate change thus risks an electoral backlash as was feared but didn't eventuate in Australia's federal election in May 2019 (Hanrahan, 2019), which was partly a contest between denialist and progressive climate policies.

These three licences are complementary in that they can work to protect both societal and environmental interests. The dynamic among these licences, however, is not frictionless, especially because each licence space itself is contested. In the case of legal licences, conflict frequently arises between opposing views on regulatory efficacy and the effective balancing of demands for community and environmental protection vis-à-vis market efficiency. For example, the desires by industry and pro-development governments to eliminate structural impediments or red tape hampering industry growth are often tempered by communities seeking protection from adverse development impacts (Brueckner et al., 2014). Further, both political and legal licences are frequently being challenged by communities on social licence grounds in situations where community well-being is deemed to be at risk or afforded insufficient protection. The unconventional gas industry, which in many countries has been able to garner political support and receive regulatory approval, continues to face fierce opposition due to community concerns about the impact of hydraulic fracturing (e.g., Rijke, 2013; Steger & Milicevic, 2014; Watson & Cadena, 2014; Luke, Brueckner & Emmanouil, 2018). Another prominent Australian example is the current contest surrounding Adani's Carmichael coal mine in

Queensland, which enjoys political and legal licence support yet faces vehement community opposition on environmental, economic, social and cultural grounds (Brueckner & Eabrasu, 2018). These tensions speak to a complex interplay among the different licences, especially in situations where social licences are contested and in conflict with political and legal licences.

Risk perceptions are critical in licence determinations as they intersect with licence stakeholders' values, priority concerns and tolerance. Thus it is useful, whilst recognising that risk itself is a contested term (Rosa, 1998), to classify, gauge and contrast different types of risk and risk perceptions (Haines, 2011) to help identify and query competing interests (Dunn, 2000). Corresponding to legal, social and political licences introduced previously, Haines distinguishes among "three independent yet intersecting ideal types of risk", namely, legal, social and political risks. There are legal risks that are commonly associated with "physical or financial threat(s)" with real harm potential (Haines, 2011, pp. 34 & 36). As associated losses can often be measured and predicted (Aven & Renn, 2009) and therefore potentially prevented or mitigated (Kaplan & Garrick, 1981), this type of risk lends itself to legal licencing. At times, however, when the impact potential of particular activities is high (e.g., unconventional gas or nuclear power), consideration also needs to be given to both social and political risks.

Social risks refer to threats to human values and social order (Rosa, cited in Aven & Renn, 2009; Haines, 2011), both contrasting and complementing legal risks. Even though social risks are subjective, emotive and value laden, following an emotional as opposed to an intellectual logic (Haines, 2011, p. 44), they reflect community concerns in ways formal rules and regulations cannot (Douglas, 1992). Effective risk governance thus needs to consider both legal and social risk dimensions. Yet, even due attention given to social and legal licensing requirements at times cannot prevent the emergence of a third type of risk in response to political pressure, especially in situations where there is persistent social risk despite regulatory attempts by government (e.g., diesel emissions, glyphosate and genetically modified crops). Political risk is defined by two competing concerns. The first concern relates to governments' potential loss of legitimacy, whereas the second concern refers to the economic accountabilities faced by governments needing to ensure appropriate resources to support the public interest (Haines, 2011). Political risk is increased when economic stakes are high as political decisions in these circumstances can come with high social or legal risks, which in turn can damage a government's political legitimacy and licence.

The licences and risks described here have been captured by Bice, Brueckner and Pforr (2017) in the social actuarial (legal) political (SAP) method (see Figure 1.2). It juxtaposes risks and licences, providing an overview of the interplay of competing demands and interests and depicting the kinds and levels of risk that licence stakeholders face compounded further by the competing risks the licences themselves carry. The analytical method has the public interest and welfare (Ho,

12 Martin Brueckner & Dyann Ross

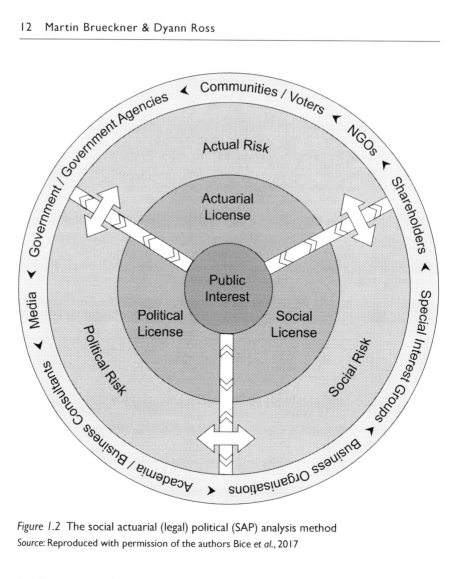

Figure 1.2 The social actuarial (legal) political (SAP) analysis method
Source: Reproduced with permission of the authors Bice et al., 2017

2013) as its central concern, ideally with all three risks and licences in balance. Social, actuarial (legal) and political risks can arise due to tensions among the social, actuarial and political licences, which speaks to both their interdependence (Morrison, 2014) and also the friction potential among them. A cast of stakeholders is shown along the periphery of the diagram, weighing into licence debates, with each representing segmented interests with differential power bases. This is what makes licence negotiations both complex and political.

The SAP method is adopted here as an analytical tool which describes the action arena of eco-activism, entailing the licence spaces activists and practitioners become involved in as well as the risks they encounter and need to balance. Chapter 9 shows how it can be a useful analytic in making sense of the multi-stakeholder interests and risks in three international examples of eco-justice concerns. Of interest here is the risk-licence interplay and the ways in which this can be affected by particular politico-economic systems. Different systems have their own distinctive ideological traditions (Pauly & Reich, 1997), institutional arrangements and political cultures which shape, as shown by research into the varieties of capitalism, a country's lawmaking (Meyer & Bridgen, 2012), its political and business institutions (Hall & Thelen, 2009; Kang & Moon, 2012) as well as its brand of activism (Bair & Palpacuer, 2012). In light of this volume's WA flavour, a brief insight will be provided into the Australian and WA variety of capitalism and development ideology. This will provide the requisite background against which ensuing chapters ought to be read and give an understanding of the risk and licence dynamics to which local institutional arrangements are prone to give rise.

Development agendas and impact on social licences

Since colonisation in the late 18th century, Australia has been pursuing an aggressive development agenda. The country is classified as a liberal market-based economy (Chester, 2012), exhibiting the kind of stock market capitalism (Dore, 2000) found in other Anglo-Saxon countries such as the United States and the UK. Fears of economic underdevelopment have occupied the minds of successive governments since white settlement, helping explain Australia's developmentalism ambitions, especially from the 1960s onwards, particularly in resource-rich states such as Queensland and WA (Layman, 1982; Kellow & Niemeyer, 1999), where development is being equated to moral progress (Trigger, 1997). Developmentalism, according to Thurbon (2012, p. 275), can largely be understood as viewing national economic prosperity and security as primary priorities of government. This in turn grants governing elites an active role in facilitating the transformation and upgrading of the national techno-industrial infrastructure. Kellow and Niemeyer characterise developmentalism in WA as a "proclivity for pursuing interventionist development policies to overcome their particular disadvantage, a tendency towards political conservatism and an ideational environment where development was seen as a panacea" (1999, p. 206). In WA, the policy priority of economic advancement since the 1820s has largely been centred on the exploitation of the state's natural assets (Walker et al., 2002) and been an "objective of all Western Australian governments" (Layman, 1982, p. 149). Unsurprisingly, WA has remained a resource-based and resource-dependent economy with its economic fortunes closely tied to those of the resource sector (Lawrie, Tonts & Plummer, 2011).

From the 1960s onwards, successive WA governments have played an important role in the development of the resource sector as one of the state's economic cornerstones (Phillimore, 2014). This has involved pursuing economic growth by committing "to resource development by large-scale private capital undertaking large scale projects with assistance at all stages by state planning" (Layman, 1982, p. 163). The state's development is said to be driven by a frontier mentality (Harman, 1982) and an urgency to "develop [natural] resources expeditiously" (Phillimore, 2014, p. 31) so as not to "miss . . . out in the global commodity race" (Barnett, cited in Maumill, 2013). For the state, development has long been a means of overcoming its isolation and remoteness (Moon & Sharman, 2003), and accordingly, industry regulation has a tendency to be soft touch, at least in terms of enforcement (Chandler, 2014), matched by tax incentives and lucrative royalty terms to encourage investment and business activity (Brueckner et al., 2014).

WA's development mantra is premised on the belief that the benefits of development can be captured by way of material diffusion through the employment and income that development generates (Harman, 1982). In other words, social benefits are seen as automatic by-products of development, whereas development impacts are regarded necessary trade-offs for progress and prosperity (Brueckner et al., 2014). As a result, social and environmental dimensions of development tend to be overlooked, downplayed or ignored (Franks, Fidler, Brereton, Vanclay & Clark, 2009; Michell & McManus, 2013), pointing to an imbalance – despite political claims to the contrary (Moodie, 2010; McHugh, 2014) – among the state's growth aspirations, community well-being and environmental health (Beresford, 2001; Brueckner & Pforr, 2011). Development impacts in WA, which are well documented (Denniss, 2007; Environmental Protection Authority, 2007; Western Australian Council of Social Service, 2009; Brueckner Durey, Mayes & Pforr, 2014; Environmental Protection Authority, 2014), speak to a strong political licence seemingly trumping both legal and social licences as will also be shown by chapter contributions in this volume. The state's political pro-development climate routinely translates into the de-facto protection of industry interests oftentimes at the expense of social, cultural and environmental concerns championed by development-affected communities. Predictably, this state of play has triggered community opposition to entrenched development orthodoxies, which is now considered to complete the contextualisation of eco-activism in WA.

WA developmentalism and activist responses

WA has a long history of development conflicts, owing to the expansion of industry into environmentally, socially and culturally sensitive areas and the desire by governments to pursue economic development, which oftentimes has been met with vehement community opposition. Some of the earlier conflicts include protests that have erupted in response to bauxite mining in the state's Southwest (Hughes, 1980; Lines, 2006) or timber cutting and wood chipping in native forest areas (Calder, 1980; Carron, 1985). More recent disputes include community opposition to coastal development (Pforr, Macbeth, Clark, Fountain & Wood, 2007; Wesley & Pforr, 2008a, 2008b) as well as mining development in places such as James Price Point (Bradley, 2011) and other parts of the Kimberly, the Burrup Peninsula (Morgan, Kwaymullina & Kwaymullina, 2006) or the state's South-West (Paddenburg, 2010; Mercer & Emery, 2012).

These disputes chiefly centre on cultural, community and environmental values, often in collision with the dominant development logic. They also highlight the ongoing questioning of the social legitimacy of certain forms of development even in situations where projects and industries garner political support and regulatory approval and despite improved corporate attention on their social and environmental performance (Franks et al., 2009) and companies' widespread espousal of the social licence (Bice, 2014). Thus, ongoing community opposition attests to a conflicted licensing terrain. The level of contestation is also illustrated by the way in which protest is responded to by governments.

In WA's rich community protest history, there are numerous examples of protester vilification by government coupled with changes to the law to curtail protesters' rights; this has become a trend that has intensified nationally (see Forst, 2016). For example, the establishment of the alumina industry in the 1970s (see Chapters 2, 3 & 4) was strongly supported by then Premier Sir Charles Court (Anon, 1976, p. 8). In the face of growing public protests, the premier passed legislation to advance the development of the industry independent of input from the state's Environmental Protection Authority (EPA). The Court government also strengthened police powers by way of changing the Police Act to prosecute protesters in an attempt to minimise disruptions to industry development (Kellow & Niemeyer, 1999). Of a similar nature has been the treatment of people protesting against the James Prize Point Liquid Gas Hub, who were publicly vilified by government (Wesley, 2014). The government also moved to compulsorily acquire the contested coastal strip against the wishes of traditional owners and local residents in an attempt to enable the development of the site (Fyfe, 2013). Also, in connection with the controversial Roe Highway extension and anti-fracking protests, the state government at the time attempted to introduce changes to highly restrictive protest laws and stood accused of excessive policing of protests and protester vilification (Australian Associated Press, 2015; CounterAct & Beeliar Legal Support, 2017). Finally, a recent attempt by the EPA (2019a) to introduce carbon offset requirements for heavy emitters in light of Australia's commitments made under the Paris Agreement and the state's continual rise in industry levels of emissions has effectively (EPA, 2019b) been overruled by the state government out of concerns for industry jobs and economy-wide impacts (Kennedy, Weber & Shine, 2019).

This demonstrative support for industry by the state government illustrates further the earlier referred to dominance of the political licence in the state and shows how this dominance has created conflicts with both social and legal licence domains. The issues at the heart of these conflicts are key focal points of eco-activism, which this volume seeks to explore. Ensuing chapters will provide rich detail on eco-social engagements in WA development conflicts, helping shed light on the nature of, and helping articulate an agenda for, eco-social work activism.

Book overview

The book is structured into two parts and is comprised of 12 chapters in total including introductory chapters for both parts and a concluding chapter. A final section called "Resources for practice" provides a selection of resources that may be useful for eco-activists. Part 1, titled "What love looks like in public", is based on eco-activist stories in which the exemplar eco-justice concerns and activism are outlined. Part 2, titled "Clarion call for social work", is a compilation of the context- and power-sensitive strategies. These strategies are presented by outlining the love ethic model and are adaptable and ready for use by eco-activists.

Chapter 2 by Dyann Ross and Vince Puccio introduces the eco-justice issues related to impact on a small WA rural community, Yarloop, by a nearby alumina refinery operated by Alcoa World Alumina, Wagerup (Alcoa). This is one of a set of three chapters about Yarloop which present different strategies by the contributors over the last two decades to highlight the multidimensional nature of the slow violence of the intrusion of mining operations on people and place. The in-depth and rich set of eco-activists' stories is possible due to a long-term engagement with many people in Yarloop, who have invited the authors to contribute in the ways discussed. In Chapter 2, Ross, a social work academic, and Puccio, the chairperson of CAPS – the local activist group – present the argument for the importance of home-grown community-based activism when a mining company loses its social licence to operate. The nature of local eco-activism is presented, drawing on research with Yarloop residents, and the challenges and achievements give credence to what is needed to address the perceived justice concerns. The concerns relate to the insufficient government regulation of Alcoa (legal licence) and the insufficient political will by successive governments (political licence) to protect the town of Yarloop, its people and surrounding ecosystems.

Marilyn Palmer is an eco-activist and social work academic who details in Chapter 3 a piece of research undertaken in the aftermath of the devastating bush fire of 2016, which almost destroyed the town of Yarloop. The research asked the participating residents about their experiences of how the disaster was managed and what leadership looked like to them. Palmer's narrative account and the research findings bring a renewed lens to the ongoing failures of political and legal licences by the key entities to protect people, the town and the environment. The chapter also shows how Palmer reflects upon the disquiet she experienced when the research was out of step with participatory approaches that can enable participants to have a greater sense of involvement in and ownership of the research.

Helen Seiver is an artist who has supported the Yarloop people over many years with community-based arts projects to engage residents and validate their experiences through the use of art. Chapter 4 shows the value of being people focused during times of threat, dislocation and natural disaster. Art for the people by the people in times of such contestation and turmoil provides a third space for residents to resist the fragmenting and disempowering pressures and losses and to keep alive a sense of community and belonging. The context of the artwork with residents is highly politicised, and as such the chapter speaks to the deep human effects of the pro-development political licence of the government and the loss of Alcoa's social licence to operate.

Michael Woodley is an elder of the Yindjibarndi People from Roebourne in the Pilbara area of north-west WA. Chapter 5 outlines the personal and community impact of a long-term legal struggle with Fortescue Metals Group (FMG), one of Australia's largest iron ore mining companies. Despite land rights legislation to protect the interests of First Nation People, the mining sector has continued to have access to land that has not been ceded and often dictate the compensation terms to impacted Indigenous communities. Woodley recounts his experiences and the nature of the legal struggle with FMG and how this has intersected with his perception that FMG has divided and fragmented his community for commercial advantage. The government is complicit with industry interests, which shows the influence of a dominant political licence for mining in sacred ancestral lands. Woodley, who is the chief executive officer of the legally approved body representing the interests of the Yindjibarndi People, explains the reasons for the absence of a social licence for FMG to operate on their land.

Danielle Brady is an academic and a member of the Beeliar Group, which is an environmental advocacy organisation. She became involved in the group's social campaign in Perth, WA, to stop the state government building an extension to the Roe 8 highway. Chapter 6 provides an insider account of what is needed for the latter period of a 30-year campaign to succeed and acknowledges the community interest groups who worked collaboratively over many years to stop the highway extension. The premise for the campaign centred on spatial issues related to the destruction of tracts of natural habitat in the Beeliar area which are highly valued by the local First Nation People and non-Indigenous people. The government lost its social licence to proceed with the highway extension, and the campaigners mobilised sufficient influence to challenge the dominant political licence of the government.

In Chapter 7, Dawn Jecks, who is a civil engineer, explains how she became an unexpected eco-activist as the leader of a 12-year-long community-based campaign. The goal was to stop a private developer gaining government planning approval to build a residential canal marina development. Point Peron was the area of contestation and is a coastal wetlands area at Rockingham, a regional city south of the capital city of Perth in WA. Jecks realised that success required people to stand together, drawing on a range of strategies and not relenting until Point Peron was protected from private development. She tells her story in a way that conveys the deeply personal nature of challenging the political and legal licence of the state government by using its own laws and appeals avenues. Engaging with, and enabling the empowerment of, a broad cross section of community members is a particular achievement of this eco-activism. The Point Peron area is now in the process of being protected against development. Jecks's chapter gives a first-hand account of what eco-activist leadership entails.

In Chapter 8, Wallea Eaglehawk, who is a sociologist, develops a species justice argument to challenge the nature and extent of harm experienced by farm animals. The objectification of farm animals is identified as a key cultural practice which legitimates the killing of millions of animals in Australia each year. Eaglehawk overviews the use of animals in large-scale agri-farming businesses with the example of the live sheep export issue in WA. This is chosen for particular attention due to the 2017 media report of deaths of sheep at sea and the resultant public debates and threats that followed to Australia's live animal export industry. She coins the term *anthropocentric harm* to describe the harm caused by humans against humans, animals and the environment. Eaglehawk suggests that the personal is political where veganism, no harm to animals, and joining social media campaigns can begin at a personal level and extend to become part of a politico-social movement to stop the institutionalised support for human use and consumption of animals.

Chapter 9 by Martin Brueckner and Lian Sinclair provides the reader with an account of how the SAP licence analytical method (Bice et al., 2017), introduced in Chapter 1, can be applied to understand three internationally significant examples of ecological harm. The examples are: the major Adani coal mine development in the central Queensland threatening sensitive ecosystems and endangered birds; Rio Tinto's Oyu Tolgoi copper and gold mine in Mongolia impacting nomadic herders and precious water resources in an arid environment; and Rio Tinto's ex-Kelian gold mine in Indonesia, where hundreds of residents were forcibly removed from their properties without compensation. The SAP method can aid eco-activists in building their political analysis capacities by reading the (con)text (Freire, 1970) and power dynamics across multiple intersecting stakeholder groups and interests.

Part 1 of the book proceeds by presenting these examples of eco-activism, showing how ecological values and ideas are enacted. In Part 2, an introductory chapter by Dyann Ross translates the informing ecological values and ideas into a love ethic practice model and set of resources to guide eco-activism in complex and conflictual contexts. In Chapter 11 Dyann Ross and Marilyn Palmer discuss the nature of leadership required to foster nonviolent, direct action strategies and group-based dialogues, drawing on insights from the eco-activist stories. The love ethic model utilises the ethics, analyses and skills required to achieve ecological democracy (Hollo, 2018) built on social, species and environmental justice and sustainability. The chapter is presented as a guide to practice for eco-activists, which is distinctive in its attention to the influence of context and power and how to work with these dynamics. The concluding chapter by Dyann Ross, Marilyn Palmer, Wallea Eaglehawk and Martin Brueckner draws the key arguments of the book together and distils the main insights from the eco-activist accounts. The "Resources for practice" section holds a range of relevant resources and web links for eco-activists.

References

Alston, M. (2015). Social work, climate change & global co-operation. *International Social Work*, 58(3), 335–363.

Anon. (1976, 10 December). $650 million alumina works plan for southwest. *The West Australian*, pp. 1 & 8.

Australian Associated Press. (2015, 18 March). West Australian anti-protest laws denounced as far too broad. *The Guardian*. Retrieved from www.theguardian.com/australia-news/2015/mar/18/west-australian-anti-protest-laws-denounced-as-far-too-broad

Aven, T. & Renn, O. (2009). On risk defined as an event where the outcome is uncertain. *Journal of Risk Research*, 12(1), 1–11. doi:10.1080/13669870802488883

Bailey, S., Hendrick, A. & Palmer, M. (2017). Eco-social work in action: A place for community gardens. *Australian Social Work*, 71(1), 98–110.

Bair, J. & Palpacuer, F. (2012). From varieties of capitalism to varieties of activism: The anti-sweatshop movement in comparative perspective. *Social Problems*, 59(4), 522–543.

Bennett, B., Green, S., Gilbert, S. & Bessarab, D. (Eds.). (2013). *Our voices: Aboriginal and Torres Strait Islander social work*. South Yarra, Australia: Palgrave Macmillan.

Besthorn, F. (2000). Toward a deep-ecological social work: Its environmental, spiritual and political dimensions. *The Spirituality & Social Work Forum*, 7(2), 2–7.

Besthorn, F. & McMillen, D. (2002). The oppression of women and nature. *Families in Society: The Journal of Contemporary Social Services*, 83(3), 221–232.

Beresford, Q. (2001). Developmentalism and its environmental legacy: The Western Australia wheatbelt, 1900–1990s. *Australian Journal of Politics & History*, 47(3), 403–415.

Bice, S. (2014). What gives you a social licence? An exploration of the social licence to operate in the Australian mining industry. *Resources*, 3(1), 62–80. doi:10.3390/resources3010062

Bice, S., Brueckner, M. & Pforr, C. (2017). Putting social license to operate on the map: A social, actuarial and political risk and licensing model (SAP Model). *Resources Policy*, 53, 46–55. doi:10.1016/j.resourpol.2017.05.011

Bigould, L. (2014). It's time to re-evaluate our relationship with animals. *TedTalk*. Retrieved from https://youtu.be/Fr26scqsIwk

Boetto, H. (2019). Advancing transformative eco-social change: Shifting from modernist to holistic foundations. *Australian Social Work*, 72(2), 139–152.

Bomsel, O., Börkey, P., Glachant, M. & Lévêque, F. (1996). Is there room for environmental self regulation in the mining sector? *Resources Policy*, 22(1–2), 79–86.

Bradley, R. (2011, 24–30 August). Battle lines are laid over pristine Kimberley. *The Epoch Times*. Retrieved from www.epoch-archive.com

Bridge, G. & McManus, P. (2000). Sticks and stones: Environmental narratives and discursive regulation in the forestry and mining sectors. *Antipode*, 32(1), 10–47. doi:10.1111/1467-8330.00118

Brueckner, M., Durey, A., Mayes, R. & Pforr, C. (Eds.). (2014). *Resource curse or cure? On the sustainability of development in Western Australia*. Heidelberg, Germany: Springer.

Brueckner, M., Durey, A., Pforr, C. & Mayes, R. (2014). The civic virtue of developmentalism: On the mining industry's political licence to develop Western Australia. *Impact Assessment and Project Appraisal*, 32(4), 315–326. doi:10.1080/14615517.2014.929784

Brueckner, M. & Eabrasu, M. (2018). Pinning down the social license to operate (SLO): The problem of normative complexity. *Resources Policy*, *59*, 217–226. https://doi.org/10.1016/j.resourpol.2018.07.004

Brueckner, M. & Pforr, C. (2011). Western Australia's short-lived 'sustainability revolution'. *Environmental Politics*, *20*(4), 585–589.

Brueckner, M. & Ross, D. (2010). *Under corporate skies: A struggle between people, place and profit*. Perth, Australia: Fremantle Press.

Calder, M. (1980). *Big timber country*. Sydney, Australia: Rigby Publishers Ltd.

Carron, L. (1985). *A history of forestry in Australia*. Canberra, Australia: Australian National University Press.

Chandler, L. (2014). Regulating the resource juggernaut. In M. Brueckner, A. Durey, R. Mayes & C. Pforr (Eds.), *Resource curse or cure? On the sustainability of development in Western Australia* (pp. 165–177). Heidelberg, Germany: Springer.

Chenoweth, E. & Stephan, M. (2011). *Why civil resistance works: The strategic logic of nonviolent conflict*. New York, USA: Columbia University Press.

Chester, L. (2012). The Australian variant of neoliberal capitalism. In D. Cahill, L. Edwards & F. Stilwell (Eds.), *Neoliberalism: Beyond the free market* (pp. 153–179). Cheltenham, UK: Edward Elgar Publishing.

Cleary, P. (2012). *Mine-field: The dark side of Australia's resource rush*. Collingwood, Australia: Black Inc.

Conde, M. (2017). Resistance to mining: A review. *Ecological Economics*, *132*, 80–90.

CounterAct & Beeliar Legal Support. (2017). *The policing of Beeliar protests*. Retrieved from https://counteract.org.au/projects/report-policing-beeliar/

Creative Spirits. (2019). *What is Aboriginal spirituality?* Retrieved from www.creativespirits.info/aboriginalculture/spirituality/what-is-aboriginal-spirituality

Denniss, R. (2007). *The boom for whom? Who benefits from the WA resources boom?* Perth, Western Australia: The Greens.

Dominelli, L. (2012). *Green social work: From environmental crises to environmental justice*. Cambridge, UK: Polity Press.

Dominelli, L. (Ed.). (2018). *The Routledge handbook of green social work*. New York, USA: Routledge.

Dore, R. P. (2000). *Stock market capitalism: Welfare capitalism: Japan and Germany versus the Anglo-Saxons*. Oxford, UK: Oxford University Press.

Douglas, M. (1992). *Risk and blame: Essays in cultural theory*. London, UK: Routledge.

Dunn, J. (2000). *The cunning of unreason: Making sense of politics*. New York, USA: Basic Books.

Environmental Protection Authority. (2007). *State of the environment 2007 Western Australia*. Perth, Australia: Western Australian Government.

Environmental Protection Authority. (2014). *Cumulative environmental impacts of development in the Pilbara region: Advice of the Environmental Protection Authority to the Minister for Environment under Section 16(e) of the Environmental Protection Act 1986*. Perth, Australia: Western Australian Government.

Environmental Protection Authority. (2019a). *Media statement: EPA releases revised guidance for proponents on greenhouse gas emissions*. Retrieved from www.epa.wa.gov.au/sites/default/files/MEDIA_STATEMENTS/EPA%20Greenhouse%20Gas%20Media%20Statement%20070319_0.pdf

Environmental Protection Authority. (2019b). *Technical guidance: Mitigating greenhouse gas emissions*. Perth, Australia: Western Australian Government.

Forst, M. (2018, 18 October 2016). *End of mission statement by Michel Forst, United Nations Special Rapporteur on the situation of human rights defenders.* Geneva, Switzerland: United Nations Human Rights Office of the High Commissioner.

Francione, G. & Charlton, A. (2013). *Animal rights: The abolutionist approach.* Utah, USA: Exempla Press.

Franks, D., Fidler, C., Brereton, D., Vanclay, F. & Clark, P. (2009). *Leading practice strategies for addressing the social impacts of resource developments: Briefing paper for the Department of Employment, Economic Development and Innovation.* Brisbane, Australia: Queensland Government.

Freire, P. (1970). *Pedagogy of the oppressed.* New York, USA: Herder and Herder.

Fyfe, M. (2013, 23 November). Kimberley Aborigines' fight for James Price point is now against WA's Premier. *The Sydney Morning Herald.* Retrieved from www.smh.com.au/national/kimberley-aborigines-fight-for-james-price-point-is-now-against-was-premier-20131122-2y1f7.html

Gaard, G. (2011). Ecofeminism revisited: Rejecting essentialism and re-placing species in a material feminist environmentalism. *Feminist Formulations, 23,* 26–53.

Gandhi, R. (2013). Gandhi's journey to ahimsa. In J. Sethia and A. Narayan (Eds.), *The living Gandhi: Lessons for our times* (pp. 101–117). New Delhi, India: Penguin Books.

Godden, N. (2017). The love ethic: A radical theory for social work practice. *Australian Social Work, 70*(4), 405–416.

Gray, M., Coates, J. & Hetherington, T. (Eds.). (2013). *Environmental social work.* London, UK & New York, USA: Routledge.

Green, S. (2018). Aboriginal People and caring within a colonised society. In B. Pease, A. Vreugdenhil & S. Stanford (Eds.), *Critical ethics of care in social work: Transforming the politics and practices of caring* (pp. 139–147). New York, USA: Routledge.

Greenslade, L., McAuliffe, D. & Chenoweth, L. (2015). Social work experiences of covert workplace activism. *Australian Social Work, 68*(4), 422–437.

Gunningham, N. A., Kagan, R. & Thornton, D. (2004). Social license and environment protection: Why businesses go beyond compliance. *Law & Social Inquiry, 29*(2), 307–341.

Haines, F. (2009). Vanquishing the enemy or civilizing the neighbour? Controlling the risks from hazardous industries. *Social and Legal Studies, 18*(3), 397–415.

Haines, F. (2011). *The paradox of regulation: What regulation can achieve and what it cannot.* Cheltenham, UK: Edward Elgar Publishing.

Hall, P. & Thelen, K. (2009). Institutional change in varieties of capitalism. *Socio-Economic Review, 7*(1), 7–34.

Hanrahan, C. (2011). Challenging anthropocentrism in social work through ethics and spirituality. *Journal of Religion & Spirituality in Social Work, 30*(3), 272–293.

Hanrahan, C. (2019, 15 May). Federal election 2019: Vote Compass finds broad desire for more action on climate change. *ABC News.* Retrieved from www.abc.net.au/news/2019-05-15/federal-election-vote-compass-climate-change/11110912

Harman, E. (1982). Ideology and mineral development in Western Australia, 1960–1980. In E. Harman & B. Head (Eds.), *State, capital and resources in the north and west of Australia* (pp. 167–196). Perth, Australia: University of Western Australia Press.

Ho, L.-s. (2013). *Public policy and the public interest.* Abingdon, Oxon, UK: Routledge.

Hollo, T. (2018). *Toward ecological democracy: Part 1.* Retrieved from https://greenagenda.org.au/2018/04/towards-ecological-democracy/

hooks, b. (2000). *All about love.* New York, USA: New Visions.

hooks, b. (2001). *Salvation: Black people and love.* New York, USA: William Morrow.

Hughes, O. (1980). Bauxite mining and jarrah forests in Western Australia. In R. Scott (Ed.), *Interest groups and public policy: Case studies from the Australian states* (pp. 170–193). Melbourne, Australia: Macmillan.

Intergovernmental Panel on Climate Change. (2018). *Global warming of 1.5°C: An IPCC special report on the impacts of global warming of 1.5°C above pre-industrial levels and related global greenhouse gas emission pathways, in the context of strengthening the global response to the threat of climate change, sustainable development, and efforts to eradicate poverty*. Retrieved from https://report.ipcc.ch/sr15/pdf/sr15_spm_final.pdf

Intergovernmental Science-Policy Platform on Biodiversity and Ecosystem Services. (2019a). *UN report: Nature's dangerous decline 'unprecedented': Species extinction rates 'accelerating'*. Retrieved from www.un.org/sustainabledevelopment/blog/2019/05/nature-decline-unprecedented-report/

Intergovernmental Science-Policy Platform on Biodiversity and Ecosystem Services. (2019b). *The regional assessment report on biodiversity and ecosystem services for Europe and Central Asia*. Retrieved from www.ipbes.net/system/tdf/spm_2b_eca_digital_0.pdf?file=1&type=node&id=28318

International Federation of Social Workers (IFSW). (2018). *Global social work statement of ethical principles*. Retrieved from www.ifsw.org/global-social-work-statement-of-ethical-principles/

Jaysawal, N. (2013). Civil society, democratic space and social work. Retrieved from https://doi.org/10.1177/2158244013504934

Jones, P. (2013). Transforming the curriculum: Social work education and ecological consciousness. In M. Gray, J. Coates & T. Hetherington (Eds.), *Environmental social work* (pp. 213–230). London, UK & New York, USA: Routledge.

Kang, N. & Moon, J. (2012). Institutional complementarity between corporate governance and CSR: A comparative institutional analysis of three capitalisms. *Socio-Economic Review, 10*(1), 85–108.

Kaplan, S. & Garrick, B. (1981). On the quantitative definition of risk. *Risk Analysis, 1*(1), 11–27.

Kellow, A. & Niemeyer, S. (1999). The development of environmental administration in Queensland and Western Australia: Why are they different? *Australian Journal of Political Science, 34*(2), 205–222.

Kennedy, E., Weber, D. & Shine, R. (2019, 8 March). WA Premier Mark McGowan attacks EPA guidelines aimed at cutting carbon emissions. *ABC News*. Retrieved from www.abc.net.au/news/2019-03-08/mark-mcgowan-attacks-epa-carbon-emissions-policy/10882946

Klinsky, S., Roberts, T., Huq, S., Okereke, C., Newell, P., Dauvergne, P., . . . Clapp, J. (2017). Why equity is fundamental in climate change policy research. *Global Environmental Change, 44*, 170–173.

Lawrie, M., Tonts, M. & Plummer, P. (2011). Boomtowns, resource dependence and socio-economic wellbeing. *Australian Geographer, 42*(2), 139–164.

Layman, L. (1982). Changing resource development policy in Western Australia, 1930s to 1960s. In E. J. Harman & B. W. Head (Eds.), *State, capital and resources in the North and West of Australia* (pp. 149–165). Nedlands, Australia: UWA Press.

Levy, B. & Patz, J. (2015). Climate change, human rights, and social justice. *Annals of Global Health, 81*(3), 310–322.

Lines, W. (2006). *Patriots: Defending Australia's natural heritage*. St. Lucia, Queensland, Australia: University of Queensland Press.

Luke, H., Brueckner, M. & Emmanouil, N. (2018). Unconventional gas development in Australia: A critical review of its social license. *The Extractive Industries and Society*. https://doi.org/10.1016/j.exis.2018.10.006

Martinez-Alier, J. (2002). *A study of eco-conflicts and valuation*. Cheltenham, UK: Edward Elgar Publishers.

Matsuoka, A. & Sorenson, J. (2014). Social justice beyond human beings: Trans-species social justice. In T. Ryan (Ed.), *Animals and social work* (pp. 64–79). New York, USA: Palgrave Macmillan.

Maumill, B. (2013, 3 February). An audience with the emperor. *Sydney Morning Herald*. Retrieved from www.smh.com.au

Mazzeo, A. (2018). The temporalities of asbestos mining and community activism. *The Extractive Industries and Society*, 5(2), 223–229.

McHugh, B. (2014, 4 February). Barnett signs mining agreement with African governments. *ABC Rural Radio*. Retrieved from www.abc.net.au/news/rural/2014-02-04/wa-signs-mining-mou-with-africa/5237060

Mercer, D. & Emery, K. (2012, 25 June). Residents unite to fight bauxite mine plans. *The West Australian*. Retrieved from http://au.news.yahoo.com/thewest/a/-/wa/14026548/residents-unite-to-fight-bauxite-mine-plans/

Meyer, T. & Bridgen, P. (2012). Business, regulation and welfare politics in liberal capitalism. *Policy & Politics*, 40(3), 387–403.

Michell, G. & McManus, P. (2013). Engaging communities for success: Social impact assessment and social licence to operate at Northparkes Mines, NSW. *Australian Geographer*, 44(4), 435–459.

Mills, C. (1953). *The power elite*. Oxford, UK: Oxford University Press.

Moffat, K. & Zhang, A. (2014). The paths to social licence to operate: An integrative model explaining community acceptance of mining. *Resources Policy*, 39(0), 61–70.

Molyneux, R. (2010). The practical realities of eco-social work: A review of the literature. *Critical Social Work*. Retrieved from www1.uwindsor.ca/criticalsocialwork/the-practical-realities-of-ecosocial-work-a-review-of-the-literature

Moodie, C. (2010, 2 August). Under corporate skies. *ABC Stateline WA*. Retrieved from www.abc.net.au/news/2010-07-30/under-corporate-skies/927390

Moon, J. & Sharman, C. (2003). *Australian politics and government*. Cambridge, UK: Cambridge University Press.

Morgan, S., Kwaymullina, A. & Kwaymullina, B. (2006). Bulldozing Stonehenge: Fighting for cultural heritage in the wild wild west. *Indigenous Law Bulletin*, 6(20), 6–9

Morrison, J. (2014). *The social licence: How to keep your organization legitimate*. Basingstoke, UK: Palgrave Macmillan.

Munro, S. (2012). *Rich land, Wasteland: How coal is killing Australia*. Sydney, Australia: Macmillan.

New Zealand Government. (1840). *The treaty of Waitangi*. Retrieved from https://nzhistory.govt.nz/politics/treaty/the-treaty-in-brief

Norton, C. (2011). Social work and the environment: An eco-social approach. *International Journal of Social Welfare*, 21(3). Retrieved from https://onlinelibrary.wiley.com/doi/abs/10.1111/j.1468-2397.2011.00853.x

Nussbaum, M. (2013). *Political emotions: Why love matters for justice*. Cambridge, USA: Belknap Press.

Our Planet. Theirs Too. (2011). *The declaration of animal rights*. Retrieved from http://declarationofar.org/

Paddenburg, T. (2010, 11 September). Community raise funds to stop coal mine in Margaret River. *The Sunday Times*. Retrieved from www.news.com.au/breaking-news/community-raise-funds-to-stop-coal-mine-in-margaret-river/story-e6frfkp9-1225918583700#ixzz2cZhUh22J

Pauly, L. & Reich, S. (1997). National structures and multinational corporate behaviour: Enduring differences in the age of globalization. *International Organization, 51*(1), 1–30.

Payne, M. (2014). *Modern social work theory*. Oxford, UK: Oxford University Press.

Pedersen, A. (2014). Landscapes of resistance: Community opposition to Canadian mining operations in Guatemala. *Journal of Latin American Geography, 13*(1), 187–214.

Peeters, J. (2011). The place of social work in sustainable development: Towards eco-social practice. *International Journal of Social Welfare, 21*(3). Retrieved from https://onlinelibrary.wiley.com/doi/abs/10.1111/j.1468-2397.2011.00856.x

Pforr, C., Macbeth, J., Clark, K., Fountain, J. & Wood, D. (2007). *The dynamics of a coastal tourism development: Attitudes, perceptions and processes*. Retrieved from www.academia.edu/31983713/The_dynamics_of_a_coastal_tourism_development_Attitudes_perceptions_and_processes

Phillimore, J. (2014). The politics of resource development in Western Australia. In M. Brueckner, A. Durey, R. Mayes & C. Pforr (Eds.), *Resource curse or cure? On the sustainability of development in Western Australia* (pp. 25–40). Heidelberg, Germany: Springer.

Poelina, A. (2019). *Economies of nature*. Retrieved from https://greataustralianstory.com.au/story/economies-nature

Rijke, K. (2013). The agri-gas fields of Australia: Black soil, food, and unconventional gas. *Culture, Agriculture, Food and Environment, 35*(1), 41–53.

Rosa, E. (1998). Meta-theoretical foundations for post-normal risk. *Journal of Risk Research, 1*(1), 15–44.

Ross, D. (2015). Social sustainability. In S. Idowu (Ed.). *Dictionary of corporate social responsibility* (p. 466). New York, USA: Springer.

Ryan, T. (2011). *Animals and social work: A moral introduction*. New York, USA: Palgrave MacMillan.

Sandlos, J. & Keeling, A. (2016). Toxic legacies, slow violence, and environmental injustice at Giant Mine, Northwest territories. *Northern Review, 42*, 7–21.

Sharp, G. (2005). *Waging nonviolence struggle: 20th century practice and 21st century potential*. Dexter, USA: Extending Horizons Books.

Starik, M. (1995). Should trees have managerial standing? Toward stakeholder status for nonhuman nature. *Journal of Business Ethics, 14*, 207–217.

Stead, W. & Stead, J. (1992). *Management for a small planet: Strategic decision making and the environment*. Newbury Park, USA: Sage Publications.

Steger, T. & Milicevic, M. (2014). One global movement, many local voices: Discourse(s) of the global anti-Fracking movement. In T. Steger & M. Milicevic (Eds.), *Occupy the earth: Global environmental movements* (pp. 1–35). Bingley, UK: Emerald Publishing Group.

Suzuki, D. (1997). *The sacred balance: Rediscovering our place in nature*. St Leonards, Australia: Allen & Unwin.

Swedish Union for Social Sciences Professionals. (2015). *Ethics in social work: A code of conduct and ethical behaviour for social workers*. Retrieved from https://akademssr.se/sites/default/files/files/ETHICS%20IN%20SOCIAL%20WORK%20w.pdf

Thurbon, E. (2012). From developmentalism to neoliberalism and back again? Governing the market in Australia from the 1980s to the present. In C. Kyung-Sup, B. Fine & L. Weiss (Eds.), *Developmental politics in transition: The neoliberal era and beyond* (pp. 274–295). London, UK: Palgrave Macmillan.

Tischler, A. (2011). Climate change and social work: Steps to an eco-social work practice. *Theses, Dissertations, and Projects, 1023*. Retrieved from https://scholarworks.smith.edu/theses/1023.

Trigger, D. (1997). Mining, landscape and the culture of development ideology in Australia. *Ecumene*, *4*(2), 161–180.
United Nations. (1948). *Universal declaration of human rights*. Retrieved from www.un.org/en/universal-declaration-human-rights/
United Nations Global Compact. (2019). *Governance*. Retrieved from www.unglobalcompact.org/what-is-gc/our-work/governance
Walker, B., Carpenter, S., Anderies, J., Abel, N., Cumming, G., Janssen, M., . . . Pritchard, R. (2002). Resilience management in social-ecological systems: A working hypothesis for a participatory approach. *Conservation Ecology*, *6*(1), 14.
Walter, M., Taylor, S. & Habibis, D. (2013). Australian social work is white. In B. Bennett, S. Green, S. Gilbert & D. Bessarab (Eds.), *Our voices: Aboriginal and Torres Strait Islander social work* (pp. 230–247). South Yarra, Australia: Palgrave Macmillan.
Walters, R. (2017). Eco-crime and green activism. In T. Bergin & E. Orlando (Eds.), *Forging a socio-legal approach to environmental harms* (pp. 220–236). Abingdon, UK: Routledge.
Watson, R. & Cadena, J. (2014). Anti-fracking initiatives: Power to the people or more of the same? *Natural Resources & Environment*, *28*(4), 44.
Wesley, A. (2014). *The socio-political construction and experience of corporate social responsibility (CSR): An investigation into the conflict surrounding the James Price Point LNG precinct, Kimberley, Western Australia*. (PhD). Perth, Australia: Curtin University.
Wesley, A. & Pforr, C. (2008a). Coastal tourism governance: Insights from Smiths Beach, Yallingup. In J. Jenkins (Ed.), *Developing and delivering industry-relevant education and research (Proceedings of the 6th Asia Pacific CHRIE conference)* (pp. 447–461). Tweed Heads, Australia: The International Centre of Excellence in Tourism and Hospitality Education.
Wesley, A. & Pforr, C. (2008b). Tourism development in conflict: Costal tourism in Western Australia. In K. Edyvane & B. Russel (Eds.), *Coast to coast collaboration: Crossing boundaries (Proceedings of Australia's national coastal conference)* (pp. 103–103). Darwin, Australia: Department of Natural Resources, Environment and the Arts.
West, C. (2011). *Cornell West: Justice is what love looks like in public*. Retrieved from www.youtube.com/watch?v=nGqP7S_WO6o.
Western Australian Council of Social Service. (2009). *The boom is busted for 400,000 of us*. Retrieved from https://wacoss.org.au/wp-content/uploads/2017/06/Microsoft-Word-Cost-of-Living-Paper-2008-FINAL.pdf
Wheeler, C. (2006). *The public interest: We know it's important but do we know what it means*. Retrieved from www5.austlii.edu.au/au/journals/AIAdminLawF/2006/2.pdf
White, R. (2017). Corruption and the securitisation of nature. *International Journal for Crime, Justice and Social Democracy*, *6*(4), 55–70.
White, R. (2018). Ecocentrism & criminal justice. *Theoretical Criminology*, *22*(3), 342–362.
World Animal Protection. (2019). *Animals in farming: Supporting 70 billion animals*. Retrieved from www.worldanimalprotection.org.au/our-work/animals-farming-supporting-70-billion-animals
Yellow Bird, M., Coates, J. & Gray, M. (2013). *Decolonising social work*. Burlington, USA: Routledge.

Chapter 2

Home-grown community activism in Yarloop

Dyann Ross & Vince Puccio

Introduction

Chapters 2, 3 and 4 present three eco-activist stories about Yarloop, a small rural town south-east of Perth in WA. This extent of focus on one town is warranted due to the long-standing, multifaceted impact from the nearby alumina refinery owned by Alcoa World Alumina, Wagerup (Alcoa). The community concerns for their town were further worsened by a major bush fire in 2016, which almost destroyed the town. In the present chapter an overview is presented of the authors' understanding of Yarloop's issues with Alcoa and the compounding losses from the bush fire. The aim is to explain why activist groups are crucial to ensure businesses such as Alcoa are accountable when they do not uphold their legal and social licences. The chapter outlines the creation and history of the local activist group, CAPS, to show why some community members came to undertake activism. It also provides some examples of their proactive and resistive strategies over an extended period of conflict in a slow violence situation (Nixon, 2011). Chapter 3 explores issues of leadership in the aftermath of the bush fire and some of the author's challenges in undertaking the research. Chapter 4 shows how community art with a justice sensibility can provide a caring and creative space for residents to share their experiences in two impactful periods of Yarloop's history.

The CAPS story, within the larger story of Yarloop, provides an example of the role of communities in conflict situations when there is a lack of social responsibility by the mining company and the government. The idea of CSR, whilst contested in meaning (Okoye, 2009), is typically defined by industry to describe their positive social contributions to local communities (Galbreath, 2010, p. 411). CSR approaches by industry are often found to be instrumental and transactional in nature (Williams & Walton, 2013). Nevertheless, CSR is generally regarded as integral to having a social licence to operate by gaining community approval (Wilburn & Wilburn, 2011). In this sense, the granting of a social licence to operate is seen to be contingent on a company acting in the public interest (Bice, Brueckner & Pforr, 2017). The lack of CSR, as understood from a community perspective, affects the company's social licence and arises when members of a community consider the industry impacts and their grievances are not addressed and the public interest is not protected.

CAPS is an incorporated community organisation whose members either live in or have connections remaining to Yarloop. The second author of this chapter, Vince Puccio, is the chairperson of CAPS. Vince has lived in Yarloop almost his entire life, raised his family in Yarloop and worked for Alcoa for many years, until recently retiring. The CAPS website provides extensive documents and information about their concerns and activism for the last 15 years (CAPS, 2019). The group's activities are directed towards the WA state government and Alcoa which is a US-owned multinational corporation operating a nearby alumina refinery and bauxite mine. CAPS has worked to obtain accountability from their state government and their corporate neighbour relating to a range of adverse impacts attributed to the company. This struggle has intensified after the bush fire which compounded the pre-exiting issues and added more challenges as Yarloop was almost totally destroyed.

Dyann Ross has had an ongoing connection with Yarloop since the early 2000s, when she led a research team from Edith Cowan University in a participatory action research approach with the community and Alcoa (Ross, 2009). Part of the research involved a collaboration between the parties to negotiate some of the issues relating to health impacts from the refinery's noise and air pollution and the impact of Alcoa's purchases of local private properties (Ross, 2003). The testimonies from Yarloop residents, which form the basis to the chapter, were obtained as part of a formal larger research project. Ethics approval was obtained from Murdoch University in Perth, WA, by the authors' colleague, Martin Brueckner in 2016 and was later extended in 2017 to include Dyann Ross. The research was an exploratory study using interviews with participants to understand their experiences of Alcoa from 2002 and in the aftermath of a major bush fire in 2016. Excerpts from the research participants' transcripts are presented in anonymous form by referring to a "Member, CAPS" or "Yarloop resident" and using pseudonyms if a name is used.

The effect of activism by CAPS for their town over many years has been twofold: a) rendering CAPS the watchdog of the supposed government's role as a watchdog to industry as well as b) highlighting the role of community activism in bringing about corporate and government social responsibility through community pressure. Arguably, community activism might even be seen as a necessary precondition for ensuring social responsibility of entities with vested interests in the mining operations. The CAPS experience shows that consideration needs to be given to how to protect communities and ecosystems in situations of conflict where there is a failure of CSR by mining companies and insufficient government oversight of mining operations.

The impetus to establish CAPS

The conflict began in the late 1990s with health concerns about emissions from Alcoa's alumina refinery at Wagerup, just two kilometres from the northern outskirts of Yarloop. Alcoa refused to accept that their emissions were causing health issues for Yarloop residents and the surrounding area. A Yarloop resident speaks of Alcoa being "like someone invading my home basically telling me to leave town". The resident goes on to say that everyone seemed to have forgotten that the people of Yarloop "were here first long before Alcoa and the government decided to plant this toxic industry on our doorstep" (Yarloop resident). Alcoa was established on the town's doorstep in the 1970s by a real estate company buying farmland under the pretence of establishing a sunflower seed farm. Once the land was acquired, it became public knowledge that the real estate company was acting on behalf of Alcoa, which intended to build an alumina refinery. In the beginning, the arrival of Alcoa was seen as positive around Yarloop as no one knew of the health or environmental impacts involved. When Alcoa began to expand and built the liquor burner (equipment that increased the value of the raw materials but did so using toxic chemicals), people's health and well-being became affected. It was at this point that "Alcoa showed its true colours. [Alcoa's] only interest was the bottom line of profits and they [didn't] give a damn how they achieved that" (Member, CAPS).

The problems escalated for the community when a number of Alcoa employees became sick and Alcoa would not accept it was work related. The workers were eventually given ex gratia payments in acknowledgement of the work-related health impacts. The conflict between the workers and Alcoa management spilled over into the surrounding towns through word of mouth, and as a result concern for the health of people and animals escalated. Attempts by some residents to get answers from Alcoa were rebuffed, and in 2002 a major national newspaper report titled "The stink of Uncle Al" (Mayman, 2002, p. 19) made public the conflict that was building. Alcoa believed it was not causing air and noise pollution and that the health concerns were unfounded. However, many residents' own experiences were of health and safety concerns (Brueckner & Ross, 2010). In this context of uncertainty and distrust, Alcoa decided to implement a property buy-up plan to protect their commercial interests and paid property owners immediately surrounding the refinery a percentage on top of property market value and removal costs (Alcoa World Alumina (Australia), 2002). Alcoa was reluctant to buy other properties in the older part of Yarloop farthest from the refinery but brought some at market value only. The properties purchased at the higher-value formula by Alcoa became what was called locally the "buffer zone", but it was not legally established through formal planning approvals. It is common practice that mining operations require an area of land where there are no private dwellings around the perimeter to ensure there is no impact on nearby communities. This was not undertaken when Alcoa built the refinery and mine site. According to residents, Alcoa knew from the beginning that they required a buffer zone around its operations. Alcoa commenced meetings with local residents to gauge possible resistance to the buying up of properties. In this situation, it meant that there would be dwellings and people living in Alcoa's buffer zone, even though increasingly the properties were owned by Alcoa. It was through this process that the broader community became uncertain of Alcoa's intention for

Yarloop. The community sentiment about Alcoa was "fix your problems and leave the bloody town alone!" (Member, CAPS). The social impact increased with Alcoa's property buy-up plan, when many residents sold their property in a situation of fear and uncertainty. A resident, who later joined CAPS, said "This marked the start of the division of our community and the beginning of the end for Yarloop". Another resident described what happened as "criminal". Further, they added that Alcoa went out of its way to "destroy, intimidate, create fear, abuse and make fun of people who complained, or were concerned about their health" (Member, CAPS). Because Alcoa was the only buyer of properties that were now devalued because of their proximity to the refinery, some residents had to negotiate for as long as nine months amidst health concerns and community tensions. One community member saw this as "Alcoa teaching a lesson to other residents that if you don't play by the rules this is what happens" (Yarloop resident). All those who didn't play by Alcoa's rules had their suffering drawn out, despite it being Alcoa that wished to purchase the land in the first place.

There is extensive material on the public record including media releases (see the CAPS website, 2019) and the Australian Broadcasting Commission's Four Corners documentary (McDermott, 2005) on the pollution and social impact caused by Alcoa during this period. It led to the WA state government establishing a parliamentary inquiry. The inquiry found that Alcoa was acting outside state planning legislation in instigating its own purchase plan of private properties around the refinery (Sharp, 2004). Alcoa maintained it was buying properties for its commercial interests, merely citing land-use incompatibilities, and did not acknowledge that many people were selling due to their fears for their health and the safety of their children (Ross, 2003). Alcoa's own medical adviser admitted that Alcoa had created a problem and needed to fix it, but building high stacks to disperse the emissions and other technical improvements to the refinery did not solve the problem (Miraudo, 2002).

The international and government research evidence at the time was inconclusive with regard to health impacts from alumina refineries. In 2002 production at Alcoa's Wagerup refinery increased from 1.75 to 2.35 million tonnes despite a record number of public submissions against production increases. In 2004, Alcoa applied for an expansion to its refinery in the context of calls against any expansion from respected advisory groups such as the Medical Practitioners Forum (Holman, Harper, Somers, Galton-Fenzi & Phillips, 2005). The expansion was approved by the state government, but to date Alcoa has not undertaken the expansion. Nevertheless, at the time it was part of the community's concern for the safety and future of their town, and it fuelled the perception that they were abandoned by their own government. Alcoa's production level is now 2.85 million tonnes per annum, an increase of 0.5 million tonnes due to incremental increases with each licencing approval. A CAPS member explains that for the company's head office in Pittsburgh, Pennsylvania, "The bottom line [of profit] comes first no matter what damage, what impacts or whether they completely destroy the community. None of this is part of their equation. The bottom line comes first".

Conde explains that communities tend to resist mining operations when they "perceive a threat to their health or livelihood" (2017, p. 80). The political context though is one of unequal power and financial resources between communities, mining corporations and the government regulator. It is therefore a tall order to mount a concerted, locally based resistance to adverse impacts and to attempt to hold the more powerful entities accountable. Mining corporations and governments are typically intolerant of social resistance to their operations and decisions. From an international perspective, Global Witness provides statistics of the cost of resistance to mining:

> Nearly four people were murdered every week in 2016 whilst protecting their land, forests and rivers from mining, logging and agricultural companies . . . At least 200 people were killed in 2016. . . . Severe limits on available information mean the global total is likely far higher. Murder is the sharp end of a range of tactics used to silence defenders, including death threats, arrests, sexual assault, abductions and aggressive legal attacks.
> (Harrison, 2017, n.p.)

The main impetus to CAPS forming in 2004 related to the inaugural members' concerns as they continued to hear of the town's people having their lives intruded upon in what they describe as the divide-and-conquer strategy of Alcoa. "I don't like corporations, simple as that", one of the CAPS members said, "and I don't like people who throw their weight around, especially those who try and put the little people down". The otherwise settled population of 600 people in Yarloop changed dramatically in a few short years and after the bush fire in 2016; approximately only 10% of Yarloop's original residents remain in the town (compare Australian Bureau of Statistics, 2006, 2016). Since 2002, Alcoa has purchased most of the area around its industrial footprint and post-fire was able to buy the remaining land with destroyed or scorched dwellings even more cheaply, further compounding the losses for remaining residents.

On reflecting how they came to take the leadership role they did by creating CAPS in 2004, one of the CAPS members noted how their commitment changed as the conflict went on. They explained how, when the conflict began to unfold, "we were witnessing the destruction of our community by Alcoa's divide and conquer tactics and the government's inaction". This was the catalyst to become home-grown activists to fight Alcoa on all fronts by "taking a holistic approach to all of the Alcoa issues" (Member, CAPS). This led the organisation to adapt and change their tactics as needed to counter Alcoa's and the government's moves which, almost without exception, continued to disadvantage Yarloop. Another member explains that CAPS had such a strong following because they were not asking Alcoa to shut down; what they wanted was accountability, transparency and for Alcoa to do right by the community

(Member, CAPS). These goals were sustainable and achievable, and because of that more people joined or approached CAPS. They "looked to us for a resolution" as the community was becoming more desperate to find a way out (Member, CAPS).

An unrelenting desire for justice

An unrelenting desire for justice for their people has sustained CAPS members for more than a decade to the present time. A CAPS member explains, "we believe that the government is colluding with industry and small towns like Yarloop are sacrificed in the name of the dollar disguised as progress". In Chapter 1 Brueckner and Ross outline some pertinent examples of the WA government's reaction to activism. This locates the Yarloop experience in what is a continuation of the government protecting big business. Internationally, Conde found that there is an "increasing use of repressive measures, the criminalisation of protest through new legislation and the prosecution of leaders in resistance movements" (2017, p. 86). This backlash power dynamic against public protests is a form of structural violence or "routine inequality" in which the effect of no challenge to business as usual is to "normalise the process of plunder" (Butler, 2015, p. 287). Butler explains that it occurs in a "rationalised, routine, unspectacular manner in which systemic harm occurs, garnering little media attention and even less consistent public concern and outrage" (2015, p. 287). This description by Butler (2015) captures CAPS's understanding of the situation. Analogously, the pro-development stance of successive state governments in WA has also resulted in the passing of legislation that aided industrial development whilst restricting avenues for public protest and appeal. For example, the government brought changes to the Police Act to prosecute protesters in an attempt to minimise impediments to the construction of Alcoa's Wagerup refinery (Kellow & Niemeyer, 1999).

Thomas and Mitra consider that it is a matter of concern for global civil society to address the inequalities that occur due to these types of issues which they call "ecological distribution conflict" (2018, p. 55). Yet they recognise the limits of grassroots organisations which often see local activism fail (Thomas & Mitra, 2018). The research literature shows that community activism strategies are more successful if short term, focused with a clear goal and able to garner broad public interest and media coverage and to foster links between local efforts to broader alliances often beyond national boundaries. This begs the question of what happens in conflict situations such as Yarloop, where over a long period of time, there has been a significant disruption of the population, a collapse of social capital and reduced capacity for community resistance.

The conundrum becomes one of the people being impacted also being the people waging hard to win struggles between people, place and profit (Brueckner & Ross, 2010). Therefore, those who create what are called "landscapes of resistance" (Pedersen, 2014) may experience a double "*in* jeopardy". For

Yarloop, the double in jeopardy relates to impact from the industry and impact from the challenges of mounting the resistance to stem the adverse impact. Jeopardy is defined as "risk of loss or injury, peril or danger" (Farlex, 2018). The idea of "*in* jeopardy" seeks to accent the locatedness of danger in: time and place; the material effects such as impact on income and property values; and its embodiment in people, animals and landscapes. It interlinks with Butler's (2015) idea of structural violence, which is experienced as adverse circumstances not of peoples' choosing and beyond their collective efforts to protect themselves. It has a correlation for present purposes with the failure to enact environmental and social precautionary principles by the industry regulator, that is, by the government, where dangers are being voiced by local communities (Ross, 2017).

The heavy costs of being an activist with no choice over the circumstances brings the politics into the home and community spaces and can cause interpersonal and local tensions and conflict. In a study with women who are anti-mining activists in Peru and Ecuador, Jenkins writes:

> A sense of community fragmentation is a prominent feature of the women's accounts, underlining how community spaces, dynamics and power relations have been re-shaped over a period of many years of conflict within the women's communities, reinforced by the divisive nature of mining company activities. Common to many of the women's narratives was a discussion of how their activist identities were forged through every day, low level confrontations within their communities, usually with members of the community who were in favour of the mine rather than with external actors.
> (2017, p. 1148)

The Jenkins (2017) quote could be referring to Yarloop. Thus, the backlash by mining corporations and governments can combine with local backlashes creating a cocktail of power dynamics. Compoundingly, a triple "*in* jeopardy" can arise relating to the costs of trying to protect local ecosystems and animals. The scientific and specialist knowledge and research needed to provide evidence of harm to air, land, water, flora and fauna can require resources beyond the reach of a small community. The call to eco-activism may well hide a range of costs and challenges for the community that can combine to limit what is possible in complex situations. Research shows, for example, that the social costs include financial impost to fund the ongoing activist work; property blight; loss of neighbours and friends either through population decline or due to the tensions arising from the conflict; health; and separation from partners and family (Brueckner & Ross, 2010).

Home-grown activism in Yarloop

This section conveys some of the home-grown activism by Yarloop residents to highlight the activist skills and strategies employed to protect the interests of their town from the mining operations. It also highlights the personal resilience needed to survive and endure when they experienced devastating losses from the bush fire. Eco-activism forms out of collective outrage relating to social and environmental injustice and harm. In the business literature, outrage refers to the emotional intensity that occurs in a hazardous situation and is used to gauge the level of risk for a corporation (Sandman, 2003). In this chapter it is used to refer to the highly focused use of the anger that occurred due to the harm and injustice experienced by many people in the Yarloop community. Their outrage was strong enough to make some of them stand up and challenge Alcoa and the government for more than a decade. Rees (2016) explains that activists need to ensure their outrage is based on facts and not the emotionality of the issues alone. CAPS became skilled at gathering the facts. CAPS developed the advocacy skills needed to represent the facts at opportune points on a trial-and-error basis. Their efforts have resulted in a sophisticated network of supporters and experts, significant wins and a set of letters, reports and other documents which are testimony to the long-term strategic value of CAPS's informed and sustained outrage.

For example, at the time of writing, CAPS continues to lobby the government for a legally approved industrial buffer zone around the Alcoa refinery at Wagerup. In 2002, the legal process was side-stepped by Alcoa implementing the already mentioned property buy-up through its Land Management Plan (Alcoa World Alumina (Australia), 2002). CAPS came to believe that a positive solution after the bush fire was for the government to formally approve the establishment of a buffer that extended on Alcoa's property purchases to encompass the whole town of Yarloop. Should they wish to leave, this would give remaining residents fair compensation for their properties at arm's length from Alcoa. When CAPS approached the government to advocate for a formal buffer around the refinery in 2016, the premier of WA responded by pointing to an existing buffer. This blurring of lines of truth was challenged by CAPS with the government then referring to a land management area that effectively acted as a buffer. A CAPS member recalls it in terms of the material impact on their family and finances stating that if there was no official classification of a buffer zone "between now and Christmas [2016] I will have to cut my losses and take some money out of my superannuation to buy another dwelling". There is evidence now available on the public domain that records the paper trail of confusion and ineptness at least and possible collusion between Alcoa and the highest levels of government. One Yarloop resident explains, "We've heard [government] employees of the Department of Environment refer to the department as the Department of Alcoa Protection" (Brueckner & Ross, 2010, p. 172).

The close relationship between the government and Alcoa is deeply troubling to CAPS members when other issues in the conflict are considered. For example, during the early 2000s, Yarloop residents who experienced adverse effects from the Alcoa refinery emissions would report it to the refinery, but Alcoa refused to accept there was a pollution issue causing their ailments.

CAPS challenged Alcoa's practice of monitoring emissions from its refinery as it lacked independence. They believe that corruption is possible when an industry is left to self-monitor. There was no government oversight or separate monitoring of the industrial emissions. CAPS established their own method of gathering emission samples based on American experiences. The so-called bucket brigade involved specially sealed canisters that could be taken to locations around the town when there were pollution events occurring. The residents would capture some of the air, and the whole sealed canister was then sent to be analysed. The community paid for the equipment, training in its use and the initial independent testing in an American laboratory until the government negotiated a memorandum of understanding with CAPS. The result was that CAPS shared its captured emission samples with the government's Air Quality Branch (Galbally, 2004). This was followed in 2006 by a government study known as the Winter Study which:

> Proved the link between the Yarloop complaints and Alcoa's emissions. This win established some credibility for the community and CAPS. The study found that Alcoa's reporting was flawed because they were only measuring air from part of the refinery, not the whole refinery.
> (Member, CAPS; see Winter Study, CAPS, 2019)

Over the years, CAPS has written scores of letters and emails to politicians and government officials, in particular, the heads of Departments of Health, Environmental Protection and Planning. The CAPS website is filled with paper trails that if studied would be cause for public alarm at the slow violence (Nixon, 2011) that is occurring in and around Yarloop. The systematic researching of public documents and international studies and strategies has also been a key component of the advocacy role undertaken by the CAPS "everyday activists" (Jenkins, 2017) on behalf of the people and place of Yarloop. Their home-grown activism highlights the importance of being well informed and of sustaining a focused outrage towards the government, who can hold Alcoa accountable.

There have been a range of challenges and complexities for CAPS members relating to: issues of who they represent in their community; limited financial resources; the effort of sustaining active membership and leadership; the family impact and how their own homes are affected; and being in and of the community and simultaneously needing to be focused away from these relationships. All these factors intersect in different ways for the community activists and can result in compounding stress, health issues and personal costs over the years that are impossible to quantify because they are such a significant burden. For example, CAPS members would feel disappointed when a family sold and left, but at the same time they understood the complexity of the health impact and the bleak outlook for Yarloop's future. A CAPS member explained that "the friction and fear caused by Alcoa's unwelcome intrusion into the town occurred within families and between friends". It caused many ardent Alcoa workers and loyal community members to leave town to save themselves and their families.

The personal and financial costs borne by members of CAPS were reluctantly accepted as part of the price to be paid for trying to protect their community. Further, they often were directly impacted and had to bear witness to the adverse impact of industry and more recently the bush fire on their neighbours and town. Vince was home on his small acreage property on the day of the bush fire and had to evacuate as the fire approached his home, taking only his dog and years of CAPS records with him. The bush fire swept through large tracts of forest and farmlands and went close to the perimeter of the Alcoa refinery. The town of Yarloop was hit hardest with significant loss of infrastructure, including heritage cottages, the town hall, a hotel, the guest house and the railway workshops museum. Two people died in their homes (see Yarloop fire, CAPS, 2019). Chapter 3 explains how many locals linked the destruction to the conflict with Alcoa and the neglect of the town by the government. Vince's home was saved, but some of his neighbours and friends lost their properties or put their lives at risk to save them.

A CAPS member, who talked to the authors soon after the fire, explained the impact the life-threatening fire had on them, their neighbours, homes and town. Their neighbour, Jim, had been fighting fires all through the night and hadn't had any sleep for more than 48 hours. Upon returning to his house Jim noticed his older neighbours were still in their place, one of whom had emphysema, with two grandchildren in their care. Jim reportedly said, "what the bloody hell are you doing here"? and drove them out to safety through the charred, still smoking landscape. "He reckons it was horrific", the CAPS member–neighbour recollects. By the time Jim came back to his own home, it was gone, but like the true Aussie-battler, "he reckons he could have saved it" (Member, CAPS).

In the days after the fire, there was a deafening silence from the town's nearest neighbour, Alcoa, and the state government. Although Alcoa's refinery resumed full operation only one week after the fire (de Landgrafft, 2016), questions to government about the future of the destroyed town were rebuffed with statements by the premier of it being "too early to make the call" (Anon, 2016). Jackson, a resident, describes some of the intense pain of the disaster after years of struggle to protect the town. His house was gutted, nothing left, but he and his partner, Carly, had to return home daily to feed their animals because some had survived. "We should have put all our valuables in the chook house", he remarked. "This particular day after the fire, Carly had gone down the back to feed the animals. . . . I went out the back and I just walked up the hill". Jackson continued to walk past devastated properties and families standing at their front gates going through a similar shock process; one neighbour asked him, "are you alright?" A little later on he was stopped and given a bottle of water. Jackson was inconsolable as he walked all the way to the top of the hill with a steep cliff, where he had decided to jump off. He was exhausted, spent. Jackson recalls as he turned off the road to "head bush", a little girl who was walking ahead of her family whom he knew approached him to see how he was; "she rescued me [because] when I saw her I knew I had to pull myself together". They stood on the roadside, both in tears for their homes and town.

These same people were called upon in the days and months after the fire to be there for their community, and when Dyann visited the town later that month, Vince and other CAPS members were already working on the submission for a parliamentary inquiry into the fire. Resilience isn't the right word for what it takes to care about your town and people and to want justice for them. The authors suggest that too much is expected of unsupported and unresourced communities who have no choice but to continue fighting for justice even as it seems to slip further away and even as it gets harder to keep on with the struggle.

Conclusion

The main outcomes from the activism by CAPS for more than a decade relates to the state government upholding some of CAPS's appeals against Alcoa's licence applications. This has resulted in more stringent industry controls due to the well-researched independent evidence gathered by CAPS. Community activist groups such as CAPS are crucial as Alcoa would not otherwise be required to lift the bar on its legal obligations and broader CSR performance. In some aspects CAPS has found there is a legal licencing void where there is still a role for CAPS in ensuring the tightening of licencing requirements. As the CAPS chairperson, Vince will have the final say in the chapter. He believes there is an intractability on the part of the powerful stakeholders after originally failing to engage the community as respected stakeholders. The unfortunate part about this long and sorry saga is that these multinational corporations (Alcoa) who have the money and the power to sway or threaten governments believe they can basically do what they want without any recrimination from governments. This corporate behaviour has bought about the destruction of Yarloop and displacement of its people. The failure to engage with the community as a respected stakeholder demonstrates Alcoa's unwillingness to jeopardise their shareholders' bottom line. Vince believed then (2002) and today that much of the harm and havoc could have been avoided if Alcoa and the government were open and transparent, treated the community on the same level footing, and stated the facts and what the impact on the community and the environment would be.

Such an approach would then demonstrate to the community that both government and industry have the community interest at heart. By including the community and discussing the requirements of industry and the possible impact on the community and the environment, a more amicable and fairer outcome would be possible. If Alcoa, the government and community had a common understanding of alumina refinery operations and its impact, it would enable Alcoa to implement a buffer zone with minimal resistance knowing that all parties would be protected. Industry would have certainty and be able to continue with its business, government workload would be reduced and the community members could be fairly compensated for their properties and could continue on having a similar lifestyle in a new town. This would alleviate a lot of heartache for the communities and time and money for industry.

To summarise, the authors believe the research material alongside the experience of CAPS over many years has demonstrated some of the adverse impact for their town and the local ecosystem. This complexity of adverse impact by Alcoa's refinery at nearby Wagerup and the inadequate protection and support of the community by the government has been a slow but deep and devastating violence. The story of CAPS, a community-based eco-activist group, provides important insights into what is needed to hold big business and government accountable, the challenges that can arise and the personal costs that may be experienced.

Dedication

The authors wish to dedicate this chapter to Bill Smallgange and Merv McDonald, their families, and all the people who love Yarloop.

References

Alcoa World Alumina (Australia). (2002). *Wagerup land management policy*. Wagerup, Australia: Alcoa World Alumina.

Anon. (2016, 20 January). WA fires: Waroona-Yarloop blazes to be investigated by Victorian expert Euan Ferguson. *ABC News*. Retrieved from www.abc.net.au/news/2016-01-20/waroona-yarloop-blazes-to-be-investigated-by-victorian-expert/7102150

Australian Bureau of Statistics (ABS). (2006). *2006 census quickstats: Yarloop (state suburb)*. Canberra, Australia: ABS.

Australian Bureau of Statistics (ABS). (2016). *2016 census quickstats: Yarloop (state suburb)*. Canberra, Australia: ABS.

Bice, S., Brueckner, B. & Pforr, C. (2017). Putting social license to operate on the map: A social, actuarial and political risk and licensing model (SAP Model). *Resources Policy*, 53, 46–55.

Brueckner, M. & Ross, D. (2010). *Under corporate skies: A struggle between people, place and profit*. Fremantle, Western Australia: Fremantle Press.

Butler, P. (2015). *Colonial extractions: Place and Canadian mining in contemporary Africa*. Toronto, Canada: University of Toronto.

Community Alliance for Positive Solutions, CAPS. (2019). *The Yarloop story*. Retrieved from caps6218.org.au

Conde, M. (2017). Resistance to mining: A review. *Ecological Economics*, 132, 80–90.

de Landgrafft, T. (2016, 15 January). Alcoa resumes production a week after bushfires sweep through WA's south west. *ABC Rural*. Retrieved from www.abc.net.au/news/2016-01-15/wach-alcoa-fire-recovery/7092084

Farlex. (2018). *The free dictionary*. Retrieved from www.thefreedictionary.com/jeopard

Galbally, I. (2004). *Wagerup air quality review, report C/0936*. Canberra, Australia: CSIRO Atmospheric Research.

Galbreath, J. (2010). How does corporate social responsibility benefit firms? Evidence from Australia. *European Business Review, 22*(4), 411–431.

Harrison, A. (2017). *Worst year ever for environmental and land rights activists*. Retrieved from www.globalwitness.org/en/press-releases/worst-year-ever-environmental-and-land-rights-activists-least-200-killed-2016-crisis-spreads-across-globe/

Holman, D., Harper, A., Somers, M., Galton-Fenzi, B. & Phillips, M. (2005). *Wagerup refinery unit three expansion: Letter to the environmental protection authority*. Perth, Australia: Government of Western Australia.

Jenkins, K. (2017). Women anti-mining activists' narratives of everyday resistance in the Andes: Staying put and carrying on in Peru and Ecuador. *Gender, Place & Culture, 24*(10), 1441–1459.

Kellow, A. & Niemeyer, S. (1999). The development of environmental administration in Queensland and Western Australia: Why are they different? *Australian Journal of Political Science, 34*(2), 205–222.

Mayman, J. (2002, 11 and 12 May). The stink of Uncle Al. *The Weekend Australian*.

McDermott, Q. (2005). Something in the air. *ABC Four Corners*. Retrieved from https://youtu.be/3iMzuljeUgI

Miraudo, N. (2002, 24 February). Alcoa expert links illness to refinery. *Sunday Times*. Retrieved from https://caps6218.org.au/news-media-alcoa-page/page/6/

Nixon, R. (2011). *Slow violence and the environmentalism of the poor*. Cambridge, UK: Harvard University Press.

Okoye, A. (2009). Theorising corporate social responsibility as an essentially contested concept: Is a definition Necessary? *Journal of Business Ethics, 89*(4), 613–627. doi:10.1007/s10551-008-0021-9

Pedersen, A. (2014). Landscapes of resistance: Community opposition to Canadian mining operations in Guatemala. *Journal of Latin American Geography, 13*(1), 187–214.

Rees, S. (2016). Encouraging outrage in social work: Palestine and Ebola. *Ethics and Social Welfare, 10*(2), 140–148.

Ross, D. (2003). *Reviewing the land management process: Some common ground at a point in the process: A report in collaboration between Alcoa Wagerup and Yarloop/Hamel property owners*. Bunbury, Australia: Edith Cowan University.

Ross, D. (2009). Emphasizing the 'social' in corporate social responsibility: A social work perspective. In S. Idowu & W. Leal Filho (Eds.). *Professional perspectives of corporate social responsibility* (pp. 301–318). Frankfurt am Main, Germany: Peter Lang.

Ross, D. (2017). A research-informed model for corporate social responsibility: Towards accountability to impacted stakeholders. *International Journal of Corporate Social Responsibility, 2*(8), 1–11.

Sandman, P. (1993/2003). *Responding to community outrage: Strategies for effective risk communication*. Fairfax, USA: American Industrial Hygiene Association.

Sharp, C. (2004). *Report for the standing committee on environment and public affairs in relation to the Alcoa refinery at Wagerup inquiry*. Perth, Australia: Government of Western Australia.

Thomas, D. & Mitra, S. (2018). Global civil society & resistance to Canadian mining abroad: Building and enhancing the boomerang model. *Studies in Political Economy, 98*(1), 48–70.

Wilburn, K. & Wilburn, R. (2011). Achieving social license to operate using stakeholder theory. *Journal of Business Ethics, 4*, 3–16.

Williams, R. & Walton, A. (2013). *The social licence to operate and coal seam gas development: A literature review report to the gas industry*. Canberra, Australia: Social and Environmental Research Alliance.

Chapter 3

Researching disaster recovery
The case for an activist participatory design

Marilyn Palmer

Introduction

The chapter illustrates how activist research in the area of emergency management can help fulfil social work's obligation to facilitate transitions towards just and sustainable communities. I researched the nature of leadership following the 2016 Yarloop fire and identified a number of limitations in the post-fire emergency response. The research participants described how the formal leadership was closely controlled by the state government during the recovery process. They reported that the government's failure to proactively engage with and use the local knowledge and social capital in the town became an added level of challenge for them. The research showed that Yarloop residents placed a high value on the informal leadership provided by volunteers, mainly local government and non-government workers, who supported the community in diverse, practical and creative ways. The research raised questions about the nature of leadership in disaster management and its impact on the community.

Writing this chapter two years later, I have deconstructed the research experience to better understand my sense of disquiet about the research design and process. The disquiet relates to a disjuncture between my intention (to support the people of Yarloop) and the research design, which lacked an engagement with participants as equal co-researchers in designing the study and guiding the process. I consider how my research might have benefited the community had the intent and design been more explicitly informed by activist research (Hale, 2001) using a participatory action or collaborative inquiry approach as endorsed by Godden (2016). My reflections about the nature of leadership show the challenges for eco-activist practice; they also illustrate the importance of building and sustaining equal, mutual relationships with a community, whether you are leading a disaster recovery process or researching it.

The backstory: my connection with Yarloop

I live in Bunbury, a coastal regional centre south of Perth, the capital city of WA. I was away when I first heard about a bush fire raging in the South-west in early 2016. Two days later, on my way home from Perth, I heard that there had been two fatalities and most of the homes, as well as commercial and heritage buildings, in Yarloop had been destroyed. The fire had burnt through forest, bushland and rural properties, causing extensive damage and farm animal loss. The main highways from Perth to the South-west were closed, and so I drove the long way home, further east and around the fire. The fire continued to burn, threatening more townships, and over the next two weeks it flared and abated until it was eventually extinguished. My involvement with Yarloop residents dated from the early 2000s, when I was part of a research team from Edith Cowan University (ECU). At the time we were working in collaboration with the community, Alcoa World Alumina, Wagerup (Alcoa) and the government to enable dialogue (Ross, 2009) around issues of health, property and social amenity impacts from the nearby Alcoa refinery (Brueckner & Ross, 2010). It was devastating that the town had almost been destroyed after a long, tumultuous struggle to survive industry intrusion, population loss and infrastructure decline over the past two decades.

In the weeks following the fire, community concerns about the government's apparent lack of commitment to rebuild and repopulate the town were emerging (see Yarloop fire, CAPS, 2019). There was also controversy about the management of the fire by state fire and emergency services which prompted a formal government inquiry. In anticipation of the call for submissions to the inquiry, I helped prepare some of the materials with the community activist group in Yarloop – Community Alliance for Positive Solutions (CAPS) (see Chapter 2). I documented for the public record some of the troubling points about Yarloop's history with Alcoa: the refinery's installation of a liquor burner in the late 1990s where this equipment upgrade seemed to immediately precipitate community health complaints; Alcoa's land management policy that had set the rules for buying local properties to create a buffer around its operations (Alcoa, 2002), undermining the town's social cohesion, safety and property values (Sharp, 2004); the Edith Cowan University (ECU) community-industry dialogue building research project (Ross, 2009); and most recently, the fire. This history also provided a context for a list of recommendations CAPS wanted to submit to the state government about the future of the town. Two months after the fire, some members of CAPS gave an oral submission to the inquiry led by Euan Ferguson, and I accompanied them to take notes at the meeting. CAPS believed the fire management issues during the crisis mirrored the ongoing neglect by government of Yarloop's safety given the proximity of a major industry.

In the months immediately after the fire, I visited the town several times talking to Vince Puccio, the CAPS chairperson, and other locals who had been affected by the fire. I also attended some public meetings to explore a focus for a possible research project or other ways ECU might be of service to the town. Some people continued to live in the town despite the roadblocks established for the duration of the government-sponsored asbestos decontamination process, which closed the town to the public for months. Other locals, like Vince, lived beyond the roadblocks but visited the town centre regularly. There were a range of theories circulating after the fire: Alcoa and the government had conspired to let the town burn; there were no warnings or capacity to fight the fire because of negligence or incompetence by firefighters who had ignored requests and advice from local volunteers; and firefighters had prioritised the refinery, leaving Yarloop exposed, to prevent the stored fuel onsite from igniting and destroying the refinery. An explosion of this order may have accelerated the fire south towards the town of Harvey, the industrial park of Kemerton and the more heavily populated Greater Bunbury regional centre. Members of the Yarloop community were using none, some or all of these theories to try and understand their situation.

At public meetings and in the media, I was struck by the silence from Alcoa. A month after the fire, they announced they would not rebuild their 35 fire-damaged rental properties, assets from the property purchase scheme. The decision by the Department of Premier and Cabinet to establish a State Recovery Coordination Group and appoint ex-Governor Dr Ken Michael from Perth as the state recovery controller (rather than a local disaster coordinating committee led by a local leader such as the shire council president) appeared to be contrary to recommended best practice and state policy for a disaster of this kind. So, by the time I applied for a small ECU research grant in July 2016, my focus had developed around the topic of leadership during the recovery process, specifically to address the question: how was leadership understood during the process of emergency recovery in the context of the Yarloop-Waroona fire? The purpose of the research was to feed back to people in Yarloop and neighbouring communities some of their reflections of leadership during the post-fire recovery period as well as to add to the academic literature on disaster recovery. Helen Seiver, who knew Yarloop from her previous work with ECU and who had maintained a connection with the town (see Chapter 4), agreed to take on the role of research assistant.

The research process and findings

At the time, I constructed the project as a small, critical ethnographic case study using qualitative methods (Quantz, 1992) gathering peoples' stories and analysing them with a lens on state power. I had ethics approval from ECU to conduct a two-stage research project involving interviews using snowball sampling and a photo-voice project advertised on local media and through flyers distributed at regular community recovery gatherings such as morning teas, sausage sizzles and farmers' breakfasts. For the interviews, Helen and I began with our initial contacts and asked for suggestions of people likely to hold a diverse range of views about leadership during the recovery process. This resulted in face-to-face interviews with 11 people. We developed a flyer using participants' comments about their experiences of leadership to advertise the photo-voice stage of the research. For this second stage we asked people to send us photographs with captions which began with the words "this photograph represents leadership to me because . . .". Sixteen people gave us photographs or asked us to come and take a photograph on their behalf. For example, we received a request to take photographs representing "red tape" and another showing "a bureaucrat sitting on their hands". A further nine people added comments on the photos when we displayed them at local gatherings.

Helen and I realised as soon as we began the interviews that the fire event was still real in peoples' lives, and as a result there was no demarcation between the fire event, immediate aftermath and the response and recovery process. Participants would always begin their stories on the day of the fire – where they were when it hit, what happened when they were evacuated (for some, more than once), their relationship to the two men who had died in the fire, their relationships with farm animals and pets, the impact of losing all that they had and, for some, the experience of being trapped on the oval (the evacuation area) with the local firefighting volunteers while the fire raged around them. When introducing the research to participants, we defined leadership as "the ability to inspire confidence and support among the people who are needed to achieve community goals", drawing from the work of Dubrin, Dalglish and Miller (2006). We realised that the construct of leadership was simultaneously esoteric and commonplace – some people interpreted leadership as formal, authoritative leadership, as in who is in charge, whereas others saw leadership as actions which had helped or inspired them regardless of who did them. The contributions we collected were rich and varied and told us a lot, although we never assumed we had collected the complete story.

The main findings from the study were threefold: firstly, the importance of recognising, building and bolstering all forms of social capital through the leadership process following the disaster. Social capital is understood as the social glue of a community, evident in the stocks of networks, norms and social trust which facilitate mutually beneficial collaborations (Cox, cited in Alston, Hazeleger & Hargraeaves, 2019). Secondly, the study findings suggested that appointed, ascribed leaders need to recognise the limitations of using a business-as-usual transactional leadership approach during disaster recovery. Finally, the ascribed leaders need to consider the likely value of a transformational leadership approach in communities to build social capital and reduce vulnerabilities (Nakagawa & Shaw, 2004; Valero, Jung & Andrew, 2015).

When Helen and I were transcribing, reading and rereading the transcripts we noted the word *step* appeared frequently to describe both positive and negative experiences with leadership. For example, participants mentioned people who had stepped up, stepped back, stepped down and stepped in at various times. We concluded that for the study participants, leadership equated with action. It was evident that many local people saw the effective leaders as local informal helpers and the recovery workers from government and non-government human service agencies working on the ground who had been proactive in providing assistance and support. The leadership of the State

Recovery Coordination Group was often criticised for being distant, indecisive and poorly communicated. These criticisms suggested a failure in the ascribed leadership to understand and perform across the four key dimensions of transformational leadership which Tafvelin, Hywonen and Westerberg identify as: charismatic role modelling; inspiring a vision; promoting creativity; and mentoring emergent leaders and organisations (2012, p. 889). Northouse identifies a fifth dimension of transformational leadership, which is to "encourage the heart . . . to achieve greater collective identity and community spirit" (2010, p. 184). This heartfelt approach was evident through the human connections made with community members by the on-the-ground recovery workers who comprised one of the following: workers who were formally assigned by government, non-government organisations, volunteering individually or through groups such as BlazeAid, the nearby town of Cookenup's Community Centre, the Country Women's Association (CWA) and local service clubs.

By the end of 2016 we no longer needed to visit Yarloop for the study, and I was writing the research report to share with the community. Although I was satisfied with the findings from the study in relation to the role of leadership and the need to support social capital in disaster recovery, I had a sense of disquiet about the research process. Helen was also troubled and acutely aware that whereas data analysis and write-up might be important to academics, our implicit reciprocal contract with the community had not been achieved. For example, although we understood more about the impact of top-down, state-controlled leadership on social capital, the research had not advanced the community's ability to prevent further harm through depopulation and the lack of a clear, shared vision for the town. Writing and editing for this volume encouraged me to engage in a reflective process using Fook's (2002) critical reconstructive process to help me identify the research limitations, given Helen's concerns and my own disquiet. This reflective process involves four steps: deconstructing what has happened; resisting dominant discourses; challenging and changing oppressive elements affecting practice; and reconstructing towards new discourses and structures (Fook, 2002).

Deconstructing: reflecting on a sense of disquiet

Through writing and reflecting, I came to see my disquiet as emanating from my reluctance to establish and clarify strategies to manage the power disparities inevitable in research related to disaster management (Smith, Mikow & Houston-Vega, 2010). I realised that I had failed to declare (from the beginning, to myself and to others) my aspiration to undertake activist research which could expose the limitations of state power during disaster recovery, something which had become obvious to me during my early visits to Yarloop. However, my aspiration sat at odds with my research proposal and grant application, which had attempted to be a credible, objective study of leadership in emergency management. My naivety in this has continued to astound me because I should have known better. Twenty years previously I had researched the human service response and recovery processes following a cliff collapse at Gracetown in the far South-west in which nine people died. I had found that similar to other disaster responses, the needs of the agents of control (such as the police and state government agencies) took precedence over the needs of the bereaved (Davis & Scraton, 1999). Further, my research found that despite emerging best practice guidelines in emergency management designed to empower local leaders, the transfer of authority and decision-making from the state to local leaders had not happened readily or easily (Palmer, 2001). This earlier study was protracted and fraught with power disparities and relationship dilemmas. It had taught me that power dynamics sit in all stages of emergency management (including retrospective research) and that any research methodology needs to be cognisant of this and clear about its intent and authorisation.

Fook's second stage in the process towards reconstruction is resistance, which she describes as "refusing to accept or participate in aspects of dominant discourses which work to disempower" (2002, p. 95). What had caused me to be so easily co-opted into undertaking a conformist research approach with findings which could easily be dismissed due to the small "sample" size and perceptions of bias? More importantly, what had prevented me from engaging in a more egalitarian and participatory research process which could leave the community with a stronger sense of ownership and empowerment as a result of the research process itself? These were not comfortable questions to consider. Inter-related with this was the need to challenge my practice, which Fook describes as the process of "identification or labelling of both the existence and operation of discourses and that which is hidden, glossed over or assumed" (2002, p. 95).

I was aware that I had resisted the taken-for-granted discourses and assumptions about the necessity for state control when I had initially visited Yarloop, and this resistance had continued. I was sceptical, like many others, about the need for an eight-month asbestos clean-up operation (which kept the town closed) and the unusual level of involvement by the Department of Premier and Cabinet. However, I had readily accepted the university requirement for the research grant to be expended by the end of the year and failed to challenge the assumption that this was realistic. In addition, I had succumbed to the disempowering discourses of objectivity in research and researcher-as-expert with its associated constructs of what knowledge is valued, how data is understood and analysed, what it means to be seen as "objective" and how research participants are engaged and treated (Stanley & Wise, 1993). These factors had the effect of separating me from the people I wanted to support and risked treating them in an objectified and instrumental way. Smith (2012) writes of the need for white, visiting researchers to decolonise their methodologies to avoid trampling on the *mana* (spirit) of the people. Her culturally sensitive principles resonate with my own values, and yet still I found myself acting differently when I stepped into the research space, out of step with my existing relationships and support for Yarloop.

Reconstructing: towards an activist research design

Fook's fourth stage of reflection is about reconstruction (change) and involves "formulating new discourses and structures" (2002, p. 96). For me this has meant formulating personal strategies to strengthen my confidence and experience with activist research such as co-operative inquiry (Godden, 2016; Reason, 1988) or community-based participatory research (Averill, 2006). Activist research involves an explicit critique of neo-liberal capitalism as an economic system underpinned by an ideology and values which entrenches competition, profit and a free market through practices such as privatisation, contracting out and small government. However, in its guises, neo-liberal governments overtly and covertly support industry and capital, purportedly in the interests of job creation, whereas job losses through automation and deregulation of the labour market are ignored (Springer, Birch & MacLeavy, 2016). Neo-liberalism is implicated in the oppression of nonhuman species and humans marginalised by the intersectionality of class, ethnicity and gender (Klein, 2007). Activist research as the logical companion of eco-social work forms part of the social movement that unifies the principles of environmental stewardship with social justice, which is also referred to as a just sustainability (Agyeman, 2013). Activist research, informed by eco-social work practices in the context of disaster response and recovery, can shine a light on the way power operates in a neo-liberal, capitalist environment to create and sustain social inequalities and ecological tragedies (Alston et al., 2019, pp. 59–78; Bell, 2015).

In hindsight, if I had a stronger sense of the significance and potential for overtly activist, eco-social work research at the time of writing the research proposal, the design would have been different. For example, a collaborative or participative inquiry group would have given me the time and legitimacy to explore how the mining and transport of bauxite to the Alcoa refinery accelerated the speed of the fire, which was noted in the inquiry report (Ferguson, 2016, pp. 16–17). Once I began to understand how the historical and political contexts of hazards (natural and human-induced) create the backdrop for slow and rapid onset disasters (Adamo, 2011; Alston, 2013), it was too late as it was outside the scope of the study as it had been designed. However, a participatory inquiry group could have become a space for local people to collectivise, discuss the implications of this information and use it on their terms, politically or legally. They would also have been contributing data and findings to contested areas of disaster research such as vulnerability versus risk as drivers of disaster response planning (Gillespie & Danso, 2010). The potential value of participative inquiry research methods, informed by critical theory (Fook, 2016) and radical humanism (Paulston, 1996), is that it can be radical, activist and transformational.

Fook describes PAR as a reflexive methodology in which knowledge is created collaboratively through the research process that allows for "researcher interaction with research participants and for research respondents to participate as researchers in a joint process of data collection" using methods which loop one to the other (2002, p. 29). It is a methodology which was used successfully for an extensive study into the disaster recovery process following the February 2009 Black Saturday bush fires in the Australian state of Victoria (Taylor & Goodman, 2015). Tehan illustrates this methodology's potential, describing the study report as one which:

> Provides in-depth analysis of systemic power relationships and politics at play during a time of extraordinary demand, need and change. It provides a new model for future emergency management that is place-based, community-led and centred on a shift to building general community resilience.
> (2015, n.p.)

Conclusion

The chapter describes a 2016 research project, funded by a small research grant from my employer, ECU. The research explored the issue of leadership in disaster recovery by interviewing interested people from Yarloop in the immediate aftermath of a devastating bush fire. The research was undertaken on the strength of my pre-existing relationships with some of the Yarloop residents and a desire to contribute to the town's recovery. The research findings confirmed my understanding of the importance of the role of transformational leadership approaches that enhance a community's social capital as an integral part of disaster response and recovery management. This finding in turn was consistent with more extensive studies in disaster management. The chapter brings a focus to the limitations of the research design, where my highly valued relationship-based way of working and being in community was not sufficiently included in the research design. I show how I came to understand the disquiet I was feeling after the research by using a reflective process of deconstruction and reconstruction.

Some of the dominant ideas about leadership, disaster response and academic research combined to limit my capacity to be consistent with my own eco-activist values and practice. An overtly activist, participative inquiry approach to the research study would have been preferable to the one I used as it would have enabled a greater sense of empowerment and ownership by the study participants. Further, it may have resulted in a clearer sense of community authorisation of the research and direction for future work in the town, which has been, and continues to be, affected by slow and rapid onset disasters. I am reminded again of the importance of reflective practice especially at the intersections of power between myself, the academy, government, industry and communities.

References

Adamo, S. (2011). *Slow onset hazards and population displacement in the context of climate change*. Paper presented at the Protection Gaps and Responses: Challenges and Opportunities Conference. New York, USA: John Jay College of Justice, City University of New York.

Agyeman, J. (2013). *Introducing just sustainabilities: Policy, planning and practices.* London, UK: Zed Books.

Alcoa. (2002). *Alcoa Wagerup land management revised proposal.* Perth, Australia: Alcoa World Alumina.

Alston, M. (2013). Introducing gender and climate change: Research, policy and action. In M. Alston & K. Whittenbury (Eds.), *Research, action and policy: Addressing the gendered impacts of climate change* (pp. 3–14). London, UK: Springer.

Alston, M., Hazeleger, T. & Hargraeaves, D. (2019). *Social work and disasters: A handbook for practice.* Abingdon, UK: Routledge.

Averill, J. (2006). Getting started: Initiating critical ethnography and community-based action research in a program of rural health studies. *International Journal of Qualitative Methods, 5*(2), 1–8.

Bell, S. (2015). Bridging activism and the academy: Exposing environmental injustices through the feminist ethnographic method of photovoice. *Human Ecology Review, 21*(1), 27–58.

Brueckner, M. & Ross, D. (2010). *Under corporate skies: A struggle between people, place and profit.* Fremantle, Australia: Fremantle Press.

Community Alliance for Positive Solutions (CAPS). (2019). *Yarloop fire.* Retrieved from https://caps6218.org.au/doccats/yarloop-fire/

Davis, H. & Scraton, P. (1999). Institutionalised conflict and the subordination of 'loss' in the immediate aftermath of UK mass fatality disasters. *Journal of Contingencies and Crisis Management, 7*(2), 86–97.

Dubrin, A., Dalglish, C. & Miller, P. (2006). *Leadership* (2nd Asia-Pacific ed.). Milton, Australia: John Wiley & Sons.

Ferguson, E. (2016). *Reframing rural fire management: Report of the special inquiry into the January 2016 Waroona fire.* Retrieved from http://apo.org.au/files/Resource/waroona_fires_2016_volume_1_final_1.pdf

Fook, J. (2002). *Social work: Critical theory and practice.* London, UK: Sage Publications.

Fook, J. (2016). *Social work: A critical approach to practice* (3rd ed.). London, UK: Sage Publications.

Gillespie, D. & Danso, K. (2010). Vulnerability: The central concept of disaster curriculum. In D. Gillespie & K. Danso (Eds.), *Disaster concepts and issues: A guide for social work education and practice* (pp. 3–14). Alexandria, USA: Council on Social Work Education.

Godden, N. (2016). A co-operative inquiry about love using narrative, performative and visual methods. *Qualitative Research, 17*(1), 3–19.

Godden, N. (2018). Love in community work in rural Timor-Leste: A co-operative inquiry for a participatory framework of practice. *Community Development Journal, 53*(1), 78–98. doi:10.1093/cdj/bsw022

Hale, C. (2001). What is activist research? Items & issues. *Social Science Research Council, 2*(1–2), 13–15.

Klein, N. (2007). *The shock doctrine: The rise of disaster capitalism.* New York, USA: Metropolitan Books.

Nakagawa, Y. & Shaw, R. (2004). Social capital: A missing link to disaster recovery. *International Journal of Mass Emergencies and Disasters, 22*(1), 5–34.

Northouse, P. (2010). *Leadership: Theory and practice* (5th ed.). Thousand Oaks, USA: Sage Publications.

Palmer, M. (2001). Doing it by the book: A paradox in disaster management. *Australian Journal of Emergency Management,* Spring, 40–44.

Paulston, R. (Ed.). (1996). *Social cartography: Mapping ways of seeing social and educational change.* New York, USA: Garland Publishing.

Quantz, R. (1992). On critical ethnography (with some postmodern considerations). In M. LeCompte, W. Millroy & J. Preissle (Eds.), *The handbook of qualitative research in education*. San Diego, USA: Academic Press.

Reason, P. (1988). The co-operative inquiry group. In P. Reason (Ed.), *Human inquiry in action: Development in new paradigm research*, (pp. 18–39). London, UK: Sage Publications.

Ross, D. (2009). Emphasizing the 'social' in corporate social responsibility: A social work perspective. In S. Idowu & W. Leal Filho (Eds.). *Professional perspectives of corporate social responsibility* (pp. 301–318). Frankfurt, Germany: Peter Lang.

Sharp, C. (2004). *Report for the standing committee on environment and public affairs in relation to the Alcoa refinery at Wagerup inquiry*. Perth, Australia: Government of Western Australia.

Smith, L. (2012). *Decolonising methodologies: Research and Indigenous People*. London, UK: Zed Books.

Smith, M., Mikow, J. & Houston-Vega, M. (2010). Teaching disaster-related practice: Postmodern and social justice perspectives. In D. Gillespie & K. Danso (Eds.), *Disaster concepts and issues: A guide for social work education and practice* (pp. 61–88). Alexandria, USA: Council on Social Work Education.

Springer, S., Birch, K. & MacLeavy, J. (Eds.). (2016). *Handbook of neoliberalism*. New York, USA: Routledge.

Stanley, L. & Wise, S. (1993). *Breaking out again: Feminist ontology and epistemology*. London, UK: Routledge.

Tafvelin, S., Hywonen, U. & Westerberg, K. (2012). Transformational leadership in the social work context: The importance of leadership continuity and co-worker support. *British Journal of Social Work*, 44(4), 886–904.

Taylor, D. & Goodman, H. (2015). *Place-based and community-led specific disaster preparedness and generalisable community resilience*. Retrieved from www.ccam.org.au/site/DefaultSite/filesystem/documents/Place-Based%20and%20Community-Led_FINAL.pdf

Tehan, B. (2015). *Sharing power to achieve shared responsibility*. Retrieved from https://vcoss.org.au/analysis/sharing-power-to-achieve-shared-responsibility/

Valero, J., Jung, K. & Andrew, S. A. (2015). Does transformational leadership build resilient public and nonprofit organizations? *Disaster Prevention and Management*, 24(1), 4–20.

Chapter 4

Just(ice) arts in practice
Processes and collaborations

Helen Seiver

I acknowledge that the work we undertook in the locality of Yarloop happened on the contested country of the Noongar People of South-West WA.

Introduction

The authors of the two previous chapters have written about Yarloop's struggle both against the impact from Alcoa's operations and also the bush fire. I extend this context by acknowledging, albeit briefly, the Noongar First Nation People's connection to land in the Yarloop area.

The place name Yarloop is Aboriginal in origin, from the language of the local Binjareb or Pindjarup people (State Library of Western Australia, 2016). Yarloop is situated in the Shire of Harvey, WA. The 2014 Shire Municipal Heritage Inventory states that specific Aboriginal stories of the area are not well-known and that further research is needed, although it can be assumed sites of Aboriginal occupation are numerous (Shire of Harvey, 2014). The continuing habitation of the Yarloop area by Aboriginal People since colonisation is evidenced in documents and living memory according to conversations with community members who recall, for example, Jack Davis the activist and playwright, Aboriginal members of the town football teams and local school attendance. Currently, there are approximately 30,000 people of Noongar ancestry who have survived colonisation (Government of Western Australia, 2018), not given up their culture or identity and continue to fight for recognition and self-determination. In 2015, some 87 years after a deputation by Noongar William Harris to parliament, Noongar Elders and state leaders met to sign agreements comprising the South-West Native Title Settlement enabling the passage of the Noongar Korrah, Nitja, Boordahwan (Past, Present, Future) Recognition Bill (Government of Western Australia, 2016). Although our research and process did not address the Noongar People's issues of dispossession or absence from key decisions about the lands and operations occurring on it, it is important to acknowledge that in the context of social justice research, there are evident parallels with Aboriginal history, contested space, power inequalities and recovery from summarily imposed events.

This chapter will speak to two periods of community arts practice with the people of Yarloop expressing those parallels. In the first instance art was used to respond to the validation and care needs of the small community in conflict with Alcoa and, more recently, with the same community, although with different members, after a devastating bush fire. The first section of the chapter explains the guiding ideas that informed my engagement with the community and industry. The second section of the chapter describes the just(ice) arts projects and my understanding of their value for the participants.

My role in the first instance, in 2002–2004, was as a community artist employed by Edith Cowan University (ECU) in Bunbury, WA. I was a member of a team of social researchers exploring respectful dialogue as a means to resolve problematic issues being experienced by this small community and the multinational mining company. The challenge for me was to realise an arts process which enabled multiple voices through community and industry collaboration. The choice of disposable cameras brought with it the freedoms necessary to express both personal viewpoint and individual voice. In the second instance, 2017, I was involved as a community artist employed by the local government in the Shire of Harvey to facilitate a series of sculpture workshops, working with materials recovered from the fire ground. The ethos of the workshops was to enable recovery and to support community resilience after the fires and the prolonged period of some nine months before residents could resume living in Yarloop.

This was a particular type of community art requiring a particular mix of capacities as the visiting artist. To be naïve about, or insensitive to, the concerns, distress and tensions in the community would have added to their burden. It was clear, as an outsider engaging people in creative expression at such profound times, that I needed an eye for justice and a heart for the people. This is an account of my time with some of the people of Yarloop, of how I came to deeply care for them and to appreciate the important role of art in justice struggles and healing from the trauma of human-made and natural disasters.

Ideas informing just(ice) art

This section outlines the ideas that were informing my arts practice during these two tumultuous periods in Yarloop's history. The connecting thread between the ideas is the value of a justice arts approach in contested places and spaces where major power disparities and harm are occurring. The ideas embedded in my practice are described in the heart section of the chapter and are presented here in a more analytical way to convey the potential value of the ideas in similar situations in other places and countries.

Traditional methods of research and data gathering were judged to be inappropriate in this complex setting. Instead, a community cultural development approach was adopted. This approach involves the creation of flexible spaces where the participants could come together and contribute. This was paramount to the respectful power sharing and meaningful dialogue in both periods. Country Arts Network Western Australia states that "the creation of settings in which people engage . . . is at the heart of the community cultural development process" (cited in Sonn, Drew & Kasat, 2002, p. 17). Although our processes were not aimed at creating a formal cultural plan, the principle of engaging people in making meaning and valuing the matters of importance to them placed culture affirmation and culture building at the centre of the arts projects. To enable this, we needed a safe space that could hold the diversity and complexity of each community member's experiences – a space where the boundaries of power, history and community all intersect but, essentially, a place of no fixed position. Bhabha states that "the boundary becomes the place from which something begins its presencing" (1994, p. 5). He further states that "it is in the emergence of the interstices – the overlap and displacement of domains of difference – that the intersubjective and collective experiences of . . . community interest, of cultural value are negotiated" (Bhabha, 1994, p. 2). This is Bhabha's idea of third space. Ross (2017), in speaking to the social justice research in Yarloop, interprets Bhabha's third space as a dialogic space where parties attend meetings without duress and in good faith to progress a power-sensitive conversation based on an ethic of love. An ethic of love involves responding to issues of social and ecological conflict by holding powerful entities accountable for the harm experienced by the impacted stakeholders (Ross, 2017; and see Chapter 10).

The aim was to engage members of the community and industry in a safe space that was constantly enabled by a supportive third party, in this instance myself in the role of a community artist. We needed an adaptable, protected setting of respect, of equality, of being heard and of having contributing voices in seeking just and sustainable outcomes. To maintain and sustain the third space, community cultural development (CCD), PAR and cultural mapping (community art) were all seen as relevant methodologies. The mix of these methods would uphold the exploration of both a negotiated agreement in the first time period and also a place to explore community grief in the second period. CCD is "quintessentially an enabling practice" (Sonn et al., 2002, p. 3) which values each community and its significance – the tangible and intangible culture, the traditions, beliefs and history of an individual community with the goal to empower and validate people. Supporting CCD, PAR is a "method which operates from the assertion that in research, those most affected by a social issue should be key players in any research" (Ayala & Zaal, 2016, p. 2). PAR involves repeating cycles of action and reflection on that action with the community members participating as co-researchers exploring topics of concern and interest to them. Finally, as a strategic process, cultural mapping via community art was employed to contribute to the building of a "vital, safe and prosperous community" (Kasat, 2003, n.p.). Cultural mapping involves exploration of processes which value and celebrate the uniqueness of a community. Additionally, participation in processes like community arts facilitates conversations and encourages critical reflexivity by participants because they are often exposed to stories and community members with whom they have had little contact. The exposure asks that they review their beliefs of themselves and the community, resulting in new relationships and stories (Madyaningrum, 2011). This creates potential for new understandings of shared experiences and issues and can result in empowerment to challenge dominant interest groups. Freire explains this process of critical reflexivity as conscientisation where "people must first critically analyse causes [of issues], so that through transforming action they can create a new situation, one which makes possible the pursuit of a fuller humanity" (1970, p. 29). The justice art processes sought to provide a space where people could feel validated and where art provided the potential for transformative action.

These approaches provided the flexibility and versatility needed to respond to the many interconnected conflicts (historical, political and social) of the community in its numerous compounded crises. The processes affirmed both the large and small histories and lived experiences of the community which saw itself as disempowered and undervalued as an excluded voice. In pursuing these practices, the unique social and cultural capital of the Yarloop community was revealed. Dekker and Uslaner refer to social capital as the valuing of social networks comprising the bonds of like-minded people and also a bridging between disparate people within normal standards of reciprocity (2001, pp. 1–8). Similarly, Bourdieu refers to cultural capital as "acknowledging a community, and their sense of collective identity and of a shared history and group positioning" (1979/1984, p. 66). These methods created a contextualised research framework which recognised and responded to the historical and social experiences and community meaning of Yarloop. Additionally, the methods were able to foster and enable community building and to create "opportunities for dialogue to break down barriers, to share understandings" (Sonn et al., 2002, p. 3). In summary, the methodologies presented responsive processes, specific and relevant to what most mattered to the people of Yarloop.

A further issue of contention was that the historical, social and economic basis of Yarloop was seen (by a large proportion of residents) to be irrelevant, and this presented as a potentially distressing lack of vision for the future. Kasat states that "the visioning process needs to be anchored in the past, recognise the present and then and only then we can begin to imagine the future" (2003, n.p.). In support of a visioning endeavour, I note that Sandcock speaks of community arts as a process to support a "way of knowing and experiencing a community [and also] a means of explicating and legitimising local knowledge" (cited in Sonn et al., 2002, p. 20). A legitimate visioning process needs to concede to local knowledges to be authentic, to be incorporated into the social capital of the community, and here the cultural mapping process revalued Yarloop's past to assist in the creation a future vision for the town and its community.

Significantly, in both time periods and scenarios, the processes worked organically with none of the processes directed towards or by an outcome, that is, they were unfettered by formal methodologies of being guided to a particular object or outcome. There was a more gradual direction finding using informal action–reflection cycles typical of PAR. However, there was an understanding on my part, from previous community arts practice, of how some of the processes could assist to progress this dialogue.

Both projects were guided by the community's responses to the materials and the loosely held methodology being presented. In the first time period, this involved the use of disposable cameras as a tool for recording and exploring, and in the second, a sculptural workshop approach was employed, using retrieved personal items after the fire. Both material-based methods were selected to fulfil the organic nature of the process. An additional critical element of the success of both periods involved my professional engagement with participants, taking time to listen and to affirm and celebrate their contributions. Also, it gave opportunity for me, the researcher, to hear and listen to a history or an issue or a life in a personal one-to-one manner with an ethical ear of justice and compassion, informed by my own life experiences of crises. Further, that the processes were successful was also due to them having been participant directed and process driven, therefore able to evolve and change with the variety of responses from the participants. Freire describes this as "the invention of unity in diversity", for when action and reflection are united, they become creative (cited in Crotty, 1998, p. 151). Both time periods also benefited from the *communitas* generated by this shared common experience. Turner (1969, p. 132) states that *communitas* involves the "sharing of a common experience, a rite of passage like surviving the bush fire" and brings everyone onto an equal level with the benefit of the "transient personal experience of togetherness" (Turner, 1974, pp. 273–274).

Creative hearts and hands: the story of just(ice) arts in Yarloop

This section will discuss the two periods of community arts practice in more detail, exploring a cultural mapping dialogue using disposable cameras in the first instance, followed in the latter period using community sculptural workshops.

A just(ice) space by means of photographic images

When I first worked with this community in crisis between 2002 and 2004, there were grave divisions not only between the community and Alcoa but also among individual community members due to the many contentious issues. These included the purchase of homes by Alcoa, wishing to create a noise barrier between the town and the nearby refinery. There was also inequitable treatment of residents by Alcoa depending on where their homes were situated as the result of an arbitrary line drawn on the town map indicating Zone A or Zone B, which catastrophically affected home valuations (see Chapter 2). Additionally, there was bitter conflict between residents who wanted to sell their properties and those who didn't and who saw the changes in the community as destructive. A further division was evident between those residents employed or not employed in the nearby refinery and also residents whose health was negatively affected by the emissions from the refinery. Many residents from these multiple standpoints felt unheard, that they had no voice – indeed they felt silenced and that they were not being treated with respect and fairness.

Yarloop was settled in the mid-1800s as part of white settlers' possession of Aboriginal land. In the last century it flourished as a timber town. Until recent times, it had been a stable, established community, with some families having four living generations bringing their traditions and customs to the society and culture of the town. This was a small, rural town of approximately 600 people with strong social and cultural capital. The conflict brought disruption, uncertainty and insecurity to this previously stable town life. Giving equal voice to the residents, whether in favour of or against the refinery and the corporation's impositions, was important to the process: it needed to give voice to everyone whatever their standpoint. Many of the initial contacts were made in the domestic spaces of Yarloop on the invitation of interested residents. This preliminary communication opened a map of the daily lived experience of residents, each offering their own unique and different point of view in the intimacy of their own homes. Listening to and affirming the stories and concerns formed a major part of the cultural mapping process. The creation of this dialogic space enabled a support framework to begin the processes of empowerment and problem-solving.

A simple but effective arts process to further the cultural map of Yarloop was to invite the residents to become contributing researchers through using disposable cameras. Community members were invited to capture images of whatever made Yarloop a desirable or undesirable place to live and work. Approximately 40 cameras were given to the community to identify and document local cultural resources. Contributions were sought from Yarloop residents, both young and old, and also the employees of the Alcoa Wagerup refinery, to complete this cultural mapping of Yarloop. After the films were developed, I sat with each of the photographers, writing on the backs of the photos the reasons why the images were taken and describing what they saw as being vital to their community and their families or their places of work. Taking time to listen and record their words was an important step in the process as it began the validation and recognition of individual voices, acknowledging that each individual voice was significant and necessary in finding a solution to the crisis. Positive photographs were taken of family and friends, pets, the town war memorial, renovated homes, beautiful gardens. Negative images were also taken of the refinery smoke stacks (emissions) and the frequent freight trains driven through the heart of the town (noise) carrying the alumina product of the refinery. The images were indicative of the disruption to what many residents saw as their previously comfortable, stable lives. The processes of mapping created a sense of we-ness as well as recording the community identity, its stories, what it held as sacred, its values, and the intangible essence of the place.

The resulting collection of photographs was attached to the interior walls of the old hairdresser's shop in Yarloop's main street, which was being used as the ECU research office. Over time this became a moving, powerful socio/geographic pictorial map, recording the community and their concerns. By the conclusion of the activity, the photographs covered all four walls and part of the ceiling. This little abandoned hairdresser's shop functioned as the safe space, a drop-in centre and meeting place for both the community and the company. It was a safe space for both sides of the dispute, an effective third space that didn't shy away from the issues of power and harm and functioned from a place of justice and loving kindness. Sharing personal stories meant being heard for perhaps the first time. Stories that included positive family memories, health impacts, the proximity to the refinery, the noise impact, loss of organic food farming status, continuing employment for the younger generation and unfair financial dealing with regard to real estate valuations. It was also a safe place to dispute or give alternative opinions and was sometimes a place of discomfort. Essentially however, being surrounded by these images of the community, taken by the community, enabled and deepened the expression of many emotions and thoughts, some perhaps too painful or without words to express.

The juxtaposition of these often disparate images was powerful – placed side by side, neighbour with neighbour, positive and negative, family space with industrial space, with all given an equal and respectful place. They illustrated a small country town with a continuing story of social competency and cultural continuity but also exposed the grief and sorrow and the cultural, economic and social impacts of the dispute. It recorded and illustrated the loss of friends who sold their properties, businesses that shut their doors, including the closure of the local service station and grocery store. This aspect of the process vividly illustrated the function of PAR in community arts. Additionally, by sitting at kitchen tables or in the garden, listening to the stories and concerns, and taking time to write those stories was beneficial not only to the photographers, who had their image choices validated, but also enabled a greater understanding for me of the depth of feeling, sensitivity and perceptive consideration needed to be of value as a community arts worker and researcher. The value for me was in the two-way mutuality of the creative work which arose from seeing the concerns represented as an image rather than only listening, hearing and then imagining.

Another dynamic use of the disposable cameras involved inviting community members and employees of the mining company writing their sentiments on an A3-size piece of paper and have a photograph taken of themselves holding that message. To give credence to this part of the project, I was first introduced to individual community members by a trusted resident. This step was important as it placed the process and ECU in a position of trust and, of course, responsibility. This was especially significant for the residents who had conflicted issues with the company as they would be clearly and publicly stating their views to both the wider community and the company. Both positive and negative concerns were written. The vision for these images was to give voice to those who felt they were silenced or ignored, and the resulting images clearly gave face and voice to those wanting to stand up and be heard. In many cases this caused further conflict (see examples in Brueckner & Ross, 2010).

An example of one unsuccessful process undertaken at this time occurred during one of the monthly Alcoa managerial board meetings to which ECU was invited at their refinery. A selection of these photographic messages was inserted into café table stands, placed on the boardroom table and located at empty chairs. The intention was to give voice to those not present or, more importantly, those not/never invited to meet and discuss their concerns at these board meetings. Unfortunately, Alcoa management refused to begin the meeting until the photographic images were packed away. This was an unashamed and political use of the images, and it failed perhaps because the company felt undermined and threatened by this form of exploration, clearly from one side of the debate.

The final collection of photographs was taken from my outsider point of view, that of the artist researcher, and included both Yarloop town and environs, the historic Yarloop Railway Workshops and the Wagerup refinery. This outsider view was an affirmation to the community that their place was significant and worthwhile from someone who had listened to and heard the complexity of the issues, earned trust and responded with consideration and heart for the people.

Further, Yarloop had lived with industry (The Railway Workshops) for approximately 100 years and survived. The purpose of placing photographs taken in the historic workshops with photographs of the refinery was to support the idea that Yarloop could survive with the current industry, that is, the refinery. It was a view of the past and the present to give rise to a vision of a sustainable future for Yarloop, especially given the social and cultural upheavals being experienced. Paraphrasing Fortune (2000), Yarloop once stood at the centre of the world's timber production and supported a quintessential WA country town and vibrant community.

Some time after I had resigned from my position in Yarloop, one of the mining company public relations officers contacted me and asked to meet. We met in a coffee shop in Bunbury, where he related what the effect of that just(ice) space, the photographs, had had on him. He related that he felt physically sick being in the space surrounded by the community concerns and also that he felt compelled to resign from his role and was now studying environmental politics. I relate this story as it eloquently speaks to the effectiveness of a discreet social and political space in a situation of conflict and community suffering.

The photographs cut through company policy to the actual lived experiences of the community and motivated personal change through awareness of shared humanity.

The main anticipated result of the long two-year process in 2002–2004 which was not achieved related to property values, namely, a guarantee by Alcoa that it would give protection of their property values for the life of the refinery. Nevertheless, the photographic project did give voice to those who did not feel heard. The photographs included and supported both criticism and praise of the complex matters being researched and discussed and also the validation of the process of how the concerns of the community of Yarloop could be heard through a respectful dialogue with such a large corporation. The photographs stand as a valuable historical document, especially in light of the town's destruction by fire, and as a valuable social justice exploration document. When a community carries out these types of activities to map their unique culture, the spin-offs for the community are rich and ongoing. For example, individuals benefited from development of personal networks, enhanced feelings of being part of a growing community, opportunities for dialogue to break down barriers, the creation of shared understandings and the potential of community building. Perceived benefits for the wider community included enhanced awareness of community resources, creation of a shared vision and a foundation for further processes which encourage the creation of common goals and purpose. Yarloop at this particular time needed vital community capacity building to not only unite the new residents with the old but also to vision a shared future for the town.

Yarloop has persisted as a contested space for those both with power and those who feel powerless and as a divided community of the socially included and the socially excluded and of the respected and disrespected.

Recovery and regrowth sculpture project

The latter period of community art involvement, November 2017, relates to the Recovery and Resilience Sculpture Workshops and exhibition, undertaken with the Yarloop community after the devastating bush fires of 2016. These fires raged for 17 days. Two residents died, 181 properties including the historic and iconic Railway Workshops, more than 69,000 hectares, including valuable beef and dairy farmland, and fencing were destroyed. The fire's perimeter was in excess of 392 kilometres (ABC, 2016).

The local government Shire of Harvey became the umbrella organisation for a variety of community gatherings over the next two years. These gatherings functioned as a place of reunion for the now scattered residents living in surrounding areas. In addition, the Harvey Bushfire Recovery Group proposed a number of creative workshops including sculpture and working with objects retrieved from the fires. The workshops took place in one of the few surviving Yarloop community buildings, the Community Resource Centre (CRC).

Placing the workshops in this survivor building was important to the *communitas* of the group as it represented not only their past social capital but now the present, sharing a common experience. The creation of a safe and supported space, a third space, was essential due to the emotional weight of not only the materials used but also the recent nature of the trauma – less than two years since the devastation. The workshop process created and upheld this safe space for talking and crying, for mourning and grieving as well as for individual creativity.

The first workshop day included one-to-one discussions, careful listening, hearing fire stories and then consideration for the recovered materials and feedback to build on design ideas. The process was organic without set methodology, allowing each participant to work spontaneously with their own memories, grief and recovered treasures, thus facilitating their own recovery. The aim was to support participants to tell their stories in their own way and to validate their voices. The small survivor objects represented the remnants of a life lived and therefore a meaningful material to explore recovery and resilience. Creating from that authentic piece of life contributed to a future whereby the newly constructed objects held both memory and vision, respecting the life that was and the life to come. Each piece of retrieved object comprised a third space: a border between and an interstice between the past and the future. The reverence with which these everyday objects were handled and spoken of transformed them into the sacred.

As the workshops evolved everyone became more confident and positive with their sculptural projects. Handling the recovered and surviving traces of their lives had a profound effect on the atmosphere of the workshop: silence at first and then conversations of memories, loss and meaning; recovered emotions and feelings through touching these objects; and shared grief not only from the loss of their homes, possessions and animals, but loss of friendships, of community and social culture, shared facilities and clubs. For some, the loss encompassed the entirety of the lives they knew. Support and comforting among the participants was sincere, loving and kind, thus enabling reflective and thoughtful reminiscence. This was not unexpected when it is realised that this handling concerned the remnant symbols of that community's shared memories, sometimes accumulated over a lifetime or even several generations. Each artefact took on an immeasurable importance as it represented a trace of their collective histories. There was shared affinity in working this way, allowing individual expression of collective experience and emotions. This resonated as a (further) expression of *communitas*.

Working with the recovered objects gave me the opportunity to hear the personal story of not only that participant's grief but also to acknowledge the authentic life which that small, burnt survivor-object represented. It was a profound way to process the aftermath of this traumatic event. An example of the positive impact of art is in a letter sent to me by a participant after the workshops. She explained that as a result of the ongoing grief and tragedies, she had been unable to be creative. However, the sculpture workshops rekindled in her a voice to express not only her grief but also kindness as experienced from strangers post-fire. An unexpected benefit from the workshops was that her husband also became inspired to create. In her words, "We are in a creative flow that just keeps going . . . it also is a journey, finding the beauty in life and carrying it with us" (with the author's permission).

What was witnessed during these workshops was a remarkable building of community capacity. It was and is a place and space to nurture and foster the community's recovery and a place to witness a community making, talking, laughing and crying together. The workshops also cemented friendships, elevated and enriched both the personal as well as community spirit and forged a determination to thrive as a community.

The Recovery and Regrowth Art Exhibition opened Friday, 5 January 2018, at the nearby Harvey Recreation and Cultural Centre. Seeing their works included in this exhibition, as well as the response to the works from the viewers, further enriched the community experience of making art. For me it both validated and endorsed the process and my own community arts practice as I heard recently that each Monday women come together in the Yarloop CRC and create.

Conclusion

What was seen during these two periods of community arts practice was the expression of emotions and private considerations in an individual and beneficial manner, of being listened to, having voice, creating from trauma, enabling a positive experience and sharing this with neighbours and friends. The community aspect of the practices contributed to the collective experience of processing the impacts of negative forces from outside the community and of creating meaning from the remnants and traces of a life lived in that community. This amounted to a common expression of not only shared grief but shared support – if you like, the nurturing of a stable continuity for the community. The works created by residents from Yarloop and surrounding communities illuminate the importance of creative expression. Seen here, art in its many forms was understood as central to people's capacity to survive and make sense of their lives in which external and unwelcome factors affected their wellbeing, their community and the local environment.

Acknowledgement

I would like to acknowledge Joshua Ledger for his invaluable shaping and critiquing of the chapter.

References

Australian Broadcasting Commission. (2016). *All clear given for devastating Western Australian bushfire*. Retrieved from www.abc.net.au/news/2016-01-23/all-clear-given-for-devastating-western-australian-bushfire/7109708

Ayala, J. & Zaal, M. (2016). Poetics of justice: Using art as action and analysis in participatory action research. *Networks: An Online Journal for Teacher Research, 18*(1). https://dx.doi.org/10.4148/2470-6353.1019

Bhabha, H. (1994). *The location of culture*. London, UK: Routledge.

Bourdieu, P. (1979/84). *Distinction: A social critique of the judgement of taste*. Cambridge, MA, USA: Harvard University Press.

Brueckner, M. & Ross, D. (2010). *Under corporate skies: A struggle between people, place and profit*. Fremantle, Australia: Fremantle Press.

Crotty, M. (1998). *The foundations of social research*. St Leonards, Australia: Allen and Unwin.

Dekker, P. & Uslaner, E. (2001). Introduction. In E. Uslaner (Ed.), *Social capital and participation in everyday life* (pp. 1–8). London, UK: Routledge.

Fortune, G. (2000). *Yarloop, there was no better place*. Mandurah, Australia: Interesting Publications.

Freire, P. (1970). *Pedagogy of the oppressed*. London, UK: Penguin.

Government of Western Australia. (2016). *Noongar Korrah, Nitja, Boordahwan (Past, Present, Future) recognition Bill*. Retrieved from www.legislation.wa.gov.au/legislation/statutes.nsf/main_mrtitle_13755_homepage.html

Government of Western Australia. (2018). *Noongar history: South West Native Title Settlement*. Retrieved from www.dpc.wa.gov.au/swnts/Noongar-Heritage-and-History/Pages/Noongar-History.aspx

Kasat, P. (2003). *Cultural planning course book*. Western Australia, Australia: Country Arts Network.

Madyaningrum, M. (2011). *Exploring the meaning of participation in a community art project: A case study on the seeming project*. Retrieved from http://vuir.vu.edu.au/9113/1/Community%20Art%20%20Participation%20(Post%20Review%20Revision2).pdf

Ross, D. (2017). A research-based model for corporate social responsibility: Towards accountability to impacted stakeholders. *Journal of Corporate Social Responsibility, 2*(8), 1–11.

Shire of Harvey. (2014). *Shire of Harvey municipal heritage inventory*. Retrieved from www.harvey.wa.gov.au/wp-content/uploads/sites/161/2015/08/Shire-of-Harvey-Municipal-Heritage-Inventory-2014-v1.2-Pages-15-94.pdf

Sonn, C., Drew, N. & Kasat, P. (2002). *Conceptualising community cultural development: The role of cultural planning in community change*. Perth, Australia: Community Arts Network WA Inc.

State Library of Western Australia. (2016). *Yarloop: A small town with a big name*. Retrieved from https://slwa.wordpress.com/2016/01/18/yarloop-a-small-town-with-a-big-history/

Turner, V. (1969). *The ritual process: Structure and anti-structure*. New York, USA: Aldine Transaction.

Turner, V. (1974). *Dramas, fields, and metaphors: Symbolic action in human society*. Ithaca, USA: Cornell University Press.

Chapter 5

The wrong side of native title, the right side of mining

Michael Woodley

Introduction: setting the scene

In 2007 Australian Liberal Senator Vanstone asked "why are lands-rich Aborigines 'dirt poor'" and pondered "why are the traditional owners of the land the poorest people living on it?" (cited in Altman, 2009a, p. 2). These questions illustrate part of the paradox of plenty, which highlights how the dependence of nations on the enormous wealth from mineral resources co-exists with extreme economic inequality (Altman, 2009a, p. 5). This issue particularly affects Indigenous People in Australia where 60% of mining occurs in remote areas adjacent to Aboriginal communities (Altman, 2009b, p. 17). The questions posed and this paradox are at the centre of the story of how my Yindjibarndi People of North-west WA are fighting Fortescue Mining Group (FMG) in the courts for the sovereign rights to our homelands.

Justice for First Nation People is a struggle that reflects the negative impact of the continuation of colonialism to the present time with governments in handmaiden relationships with powerful multinational mining companies (Bauman, Streiein & Weir, 2013). It is an ongoing challenge to sustain our community and culture in this context. Cleary (2017, p. 25) conveys the disproportionate financial gains of big business in the Pilbara by describing how the iron ore trains travelling from the mines to port for shipping overseas are two kilometres long, comprise 200 wagons of iron ore, with the income from 10 wagons paying royalties to the state government. Tellingly, of those 10 wagons, one wagon of income is paid to the traditional owners, which amounts to 0.5% royalty on the gross value of production (Cleary, 2017). The FMG mining company stands to generate tens of billions of dollars from land over which we won a Federal Court case in 2017 and secured exclusive rights after more than a decade of resistance to FMG. These exclusive rights are under challenge from FMG at the time of writing; this sits in a political context of few traditional owners succeeding in securing exclusive rights over their homelands.

My story shows the dark side of native title, where some of my people went against the Yindjibarndi Aboriginal Corporation, which has the legally authorised responsibilities in relation to Native Title, to be on the right side of the mining company.

Heart: a First Nation's leader's story

On the day of my birth my mother named me Michael, but my grandfather called me Migu, a name in my Yindjibarndi language of an emu walking off in the distance placidly. This is to say the emu has no care of the world behind him or what might be ahead as he moves along minding his own business but at the same time careful of his steps and always aware . . . known to the Yindjibarndi as Migumigu.

When I was in the sixth grade, my grandfather took me away from Roebourne into Yindjibarndi country, Ngurra, to a place where he started his work to relocate back to his homelands. He named that place Ngurrawanna, where his grandmother Wannie was born. It is classified as a remote community some 80 kilometres away from where we live today in Roebourne. My people were removed from their homelands in the early 19th century due to the pastoralist industry's growing need for more land for grazing for their sheep and cattle. The pastoralist industry in those times ruled and dominated the laws which these parts of Australia had to adhere to. The Pilbara region had some of the best natural landscapes with tall, sweet grasses and fresh-running waters. To this day it has some of the world's highest bio-diversity and pristine wilderness areas that has led to a booming tourism industry.

The home of my address, which is stated on my birth certificate, is where the Roebourne Aboriginal population lived. My people, the Yindjibarndi, who come from the tablelands (the high country) were forced into the township of Roebourne in the early 1900s. As occurred with other language groups of the west Pilbara area, we were gathered like immigrants and put into these reserve camps segregated from the rest of society and white first-class living. In 1974 the government moved the Aboriginal People from the reserve into the new residential government social housing in the town near the cemetery. It was designed for the purpose of blacks-only living; effectively we were suburbanised to split the family living structure. It was intended to fail because of closed-door policies to manage the Aboriginal expectations of self-determination. My people were not incorporated into the mainstream industrial revolution of the 1960s and 1970s that has made the Pilbara what it is today, an economic powerhouse (Cleary, 2017).

Kujura Reserve, also known to the locals as the Old Reserve, was a place where the living conditions were of a third world country. The hardships and struggles were reflected on each of the tin-shed houses we occupied, which gave a stark reminder of the realities and how my people lived. The summer sun's heat gave no favours to the Pilbara landscape. We lived through the summer in the Old Reserve with an average of more than 40 degrees Celsius temperatures, without fans or air-conditioning. Being trapped in those tin sheds and isolated to the reserve boundaries was the law of that time; at the same time development of the Pilbara iron ore industry was ramping up. Across our Nations white people were being flown in and partaking freely in a lifestyle made for a king. However, back in Kujura, leaving without permission was illegal and you could go to jail which was 100 times more dreadful than being confined to the Old Reserve. My people were forced to live in that confined, controlled environment. If one would argue, one would be made an example by imprisonment as white justice demanded. Eventually, it was agreed that Aboriginal People could spend time at the river but couldn't cross into the town centre. This made my people happy because it is what we've always done throughout history, moving close to the water among the gum and bark trees. This always cooled and comforted the life cycles of one generation to the next, and it supported our nomadic obligations, which is how we manage the Pilbara weather.

The Old Reserve tin sheds of panels, which made up each home from walls to roof, carried the unintentional and unforgiving battering of the sun's natural born features. It showed no mercy, gave no quarter and had total disregard for everyone. Old people say *Yurra nhantharri warjimagu*, the sun, is making us suffer. That is why the river comforts and protects the Ngarda from the Yurra, and although the sun gives its grief, the winter brought a whole different kind of pain. The old people would say *Muyu nhantharri warjimagu*, the winter is making us suffer; as the cold in some cases went below zero degrees Celsius. Once again my people couldn't move to combat the winter like through the summer as we would be near the river. When winter came my people would go to the Wura, a shelter place, that minimised the winter winds. Fire could burn without being hampered by the gusts that often came and stayed throughout the winter nights, chilling the bones of a dissolute people. This not only reminded us of mother nature's tough love for the land and the Yindjibarndi but also that this is your life and you have been made for it – never take it for granted. The old people's teaching is to never sink to the level of treating the land and the people the same way as we have been treated.

In my assessment, to say we lived a life of hopelessness would be an understatement. To say that life was tough would be to suggest that we had equal standing, which was morally insensitive for that particular time in our lives. But through it all the people were sober-ishly happy because we were together.

We have created a timeline on our website that gives a sense of white people's treatment of us and their intrusion into our lives and onto our lands (Yindjibarndi People, 2019). Key pieces of legislation which occurred in the 1960s and 1990s are noted in an extended timeline as follows:

1962

The federal government recognised the right to vote for Aboriginal and Torres Strait Islander People, with state governments subsequently enacting this legislation.

1967

A referendum changed the Australian constitution to remove discrimination against Aboriginal and Torres Strait Islander People, which gave Aboriginal People citizenship rights under the constitution.

Local Yindjibarndi People recall that citizenship did not improve their employment opportunities and that the introduction of equal pay for Aboriginal stockmen resulted in those still working in the pastoral industry losing their jobs. With no employment elsewhere, and no way of staying on their traditional lands, more people were forced to live on welfare rations on the Roebourne reserve.

1969

To provide water for towns and industry, the Pilbara Supply Scheme began piping water from Millstream National Park in Yindjibarndi country.

1972

A duplicate pipeline built to service Wickham and Cape Lambert port. The WA state government passes the Aboriginal Heritage Act, designed to conserve significant Aboriginal cultural sites.

1993

The Native Title Act (NTA) became law after a decade-long struggle by Eddie Mabo and his supporters to challenge the colonialist notion of "terra nullius" (Government of Western Australia, 2018), the idea that Australia was an unoccupied country at the time of white settlement.

1996

This was the start of the joint Ngarluma Yindjibarndi Land Rights claim.

2005

The First Ngarluma Yindjibarndi Native Title Decision was appealed. Intensive new developments in the mining and resource industries led to the pegging of mining leases over most of the Pilbara. Pressure was placed on Native Title holders to provide Heritage Clearances in return for limited royalties grows.

2007

Yindjibarndi People granted Native Title and limited access to 30% of their ancestral country.

2010

Pressure on the Ngardangali to provide Heritage Clearances and allowing mining on their land continues. Karratha plans a population growth from 20,000 to 50,000 people between 2010 and 2020.

New ports, rail and mining infrastructure is planned – yet most Ngaarda live in impoverished conditions, with few opportunities for improving their economic or social well-being (Yindjibarndi People, 2019).

2017

Yindjibarndi win exclusive rights over their land with a Federal High Court ruling.

FMG mount a challenge on 4 December 2017.

2019

The High Court of Australia ruling on FMG's challenge is awaited. Terms of compensation to be paid by FMG are yet to be determined.

The notions of right and fair translate even to this day. What is lost is justice, and justice is only given when you can afford it. Yindjibarndi faces one of our greatest challenges in protecting Yindjibarndi country from the mining operations of FMG. The Yindjibarndi Nation is challenging a racist ideology and a mining company's greed, a greed which seeks to reinvent the Indigenous social contemporary living norms by stripping us of any decision-making powers and to see the federal government place all Indigenous welfare recipients on a welfare card – all so it can prove that we are not capable of managing our affairs (see Forrest's *Creating parity* report, cited in Altman, 2017). We can unpack the blatant racism that follows this type of paternalism, but one should look deep into this orchestrated plan. The aim is to somehow deem Indigenous Australians as incompetent, which will then be reflected in laws and policies, for example, the Community Development Program (CDP), which requires workers to receive government payments that are currently below employment award rates (see more details in Altman, 2017, p. 6). The idea is to prove that we are disabling of ourselves and that mining royalties are not the answer for self-determining our own future. For that reason alone, they say they will not pay us any compensation.

Living in a poverty-stricken community and waking up one day to the excitement of the industrial drums beating on the doorsteps of town meant that for the first time in our history our people wanted to engage. There was a rush out of the blocks as Aboriginal People raced into the open arms of big industry.

One thing my grandfather taught me was to judge a person's character by his or her behaviour. There is no such thing as good intentions when anyone speaks about Ngurra (Yindjibarndi Country), in-particular if they want something from it. Yindjibarndi elders always say *Mirda yabalarri gaduwa winbawayi*, no one man can be boss as tragedy follows. And I would add that no one mining company can be boss of a sovereign people and their land as tragedy follows. See, the Yindjibarndi Nation were made to protect Ngurra, to preserve it for the next generation and to keep its beauty and serenity pure so that Yindjibarndi, in all manner of life and other things, can continue to be happy.

The chapter shows how corruption is like the devil's candy, where one particular Australian iron ore mining company, FMG, has been spreading it around my community and telling my people that there is more if Yindjibarndi took less. The offer by FMG was presented to the Yindjibarndi community in two patronising terms: one, that FMG wanted to be the lowest-cost iron ore producer in the world and, two, that Yindjibarndi can't handle money. To paraphrase, giving you mob Yindjibarndi a large amount of money which you can't handle means that you will only piss it up the wall. On 6 July 2007 FMG undertook exploration activities to drill and disturb important and sacred sites, getting the green light to mine without having an Indigenous Land Use Agreement (ILUA) with the Yindjibarndi (see a video of the situation in 2011, Yindjibarndi, 2011). The only alternative left for the Yindjibarndi Ngurra Aboriginal Corporation, YNAC (RNTBC) is to submit a compensation application through the Federal Court of Australia, which we intend to do once the appeal by FMG against our exclusive possession determination is heard.

Head: the white settlers, lawmakers and industrial kings

The year 1788 began the time of civilization under colonial respectability, where a man's measure was crowned by clothes and colour. The land's new powers gave selective laws and privileges to white Australians while feeding off the injustices to abolish Indigenous sovereignty. The colonialists' attempts at genocide (Australian Human Rights Commission, 1997) have not succeeded, and this chapter is part of raising awareness about my people's claim for sovereignty over our homelands. White Australians today must live with the fact and accept the reality that a black footprint belongs, and it has been reported as the longest-living culture that exists on our planet today. The land, Ngurra, is the inheritance of all First Nations for one generation to enjoy after the next.

The folly of believing that mining could be the solution to our subjugation to white people's rule is evident in the failure of land rights legislation to improve our self-determination as First Nation People. Altman explains that it was expected that "the leverage provided by prior informed consent provisions [in the legislation] . . . might result in both beneficial agreements [for First Nation People] and beneficial development outcomes" (2009a, p. 4). But the idea that we had de facto rights to the minerals on our land was not strong enough under law and has been legally contested by wealthy mining companies, with few successful exclusive ownership claims across Australia

(Cleary, 2017). Further, FMG promotes itself as a socially responsible company (Minderoo Foundation, 2019) and a friend of Aboriginal People while acting in a similar way to other mining companies by actively excluding groups who don't accept their offers of compensation or jobs (McLean, 2012).

The scale of mining in Australia is so enormous that Cleary (2012) describes it as a resources rush by mega-mining projects. As the Native Title phenomena slowly and carefully ripped through the nation, it became easier to convince First Nation People to forego their native title rights and liabilities. In most cases those native title deals became finalised and the historical deals of "nothing gained but everything's lost" occurred. This is similar to the North American trade deal of 1626 that took Manhattan for "beads and trinkets", which disappointingly became the standard and still is so in 2019.

The Pilbara is rich with iron ore and poor in Indigenous recognition. Mining companies, their investors and shareholders cash in on this section of our continent every year, which in the eyes of God belongs to the First Nation People. The industrial revolution of introducing the Pilbara to the world began in the 1960s; we are now globally recognised, and the world can't live without us. We produce and ship nearly 1 billion tonnes of Pilbara iron ore each year to the global economy, and this amount is growing. The free prior and informed consent would see First Nation People effectively rule our country through an economic means that simply recognises Just Terms Compensation (Parliament of Australia, 2010) – and how different First Nation's Australia would look to the world if we were treated with respect and recognition.

FMG, the mining company at the centre of my story, is the fourth-largest iron ore exporter in Australia with mines in the Chichester and Hamersley Ranges in the Pilbara. In 2018 they produced 170 million tons of iron ore worth $US6.9 billion in revenue (FMG, 2019). FMG's belief is that Aboriginal People whose lands their mining company exploit are better off having jobs in their company. The mining company is on the public record saying that government handouts and royalties are "yesterday's mistakes" that are "like some drug" that people come to rely upon (FMG, 2013). The problem is constructed as being the welfare dependency and idle hands of First Nation People. But I am putting mining exploitation back on the agenda and agree with Altman (2018) that a travesty of justice is occurring against our First Nation People.

As it stands we continue to be dragged along by the back heals, forcefully stripped of every right to our sovereignty and treated as outcast to the wealth that is our natural birthright. Native Title gives legitimacy to this system that continues to steal from us what is our cultural patrimony and does so by laws made in a colonial parliament. First Nation People met in 2017 and prepared the *Uluru statement from the heart*, which in part says:

> We seek constitutional reforms to empower our people and take a rightful place in our own country. When we have power over our destiny our children will flourish. They will walk in two worlds and their culture will

be a gift to their country. We call for the establishment of a First Nations Voice enshrined in the Constitution.

(Referendum Council, 2017, p. 1)

It was presented to the prime minister, who said no. The struggle to gain this recognition continues at the time of writing. Large-scale mining operations in Australia are unsustainable and have a devastating impact on people, their cultural practices, bio-diversity and the land (White, 2018). First Nation People are disproportionately impacted due to the location of the vast majority of mines on our ancestral lands (Anguelovski, 2008). Stephen argues that the economic power of mining companies has outgrown the legal structures of the host society, with domestic laws unable to "impose basic human rights norms" (cited in Thirarungrueang, 2013, p. 2). In response, Palmer (2018) calls for "sustainable-participatory social policy" as a pathway to ecological justice. We have found legislation alone is not sufficient, with major difficulties occurring in the implementation of our Native Title rights (O'Faircheallaigh, 2013; Campbell & Hunt, 2010). Further, we are not seeing Palmer's (2018) idea for a fairer social policy approach happening for our people with poor social and health indicators despite the federal government's Closing the Gap initiative (Cox, 2019).

Hand: what we have done to protect our people and homelands

Destroying our sacred Ngurra

As I have said, corruption is like the devil's candy, and FMG has been spreading it around my community and telling my people that there is more if Yindjibarndi take less. The arrogant behavior of FMG representatives did not deter some of the Yindjibarndi people who later became known as the breakaway group that supported FMG. They gave FMG support on exploration activities to drill and disturb important and sacred sites and then the green light to mine without having an ILUA with the Yindjibarndi. I focus on this splintering of our people by the mining company because it is indicative of the divide-and-conquer tactics of FMG.

The splinter group is called Wirlumurra Yindjibarndi Aboriginal Corporation (WMYAC), and it was formed to tackle one objective, and that is to take control of the Yindjibarndi Aboriginal Corporation (YAC). The YAC, of which I am the CEO, is the only body that can enter into ILUAs. YAC can only negotiate with mining proponents on behalf of the Yindjibarndi Nation when asked to by the unanimous decision of Yindjibarndi members. This is how we like to conduct our business; everybody agrees, or we all don't agree. The consensus by all Yindjibarndi is important because we have never in the past done anything in contradiction or in separation from the main group. One of my elders would say that a whole hand fits into a glove and not the fingers we choose because the hand and glove are as one piece and only effective when proper and complete.

The WMYAC came into existence and incorporated as an Aboriginal corporation under the Aboriginal and Torres Strait Islander Commission in 2010. The main focus of the group was to give the Yindjibarndi supporters of FMG a base to work from against YAC. WMYAC sought to overtake and control for the purpose of entering into an ILUA with FMG so that FMG could continue operating on Yindjibarndi Ngurra without becoming liable for mining. The end result to this relationship and why WMYAC is loyal to FMG and not to their own people, the Yindjibarndi, might have something to do with the group receiving AU$120 million over a seven-year period. We find this type of dealing quite extraordinary for the reason that WMYAC does not have any authority in relation to native title issues and can't approve ILUAs with any mining company because it is not a Registered Native Title Body Corporate (RNTBC), which by law is the only body authorised to enter into agreements with mining proponents.

I personally believed that we as a strong, united Yindjibarndi Nation instilled with the values and teaching of our old people would never go estranged from our laws, language, culture, religious values, family relationships and love for our Ngurra. But I was totally unaware of, and unprepared for, what has become the single most destructive event of my adult life, that is, to be at the coalface of this cat verses mouse, corruption verses collectiveness, power and money verses uncertainty and the history of a deprived people. The faith of Yindjibarndi was tested that day, and there is no telling whether we will survive or, like many others of our neighbours, will be overwhelmed by the pleasures of Yindjibarndi individuals and small groups advocating mining projects in service to their own interests.

The courage to hold onto our position and to stand for our beliefs was as inspiring as it was brave. We were willing to negotiate an outcome only if FMG was willing to also negotiate on the premises of a win-win and that Yindjibarndi have respect as the traditional owners of our Ngurra. It was unfortunate, though, that FMG took the destructive option, which led to the dividing of our community and families. I quickly became out of my depth. I faced for the first time in my life a situation unknown to all of YAC, a mining company with money, power and influence investing in their business agenda and using my people to deliver them the prize, our Yindjibarndi Ngurra that had a market value of AU$200 billion in iron ore.

Ned Cheedy, one of my *Yabijis* (grandfathers), was always someone we could turn to when we needed help with words of wisdom for everyday life challenges. His greatest advice and gift to me was to get me to do away with my anger and look at life as a blessing every day. The problem I was faced with was then easily solvable – just do it the Yindjibarndi way. My biological Yabiji's way was to bring the troublemakers to a community meeting and remind them of their responsibility to act for all Yindjibarndi. If they refused, then the elders would take punishment, a lesson would be taught and then there would be no more trouble from troublemakers. At first we thought that highlighting the relationship between FMG and WMYAC would make WMYAC members and followers realise that there was something more to the relationship with their people and what they were doing was in fact wrong. At the end of the day FMG would get everything, and the WMYAC would be left managing a self-created mess. As WMYAC persisted with their idealist get-rich scheme, Yindjibarndi members from all walks of life lined up for their lion's share of the FMG agreement. The Yindjibarndi population, which is made up of men, women and children is a little more than 1,000. FMG's final offer was AU$4 million dollars per year capped at 2011 inflation. We told the broader WMYAC members that this was daylight robbery and an insult to our people and generations to come but more importantly that this deal would drive every Yindjibarndi to madness and greed would capsize us all. But without any acknowledgement of the facts, they accepted the offer in belief that FMG would provide great benefits in jobs, training and business development. That jackpot was in commercial contracting and not in mining handouts. The dialogues among us as Yindjibarndi People became much more difficult because of FMG undermining of our cultural engagement principles and our leadership practices in which elders make the final decisions.

Taking our battle to the courts

I have more recently compartmentalised the main projects that we have control over, parked the ones that are seen as long-term outcomes and done away with the WMYAC and FMG issues as they don't matter anymore. We focused on the objectives to pursue our compensation claim once we have the undisputed rights to launch our application in the Federal Court of Australia. The only other alternative left for the YNAC (RNTBC) is to submit a compensation application through the Federal High Court of Australia, which we intend to do once the appeal by FMG against our exclusive possession determination is heard. The final determination on submitting our compensation claim is still being reviewed by the full bench of the Federal Court of Australia. The reason why it has taken more than a year for the decision has been due to FMG's appeal on one of their grounds that was being heard by the High Court of Australia. The High Court has now made its decision on *Tjungarrayi v Western Australia; KN (deceased) and Others (Tjiwarl and Tjiwarl #2) v Western Australia* [2019] HCA 12 (17 April 2019). This decision upholds s47B of the NTA that mining leases do not extinguish Native Title. A decision of the full bench regarding FMG's appeal is expected to be heard soon.

About Juluwarlu Group Aboriginal Corporation (JGAC)

In 1998, my partner Lorraine and I decided to leave Karratha, where we were staying at that time as I was working for Hamersley Iron, which is now known as Rio Tinto Iron Ore (RTIO). My grandfather Woodley King came to my home one evening and said that I had to go back to the community and take charge in minding it on his behalf. I was asked to manage the community on his behalf carrying out the community objectives, which were to help and care for our people struggling with alcohol addiction and assist those members who wanted to live in peace and without stress. We packed up and left Karratha in a heartbeat and never looked back. The reasons we moved back into Roebourne were because of family politics which started to undermine and encroach on the plans we had to develop the community. In response to this decision, in 2000 we incorporated JGAC (see the *Juluwarlu* video JGAC, 2016) to give form to what is important to us. Ned Cheedy, who lived to be 106 years of age, was one of our first Yindjibarndi elder employees who came to work on the days required. At that time in his early 90s, he was a reliable contributor to the recording of the Yindjibarndi cultural history. Juluwarlu's core function is the documentation and recording of the Yindjibarndi language, culture and history. It has become a home where Yindjibarndi knowledge and people are united in body and spirit, and the power of knowledge and information helps everyone in their search for belonging. The connection that Juluwarlu offers to all Yindjibarndi is not only through cultural information but family structure and reconnecting to a sense of place and pride in identity.

Conclusion

We seem to assist the white establishment even more than a century after the Aboriginal Protection Act 1869 that was supposed to normalise parts of our transitioning into colonial society. In fact, the opposite happened. Everything about freedom became only a reminder that non-Indigenous Australians had an illegal consequence, which drew self-consciousness and with that the small detail of admitting to their wrongdoings. Being good is to do good, and the matter of dispossession needed serious follow-through if compensation was the pennant which confirmed one's passage through heaven's doors.

My vision for justice is that lands and properties would have to be decommissioned and accounted for, and every piece of dirt would have to be measured accordingly for the rights of any settler to own lawfully. This recognition would put First Nation's Australians in the box seat of vetoing every transition of property before purchase. The free prior and informed consent would see First Nation's Australians effectively rule our country through an economic means that recognises Just Terms Compensation. If this was the case, how different First Nations' Australia would look to the world.

References

Altman, J. (2009a). Indigenous communities, miners and the state in Australia. In J. Altman & D. Martin (Eds.), *Power, culture, economy: Indigenous Australians and mining* (pp. 17–50). Acton, Australia: ANU Press.

Altman, J. (2009b). Contestations over development. In J. Altman & D. Martin (Eds.), *Power, culture, economy: Indigenous Australians and mining* (pp. 1–16). Acton, Australia: ANU Press.

Altman, J. (2017). *Modern slavery in remote Australia? The government's welfare reforms for Indigenous Australians look like slavery*. Retrieved from https://arena.org.au/modern-slavery-in-remote-australia-by-jon-altman/

Altman, J. (2018). *Discussion paper: Remote employment and participation*. Letter to Premier and Cabinet. Burwood, Australia: Alfred Deakin Institute for Citizenship and Globalisation.

Anguelovski, I. (2008). Environmental justice concerns with transnational mining operations: Exploring the limitations of post-crisis community dialogues in Peru. In C. O'Faircheallaigh & A. Saleem (Eds.), *Earth matters: Indigenous peoples, the extractive industries and corporate social responsibility* (pp. 198–221). Sheffield, UK: Greenleaf Publishing.

Australian Human Rights Commission. (1997). *Bringing them home report: Report of the national inquiry into the separation of Aboriginal and Torres Strait Islander children from their families*. Retrieved from www.humanrights.gov.au/our-work/bringing-them-home-report-1997

Bauman, T., Streiein, L. & Weir, J. (Eds.). (2013). *Living with native title: The experiences of registered native title corporations*. Canberra, Australia: AIATSIS Research Publications.

Campbell, D. & Hunt, J. (2010). Community development in Central Australia: Broadening the benefits from land use agreements. *Centre for Aboriginal Economic Policy Research, Topical Issue* 7. Canberra, Australia: Australian National University.

Cleary, P. (2012). *Mine-field: The dark side of Australia's resources rush*. Collingwood, Australia: Black Inc.

Cleary, P. (2017). *Title fight: The great philanthropist vs the people of the Pilbara*. Retrieved from www.themonthly.com.au/

Cox, E. (2019). *Closing the gap: Why not focus on what works?* Retrieved from www.evacox.com.au/node/83

Fortescue Mining Group, FMG. (2013). *FMG: Andrew Forrest and Noel Pearson discuss Aboriginal business*. Retrieved from https://youtu.be/A1ejFs0eH38

Fortescue Mining Group, FMG. (2019). *Annual report FY 2018*. Retrieved from www.fmgl.com.au/docs/default-source/annual-reporting-suite/fy18-annual-report.pdf

Government of Western Australia. (2018). *Mabo decision, land rights and native title*. Retrieved from www.dlgsc.wa.gov.au/achwa/Documents/DAA_RightWrongsToolkit_Part6Mabo.pdf

Juluwarlu Group Aboriginal Corporation. (2016). *Juluwarlu: Documenting and archiving our Yindjibarndi language, law and culture*. Retrieved from www.facebook.com/watch/?v=916069595224142

McLean, J. (2012). From dispossession to compensation: A political ecology of the Ord final agreement as a partial success story for Indigenous traditional owners. *Australian Geographer, 43*(4), 339–355.

Minderoo Foundation. (2019). *Walk free foundation*. Retrieved from www.minderoo.com.au/walk-free/?utm_medium=301&utm_source=www.walkfreefoundation.org

O'Faircheallaigh, C. (2013). Registered native title bodies corporate and mining agreements: Capacities and structures. In T. Bauman, L. Strelein & J. Weir (Eds.), *Living with native title: The experiences of registered native title corporations* (pp. 275–291). Canberra, Australia: AIATSIS Research Publications.

Palmer, M. (2018). Sustainable-participatory social policy. In P. Beresford & S. Carr (Eds.), *Social policy first hand: An international introduction to participatory social welfare* (pp. 262–276). Bristol, UK: Policy Press.

Parliament of Australia. (2010). *Constitution alteration (Just terms) bill 2010*. Retrieved from http://parlinfo.aph.gov.au/parlInfo/download/legislation/bills/r4362_first/toc_pdf/10155b01.pdf;fileType%253Dapplication%252Fpdf

Referendum Council. (2017). *Uluru statements from the heart*. Retrieved from www.referendumcouncil.org.au/sites/default/files/2017-05/Uluru_Statement_From_The_Heart_0.PDF

Thirarungrueang, K. (2013). Rethinking CSR in Australia: Time for binding regulation? *International Journal of Law and Management, 55*(3), 173–200.

White, R. (2018). Ecocentrism & criminal justice. *Theoretical Criminology, 22*(3), 342–362.

Yindjibarndi. (2011). *Yindjibarndi sites disturbed by FMG*. Retrieved from https://youtu.be/NI1Wt6NkKF4

Yindjibarndi People. (2019). *Our story, our people*. Retrieved from https://juluwarlu.com.au/organisation/our-story/our-history/

Chapter 6

Saying no to Roe 8

Danielle Brady

Introduction

There are many stories which could be told of how the Beeliar Wetlands, in Perth, WA, were saved from the Roe Highway development in 2017. Doubtless a tree sitter would write a different story to a social media activist. The social movement which reached its peak during the final months before a WA election in 2017 was made up of diverse participants and groups who wanted to preserve the Beeliar Wetlands for the future. Together their protest was underpinned by legal action against the state, visualised by nonviolent direct action, communicated through multiple media channels and sustained in a strong community. Following an overview, the chapter is divided into sections which describe some of the practical actions taken during the campaign. A more extensive discussion of the background and implications of the Roe 8 dispute is given by Gaynor, Newman and Jennings (2017).

The Beeliar Wetlands vs the Roe Highway

The Beeliar Wetlands are an urban bushland remnant, surrounded by suburbs, about 20 kilometres south of Perth, the capital of WA. The name "Beeliar" comes from the First Nation People of the area, the Noongar, who lived in the region prior to European settlement, and they continue to use it today. In addition to being known as an area of high biodiversity, important for threatened species like Carnaby's black cockatoo, the Beeliar Wetlands is a place specifically valued and used by people. Sections of the Roe Highway planned in the 1960s as part of the Perth Metropolitan Regional Scheme (MRS) have been built over 50 years, but Section 8 (Roe 8) remained to be completed in 2014. Its proposed pathway through the Beeliar Wetlands had long been contentious (Gaynor et al., 2017). The historical opposition to Roe 8 received new impetus leading up to signing of WA's first Regional Forest Agreement in 1999, when thousands of Perth people rallied to protect old growth forest. At the beginning of 2001 one of the first Say No to Roe mass rallies was held near the proposed site of the new section. Roe 8 was then shelved by a state Labour government that year, and many believed it was dead until resurrected by an incoming Liberal government in 2008. This threat led to the formation of the community advocacy group: Save Beeliar Wetlands (SBW). In 2014, the threat became real as Roe 8 was included as part of a larger project called the Perth Freight Link, with AU$1.6 billion funding contributed to it by both state and federal governments ("Perth Freight Link a boost for WA industry", 2014). Although intended to link northern freight yards to the port of Fremantle, it was dubbed "The Road to Nowhere" because it was unclear how road traffic would get from the end of Roe 8 through existing suburbs to the port. Various unlikely options were mooted, including a tunnel. From 2014, supporters of the Beeliar Wetlands engaged in an intense campaign to prevent Roe 8 being built. The campaign group Rethink the Link formed in 2015, eventually driving the issue to prominence during the 2017 state election. The project was halted by the incoming McGowan Labour government in 2017, but by that time, 90 hectares of irreplaceable bushland had been bulldozed through the Beeliar Wetlands.

The community challenges the state

The legal challenge to Roe 8 was the moral core of the effort to save the Beeliar Wetlands and was pursued by incredibly determined leadership from a community organisation. In 2015 the newly incorporated SBW filed a legal claim in the Supreme Court challenging the approval for Main Roads WA to construct the proposed Roe 8 extension through the Beeliar Wetlands (*Save Beeliar Wetlands (Inc) vs Jacob*). The basis of the case was that the state government's Environmental Protection Authority (EPA) had failed to take into account its own policies and guidelines when giving advice to the minister who approved the project. The guidelines in question stipulated that offsets (or purchase of replacement land of similar quality) could not be used when a critical environmental asset would be significantly impacted by a proposed project. The environmental approval had unambiguously identified the Beeliar Wetlands as a critical asset (EPA, 2003). A lay explanation of the offset guidelines is that it was not OK to bulldoze a site of agreed environmental value and buy land elsewhere for conservation, effectively sacrificing the existing plants and animals.

Underlying the technical arguments was a spatial justice claim, that use of the wetlands by wildlife and people was more important than building a road. Privileging road building over inner-city green space can be viewed through a spatial justice lens along with unfair distribution of pollutants or access to resources (Soja, 2010). The offsets purchased to "replace" the Beeliar Wetlands were 100 kilometres distant from Perth, leading to some bizarre claims in court about cockatoos being able to "fly away", later used to humorous effect by protestors. On 16 December 2015 Chief Justice Wayne Martin found in favour of SBW (Inc), and Roe 8 was put on hold. The premier immediately said that he would "redo" the environmental approvals, and all parties expected that the decision would eventually be overturned (Messurier & Campbell, 2015). Duly the State of WA filed an appeal, and on 15 July 2016 Justice Carmel McLure overturned the decision, finding the offset guidelines were not mandatory (*Jacob v Save Beeliar Wetlands (Inc)*). The effect of the appeal was that the original environmental approvals stood and the project could proceed. In August, SBW then sought special leave to appeal to the High Court on the grounds that the appeal finding may have been in error. In a parallel action, SBW also appealed the then federal minister for the environment's decision to approve the construction of Roe 8. Ultimately neither action was successful. When special leave was declined on 16 December 2016, there was no further legal barrier to work commencing. Indeed, preliminary work had already begun, and temporary fencing for clearing was being installed, despite the fact that a state election was expected just months away in 2017.

The precious two-year delay from approval in 2014 to commencement in late 2016 prevented the completion of the project in the last term of the Barnett Liberal government. The decisive action of *Save Beeliar Wetlands (Inc) vs Jacob* also bought the time required to convince a possible alternative government of community opposition to the project. A firm commitment to save the Beeliar Wetlands came late from the Labour opposition leader only in January 2017 when bulldozing was well under way ("WA Labor vows to axe Perth Freight Link", 2017). Consequently, the legal cases bought by a community organisation were the foundation for all other actions.

In addition to the real and significant effect of stopping the project temporarily, the legal cases had a huge flow on effect to the wider campaign. They were a source of critical information about the project which was used widely in the campaign, and they were also a reason for hope. Supporters gathered in numbers outside the courts during proceedings, increasing limited media coverage (Figure 6.1). The legal cases provided tangible evidence that citizens could use the judiciary to challenge decisions they believed were unjust. As the cases were executed largely by pro-bono lawyers, they demonstrated that members of an elite profession were willing to support a cause that the government of the day was trying to portray as a minority view. The seriousness of the cases was reflected in the resources marshalled by the state to defend their claim and provided a stark contrast to the dismissive treatment of large numbers of citizens as protestors.

Nisbet and Symes (2017) considered the High Court case and appeal through a social justice lens, looking at the distribution of justice across different social groups and whether people had been treated with respect in addition to procedural justice. They found that there were shortcomings in these other justice dimensions which led to anger and loss of trust. These emotions led directly to the community campaign that started alongside the cases and continued until the end.

Figure 6.1 Save Beeliar Wetlands supporters gather outside the Federal Court in Perth in 2016
Source: Photograph: G. Bartlett

Visualising protest

Many of the actions taken by protestors during the dispute would be familiar as part of the repertoire of environmental social movements (Tilly & Wood, 2009). Within the protest movement, such actions were frequently framed as nonviolent direction action (NVDA). Sharp's definition of nonviolent action as "a general technique of conducting protest, resistance, and intervention without physical violence" (2005, p. 547) describes the philosophy behind actions taken in the campaign. In practice during the Roe 8 campaign, nonviolent direct action was understood to be active in the physical present. Sharp (2005) further categorised nonviolent action into three main groups: nonviolent protest and persuasion; noncooperation; and nonviolent intervention. In the Roe 8 campaign these categories involved escalating stakes for the individual participants.

Over the three final months, thousands of Perth people participated in low-risk NVDA such as lawful assembly at mass actions near the site of clearing. A slightly broader definition of NVDA would include mass rallies in public places with permission and participating in other organised rallies as an identifiable group. Mass rallies were held outside Parliament and in Fremantle with formidable crowds chanting, "Say no to Roe" (Figure 6.2). They were also held

Figure 6.2 Save Beeliar Wetlands Fremantle Festival parade in 2015
Source: Photograph: R. Loopers

in the suburbs affected by the Perth Freight Link and concerned about funnelling of heavy traffic via the Roe 8 section. Moderate to high-risk NVDA included breaching perimeter fencing and exclusion zones, removal of survey tape, pushing over fencing and sit-ins outside politicians' offices. A smaller number of people were involved in these actions but were supported by large groups who provided food, supplies, technical advice and emotional support. There were also organised roles of legal observers and police liaison. Individual protestors borrowed from the activist repertoire pioneered in Australian forest disputes, trespassing into clearing zones, tree sitting and locking themselves onto equipment (Bible, 2018).

At face value, NVDA is a physical attempt to stop an unwanted event. However, it is also a visualisation tool converting the unseen opposition of citizens into something that can be seen and reported upon. The Roe 8 protest was enhanced by a form of branding, utilising colours and slogans identifiable with the campaign. Today many Perth people would recognise the black cockatoo head on a blue background as the symbol of the campaign to Save the Beeliar Wetlands (see Figures 6.1 & 6.2). Thousands of blue T-shirts with the *Say No to Roe 8* slogan were printed and worn by supporters not only at protests but at workplaces, conferences and social occasions. By 2016 the sky-blue colour alone could be used to link to the campaign. A creative campaigner suggested wearing small blue squares of roughly cut cloth to represent the urban bushland fragment at threat. Beeliar blue patches were ideal to show support in workplaces and other venues where an in-your-face T-shirt was not appropriate. The patches appeared in Parliament, in court and at other environmental protests – showing support and linkage to Save Beeliar Wetlands. From 2015 Rethink the Link orange signs appeared across Perth and mass rallies (Figure 6.2).

Mass action protests were a feature of the campaign from the commencement of bush clearing in January 2017 after the legal avenues had been exhausted. Mass actions were able to transform the invisible complaints of protestors into spatial opposition. At the first mass protest held in January 2017, more than 1,000 people gathered outside the temporary fencing along the road reserve, later pushing over the fencing and swarming around clearing equipment (Rimrod, 2017). Mounted police eventually drove them back across the boundary by cantering into the crowd, and a heavy police presence was required thereafter (Figure 6.3). In this, and other mass actions protestors contested the claim to build the road by the presence of their bodies in the space that was still bushland but was to become road. Mass actions can display what has been described as the worthiness, unity, numbers and commitment of a social movement (Tilly & Wood, 2009). Additionally, the spatial practice of protest through mass action can also be considered as the formation of a collective body making a spatial claim (Navickas, 2016; Sewell, 2001). The place of the Beeliar Wetlands was central to that spatial claim because as Endres and Senda-Cook have said, "the very place in which a protest occurs is a rhetorical performance that is part of the message of the movement" (2011, p. 258). Through the numerous on-site

Figure 6.3 Mass protest at the road reserve boundary during the Roe 8 campaign
Source: Photograph: N. Miles Tweedie

actions over the months that followed the road reserve was never able to be considered simply a clearing and construction site, other meanings of the space were attributed to the place of Beeliar through continued spatial action.

Actions taken by individuals and small groups were part of the extended repertoire of the movement. A closer look at one widely reported Roe 8 protest action reveals the multiple levels on which creative NDVA can operate by enacting key messages and amplifying media reportage. Three days before the WA state election, a giant black cockatoo interrupted a weary premier having coffee in a shopping centre meet and greet. The activist in the cockatoo suit addressed his questions in a squawky voice, effectively forcing the premier to interact or appear churlish, while media looked on agog. The cockatoo was holding a sign saying "My home was bulldozed. Which way to my offset?" that referred to the contentious acquisition of land 100 kilometres from the city to offset the lost section of the Beeliar Wetlands. As discussed the problem of offset guidelines not having been followed was used in the SBW Supreme Court case. Although the "rogue cockatoo" incident was carnival-like in presentation, it addressed a core issue of justice in the campaign. It provided a visual explanation of offset, allowed viewers to consider the problem from the perspective of wildlife and brought the spatial justice issue right into the city. The humour of the situation was irresistible to even unsupportive media, and their resulting reportage revealed the premier's attitude to WA citizens and beyond ("Cockatoo chirps at WA premier", 2017). It turned the tables on the usual reportage in which the premier could denigrate protestors in their absence. The reversals of power, albeit temporary, were important motivational encounters for protestors caught up in a social movement with an uncertain outcome. Photographs, videos, newspaper articles and commentary about the incident were widely shared on social media, increasing the penetration of the wildlife and offset issue.

Building confidence and capacity

The task of providing so many people with the confidence to participate in mass protest actions was a testament to the leadership and organisation of the community groups involved. A key capacity building strategy proved to be introductory NVDA workshops offered to supporters on a weekly basis from December 2016 by skilled and empathetic trainers. Over the following three months it is estimated that hundreds of people of diverse backgrounds received the training. In addition to explaining the key concepts of nonviolence, workshops covered information about rights and responsibilities in protest activity. Participants were able to act out some simple nonviolent actions in groups. Those involved in NVDA training had considerable experience in previous environmental disputes in WA. Their knowledge, experience and generous contribution of time increased the effectiveness of protest, particularly as so many people were new to the activity.

NVDA training asked individuals to consider how far they were willing to go, ahead of time, particularly in relation to being arrested. Some participants had never had cause to expect arrest, and this training was crucial in preparing them to make good decisions under the stressful conditions which could occur in onsite actions. Training caused participants to consider their bodies in space and their role as active agents in a broader social movement. The content of workshops changed to accommodate the needs of protestors as the campaign unfolded and knowledge about the kinds of responses from police being taken was acquired. Participants were encouraged to work in affinity groups, which became a loose unit of organisation in the campaign. Although the original idea was having a small group of known individuals for nearby support in a critical incident, there was huge diversity and varying success in how such groups operated, but they allowed campaigners some autonomy in planning their actions and volunteering their time. Some groups were skill based, for example, medical support; others were simply groups of people who had met at NVDA training. Most participants were probably unaware of the long history of affinity groups in protest movements (e.g., Kauffman, 2017).

The majority of protestors stuck to their nonviolent stance, even when provoked. More than 100 people were arrested, but most received spent convictions. Those charged during the campaign were supported with free legal advice, fine donations, in-court backup by fellow campaigners, even massage and healing sessions. The complex activities around NVDA were part of the community building which occurred during the Roe 8 campaign and NVDA training to such a large group of people is a lasting legacy. In addition to learning practical skills which could be used in the future, NVDA training gave law-abiding citizens a more nuanced understanding of the blurred lines between civil disobedience and unlawful activity, a new perspective on how the police can be used to support the interests of powerful state actors and a new sense of their own agency. By using skilled and experienced people to train new campaigners, and providing support and encouragement on site, harm to protestors, workers and the police was minimised. The cost of policing the Roe 8 dispute was later revealed to be AU$1.5 million, a huge impost which was to be reimbursed to the State by Main Roads WA (Kagi, 2017). Some believe that NVDA was a failure because it did not stop the bulldozing and only slightly slowed the pace of work. However, it is impossible to separate NVDA as an activity from the visualisation of protest, building of community and changed meanings of place which came about through collective spatial action.

Making your own news

The campaign made use of multiple social media fora to disseminate information, to challenge mainstream media reportage, to recruit new supporters and to organise. Facebook was the primary social media platform for the wider campaign, although NVDA activists later used the encrypted Telegram to discuss operations. The SBW Facebook page had garnered 7,000 followers in 2017. Main posts outlining key developments were made by the SBW convenor, and comments were closely moderated. Alternatively, the Community Noticeboard for Beeliar Wetlands was an open post page and only lightly moderated. Wildly variable aspects of the campaign were openly discussed on the page, images and videos shared and doubtless police and security also read the page. The Rethink the Link Facebook page disseminated information to around 10,000 people and advertised most of the mass actions. These major pages spawned numerous niche Facebook pages and groups with objectives ranging from reporting on activities on site to fundraising.

An underappreciated feature of social media is the ability of geographically dispersed individuals to work together as a team. Supporting a strategy team who met regularly in person to plan activities was a media response group which operated privately and entirely online. Members could post links to articles about Roe 8 or alerts to live radio broadcasts for other members to respond to quickly. A simple strategy of avoiding engaging in negative or pro-Roe 8 comments and liking positive comments aimed to move arguments against Roe 8 up comment lists. Members became adept at writing persuasive, pithy comments, often using humour and satire but avoiding emotive language. Some supporters who were not able to attend on-site actions made strong commitments to this media work. They developed skills which could be described as textual analysis, deconstructing news articles, identifying flaws and contradictions and selecting from a basket of arguments to refute claims. The group was quick to spring to action when a new pro-Roe 8 media item was posted by a member with the note "positive comments needed here".

Another important function of the social media work was bringing the action closer to keep a wider group of people informed and motivated. This was vitally important given the plainly stated bias of the local *The West Australian* newspaper ("No place for the disruptive protests at Roe 8 project site", 2017). Following on from site actions, photos, images, estimates of numbers of participants and media articles were posted back to Facebook so that supporters could see the action and some of its impact. They could witness from a distance but feel connected to the campaign. Images and video were sometimes picked up by mainstream journalists, but the huge reach of Facebook pages became a viable, independent source of information. In addition to amplifying the limited mainstream media, the combined resources of the protest groups were able to provide from within: facts, humour, visuals, human interest, criticism and commentary.

The social media work and NVDA were interconnected components of the campaign, which is shown by the impact of banner drops. The practice of banner dropping involved nonviolent physical action that often occurred at night and involved trespass. However, the resulting banners were an important form of communication in the campaign and enabled resistance to Roe 8 to be viewed by a wide audience, usually car drivers. Banners were dropped from trees, on fences, pedestrian overpasses and the Narrows Bridge which crosses the Swan River and the major entry point to Perth. Although traditional media outlets refused to cover Roe 8 in detail and often focused on protesters as a nuisance, banners across the city showed that the dispute was more than a not in my backyard (NIMBY) concern. Images of the banners were quickly snapped by supporters and widely circulated even when the banners had been removed. The creativity and daring of the banner drop activists was a source of inspiration to the broader movement and a component of community building.

Sustaining community

A strong sense of a connected community was an important feature of the Roe 8 campaign, and not all actions were directed towards an audience. Throughout the campaign, music, poetry, reflective writing and videos were shared within the community. A closer look at one event shows the ways that connections between Indigenous custodians and non-Indigenous people were affirmed. The Beeliar Regional Park contains mythological sites of significance for the Noongar People of the South-west of WA (Bennetts, 2017; EPA, 2003). Removal of heritage registration of Aboriginal sites within the road reserve to facilitate the project was contentious and challenged, unsuccessfully, by a traditional custodian (Ceranic, 2016; Wahlquist, 2015). As clearing along the road reserve continued unabated, women of different cultural backgrounds participated in a women's-only event in the heart of the Beeliar Wetlands (Figure 6.4). In February 2017, they walked onto the then dry ground of the seasonal swamp,

Figure 6.4 Women gathered at the Beeliar Wetlands in February 2017
Source: Photograph: L. Clifford

removing their shoes as a sign of respect and together sang a song/poem written in Noongar language which had been privately circulated before the event.

The Beeliar Wetlands was already a significant place to both Indigenous and non-Indigenous people at the time of this event. The spatial action showed that removal of Aboriginal heritage registration ahead of road construction had not removed Indigenous claim to place. By walking onto the land and singing in Noongar together, guided by local Indigenous women, they enacted their joint custodianship of the land. Sewell (2001) described the effects that protest actions can have on meanings of place as a type of sacralisation. The women's private event spatially enacted their mourning for the lost bushland and lack of respect for heritage but also their commitment to defend the place. To those who participated, the place of Beeliar became a space of shared cultural meaning and agency, a sacred space. Women involved in different aspects of the campaign came together, deriving strength to continue through the last weeks of the campaign, and the memory of this event held at the heart of the Beeliar Wetlands remains potent.

Persisting to the end

Towards the end of the campaign, many protestors were despondent and exhausted, but they turned their attention to the coming state election, focusing on other issues to draw attention to the failings of the Liberal government.

These perceived failings included excessive infrastructure spending, including Roe 8, and a preference deal with the controversial, conservative party One Nation. Campaigners began using the hashtags #putlibslast and #drowningindebt on social media and banners. Still struggling to garner media attention NDVA activists cast around for creative ideas. Jasper (1997) has referred to artfulness as a form of agency by protestors which arises from their individuality. He says, "much of what protestors do can be understood as experiments aimed at working out new ways of living and feeling" (Jasper, 1997, p. 65). This exactly describes the weary group who decided late on a Friday night to posture as competitors at the annual Rottnest Swim, a swimming race to a coastal island, in February 2017. Getting up before dawn they were in their bathers on the beach in the premier's electorate where he was to start the race. They asked for a photo, to which he obliged, and the resulting image was one of the most widely shared of the whole campaign. With winning smiles they posed, their arms inked with the #putlibslast and #drowningindebt slogans, apparently indistinguishable to the premier from the race numbers on the real competitors (Figure 6.5). Even without the Beeliar Blue patches, viewers might

Figure 6.5 Roe 8 protestors posing with the WA Premier at the Rottnest Swim 2017
Source: Photograph: K. Dravnieks

have guessed the community to whom these indefatigable protestors belonged. The impact of this photo was acknowledged after the election with *The Sunday Times* newspaper's chief political reporter awarding it the best photo in his unofficial election campaign awards (Adshead, 2017). The new premier understood the impact of Roe 8 and committed to stopping the project, reassigning contracted work to other road projects, in his first press conference (Davey, 2017).

Conclusion

If a new government immediately halting a project can be considered a success, there are lessons from the Roe 8 campaign for others. Opposition over a long lead time resulted in a wide age range of participants and a body of knowledge about the project to be shared. Confident leadership and conviction to the justice of the cause spearheaded a legal challenge to the state. The legal challenge bought essential time to prevent completion of the project, to lobby an opposition party to commit to halting the project, and provided hope to the wider movement. Persistent, creative and varied NVDA, underpinned by quality training and support, changed the spatial meaning of the Beeliar Wetlands and visualised the widespread opposition to Roe 8. A large, diverse and connected community harnessed extensive multimedia to organise activities, communicate developments and resist dominant narratives. Through strong internal connections, this community was able to sustain itself in the face of continual disappointment and lack of immediate impact to ultimately achieve a stop to the project.

Although construction of the highway section became ultimately untenable, clearing of the road reserve continued throughout the campaign. At the time of writing, state funding has been set aside for rehabilitation of the road reserve, but land tenure remains uncertain. Legislation to remove most of the Roe 8 reserve from the Perth MRS has been introduced but faces a difficult passage through Parliament. Supporters of the Beeliar Wetlands learned in 2014 that an outdated and long dormant project could be resurrected with the right political incentive, regardless of the history of opposition or current public opinion. Without removal from the planning scheme, Roe 8 could rise again. The reality for Roe 8 protestors, as for many environmental activists, is continual vigilance and being prepared to fight for the same place again.

References

Adshead, G. (2017, 12 March). Best of the worst: Our unofficial campaign awards. *The Sunday Times*, p. 17.

Bennetts, S. (2017). Never again? Aboriginal heritage approvals and Roe 8. In A. Gaynor, P. Newman & P. Jennings (Eds.), *Never again: Reflections on environmental responsibility after Roe 8* (pp. 205–232). Crawley, Australia: UWA Press.

Bible, V. (2018). *Terania Creek and the forging of modern environmental activism*. Melbourne, Australia: Palgrave Macmillan.

Ceranic, I. (2016, 24 August). *Perth Freight Link: Roe 8 Aboriginal heritage appeal thrown out*. Retrieved from www.abc.net.au/news/2016-08-24/roe-8-perth-freight-link-aboriginal-heritage-appeal-thrown-out/7780698?pfmredir=sm

Cockatoo Chirps at WA Premier. (2017). *[video]*. Retrieved from www.smh.com.au/video/wa-news/wa-election-2017/cockatoo-chirps-at-wa-premier-20170308-4rg28.html

Davey, M. (2017, 13 March). *Mark McGowan stops Perth Freight Link in first move as WA premier*. Retrieved from www.theguardian.com/australia-news/2017/mar/13/mark-mcgowan-stops-perth-freight-link-in-first-move-as-wa-premier

Endres, D. & Senda-Cook, S. (2011). Location matters: The rhetoric of place in protest. *Quarterly Journal of Speech, 97*, 257–282.

EPA. (2003). *Environmental values associated with the alignment of Roe Highway (Stage 8): A Report by the Environmental Protection Authority under Section 16(j) of the Environmental Protection Act 1986: Bulletin 1088*. Perth, Australia: Environmental Protection Authority (EPA).

Gaynor, A., Newman, P. & Jennings, P. (Eds.). (2017). *Never again: Reflections on environmental responsibility after Roe 8*. Crawley, Australia: UWA Press.

Jasper, J. M. (1997). *The art of moral protest: Culture, biography and creativity in social movements*. Chicago, USA: Chicago University Press.

Kagi, J. (2017, 11 April). *WA Government to foot $1.5 million police bill for Roe 8 police presence*. Retrieved from www.abc.net.au/news/2017-04-11/wa-government-to-foot-1-5million-police-bill-for-roe-8/8434418

Kauffman, L. A. (2017). *Direct action: Protest and the reinvention of American radicalism*. London, UK: Verso.

Messurier, D. & Campbell, K. (2015, 16 December). *Supreme Court rules on fight to stop Roe 8 wetlands extension*. Retrieved from www.perthnow.com.au/news/wa/supreme-court-rules-on-fight-to-stop-roe-8-wetlands-extension-ng-0b1e91fed352c704bac28489538567f9

Navickas, K. (2016). *Protest and the politics of space and place, 1789–1848*. Manchester, UK: Manchester University Press.

Nisbet, T. & Symes, G. J. (2017). No way to build a highway: Law, social justice research and the Beeliar Wetlands. *Environmental and Planning Law Journal, 34(2)*, 162–175.

No Place for the Disruptive Protests at Roe 8 Project Site. (2017, 13 January). *Editorial*. Retrieved from https://thewest.com.au/opinion/editorials/no-place-for-the-disruptive-protests-at-roe-8-project-site-ng-b88353608z

Perth Freight Link a Boost for WA Industry. (2014, 1 July). *Media statement government of Western Australia*.

Rimrod, F. (2017, 12 January). *Roe 8 protests ramp up as activists clash with police*. Retrieved from www.watoday.com.au/wa-news/roe-8-protests-ramp-up-as-activists-clash-with-police-20170111-gtpxcq.html

Sewell, W. H., Jr. (2001). Space in contentious politics. In R. R. Aminzade (Ed.), *Silence and voice in the study of contentious politics* (pp. 51–88). Cambridge, UK: Cambridge University Press.

Sharp, G. (2005). *Waging nonviolent struggle: 20th century practice and 21st century potential*. Dexter, USA: Extending Horizons Books.

Soja, E. W. (2010). *Seeking spatial justice*. Minneapolis, USA: University of Minnesota Press.

Tilly, C. & Wood, L. J. (2009). *Social movements 1768–2008* (2nd ed.). London, UK: Paradigm.

Wahlquist, C. (2015, 23 September). *Indigenous site 'older than pyramids' in Perth freeway's path taken off heritage register*. Retrieved from www.theguardian.com/australia-news/2015/sep/23/indigenous-site-older-than-pyramids-in-perth-freeways-path-taken-off-heritage-register

WA Labor Vows to Axe Perth Freight Link. (2017, 4 January). Retrieved from https://thewest.com.au/politics/wa-labor-vows-to-axe-perth-freight-link-ng-s-1653414

Chapter 7

Hands off Point Peron

Dawn Jecks

Introduction

I could write a book, and it would be really interesting. I heard about this harebrained scheme to hand over a big chunk of Rockingham Lakes Regional Park at Point Peron to a private developer for a marina about 11 years ago, and that was the beginning of my story.

The chapter describes my story of leading a community-based campaign in the tradition of community development (Ife, 2016) and progressive community organising (Pyles, 2009). The campaign had a singular aim which is crucial to a campaign's success (Conde, 2016). The aim was to protect a high-value ecosystem and the Little Penguins who live at Point Peron. The distributive leadership approach, where leadership is a collaborative process not an individual quality (Crevani, Lindgren & Packendorff, 2010, p. 79), meant working in inclusive ways with a wide cross section of people and groups as leaders in their own right over many years. In a similar way to Gandhi's nonviolent activism, leadership was based on "a strategy in which practicality and morality were complementary" (O'Toole, 2013, p. 161). Thus, my leadership had a transformative component embedded in it. We worked to deconstruct dominant views that reinforced the interests of the state government and the developer, offering a balance of critique and practical ways to achieve a just outcome (Shields, 2011). This enabled the fostering of goodwill and the social capital needed to sustain the campaign and to respect and empower activists. Social capital refers to "networks together with shared norms, values and understandings that facilitate co-operation within or among groups" (Organisation for Economic Co-operation and Development (OECD), 2019, p. 103). It is about the interconnectivity among people as a resource that is integral to the relationship approach to eco-activism. The use of social media to keep the public informed was a dynamic medium that was also used to mobilise and adapt tactics and strategies as needed (Macetela, 2016). Key capacities of the campaign involved undertaking the behind-the-scenes research to access evidence-based knowledge and to write submissions and media releases.

These ideas guided my involvement in the campaign, which came to be known as Hands off Point Peron (HOPP). A timeline for the campaign is provided at the end of the chapter with links to our web page. Point Peron is the name for a headland on the southern end of Cockburn Sound in WA. It is a place of treasured memories for many West Aussies (Australians) who spent their childhoods playing among the limestone cliffs and on sheltered beaches, swimming and snorkelling around the reefs. The developers wanted the Crown (public) land at Mangles Bay, which had been transferred by the commonwealth to the people of WA in 1964. The condition of transfer was that its future use was restricted to purposes of public recreation or parklands. I use the term *Crown land* reluctantly as it implies an acceptance of the invasion and colonisation of Australia by the British. I recognise the traditional owners of Point Peron, which is part of the land of the Wadjuk People of the Noongar Nation. There was no treaty with the Crown, and this land was never ceded.

The understanding was that once the small existing holiday-camp leases expired, the entire area would become an A-class reserve (Standing Committee on Environment and Public Affairs, 2006). Giving developers this land for a marina just didn't sit right with me from the beginning, so I decided to find out more. The more I found out, the more outraged I became that anyone would try and pull such a swiftie on the unsuspecting public – essentially trying to steal what belongs to the people and destroying it while they were at it. The Cape Peron Tourist Precinct Steering Committee was established to develop the proposed marina-based tourist and residential precinct within the Mangles Bay area of Cape Peron in April 2005.

Even at the start, with little investigation, it was obvious why it needed to be stopped. As the years went by, the case for saving this area from destruction and greed became stronger as more information came to light. The reasons for stopping the development include damage to seagrass beds and ecosystems; inevitable, substantial and long-term maintenance expenses which would be borne by ratepayers or taxpayers; and finally the loss of the land's current status as a regional park and the dishonouring of the 1964 Point Peron land transfer agreement. This development plan had it all and the saying "privatise the profits and socialise the losses" summed it up.

Getting active

It soon became clear that there were people within the local and state governments who were keen to see this project get up. The developers were promoting the project as an amazing thing when it was obvious to those of us who lived in the area and had looked into the facts and details that it wasn't at all. Having worked for decades in the civil construction sector myself, I understood the scale of disruption that would be inflicted on the landscape from a project of this size. In short, from my work experience I knew a thing or two about digging huge holes in the ground.

Given that there were people in positions of power pushing for this project, it was clear the only defence we could mount was by getting the community to become aware of the facts about what was actually on offer as opposed to what was being touted through advertisements in our local newspapers. We needed to shake off the perception that it was only an environmental issue. That is, we needed to make it mainstream so we couldn't be fobbed off as just a bunch of environmentalists who didn't want development in our own backyards (Wexler, 1996). We had to make sure everyone in the City of Rockingham and wider WA knew what was actually at stake and to educate them as to what the project entailed and what the detrimental effects would be.

Staying the distance

After about a year and not seeing much happening to stop the development, I set up a Facebook page and the HOPP campaign commenced in 2008. One of my first jobs as the HOPP spokesperson was to start organising rallies and writing letters to the editor of the local paper. I also started putting out media releases. I had some schoolteacher friends and access to a printer from the Greens political party. I had different people who could draft documents for me, and I did some of it myself. We letterboxed surrounding streets. It is important to get people motivated and actively involved. At the first rally we had a sign-up sheet for volunteers, and I started to build a database, and each rally got bigger than the previous one. At the first one there were about 80 people, then we got 200, then we had one with 500 people. Recruiting volunteers was crucial because to get the message out to the broader public, we needed people power.

I didn't want to have to do so much work for so long, but I had no choice; I got caught up in it. I figured as a human being on this planet, I have a moral duty, which for me means that when I see a wrong, I have a duty to act. Over the years I've had different people come and go on the campaign. The most important addition was Ambrose Cummins, a lawyer and a local. Ambrose got involved to help with strategy and planning. I kept organising these rallies. People see the campaign has been going for a long time, and then they say, "I should join you". So, I ended up with huge community support. As well as the rallies and public stall events, I started holding public meetings at the community centre, the biggest meeting venue in Rockingham. At the last one, in January 2018, there was standing room only; it was packed with people sitting on the floor.

It was people like Ambrose who were able to help with messaging, strategy and the legalities of planning approvals. Once we got to the planning aspect of the issue, we knew we'd be on more solid ground. Planning laws have more teeth, not like the environmental protection laws, which are weak and are applied in ways that tend to favour proponents over the environment and the community. For example, the federal government defined the level and scope of assessment in a way that allowed environmental approval without proper evaluation by excluding the Little Penguins (Eudyptula minor) from the study, as if they didn't exist. But Mangles Bay, the site for the proposed marina, is the key foraging point for the Little Penguin. And Mangles Bay is shallow. This gave rise to a key planning and economic management issue where we knew we could get traction. The site was simply unsuitable; there would need to be constant dredging. The final leg of the campaign was based on making it clear the ratepayers would have to pick up the tab for the ongoing dredging.

The City of Rockingham was another key stakeholder in this proposed development. The proposal was for a canal estate, even though the developers, Cedar Woods Properties Limited (in partnership with the state government agency LandCorp), were calling it the Mangles Bay Marina Based Tourist Precinct. But it was basically a canal estate and an artificial waterway. The proponents were portraying it as a marina in the ocean like the one in Perth's northern suburbs, which locals knew about and liked. We had to run a whole campaign to educate the local people that it was a canal estate and to get them to look at the failed canal estates in other places. We letterboxed about 150,000 flyers in the City of Rockingham over the years on different issues, depending on where we were in the campaign and where we were in putting the process through the government entities. We had online petitions. It never stopped. We rallied outside local government council offices for every monthly council meeting for about 18 months with placards and speeches, taking photos of what we were doing and posting them on social media.

We were trying to pressure the City of Rockingham about the fact they would end up being the waterways manager. With canal estates and artificial waterways, local governments take on the waterways management. In fact, when I first heard about the proposal, I knew the site was unsuitable because it is naturally shallow and would need dredging forever – at great pains to everyone and at ratepayers' expense. We made sure the people of Rockingham knew what was going on. There was no way that my rates were going out to pay for this flawed proposal in the wrong place.

Bringing it home

In January 2018, a person I shall call Jason from WA's peak conservation lobby group walked into this huge meeting. I hadn't seen him for some years when at the beginning of the HOPP campaign he had commented that he didn't think it was a winnable issue. The meeting had already started, and Jason took one look at that room with people standing and sitting on the floor; the atmosphere was palpable. We had timed the meeting specifically because a decision by the state government planning minister would be announced any day. Therefore, we had this big meeting on purpose to get maximum media exposure to pressure the government into making the right decision for the community. At the end of the meeting Jason came up to me and said that their conservation group wanted to do something to support HOPP. That was a final turning point. The next day Jason contacted me and offered to assist by campaigning on the penguins. Through their networks and database they then launched a campaign highlighting the threat to Rockingham's iconic Little Penguins, who forage in and around Point Peron and Mangles Bay. The conservation group got on board, they got Sea Shepherd on board, and then all these other groups got on board too. You know how with a lot of issues, when it comes to crunch time, a lot of groups come together because they have common ground. We kept pressuring the planning minister and threw fuel on the fire. Sea Shepherd was emailing all their people. I had been saving donation money for years so that when we needed it, we could finance big strategies. We ended up with a full-page advertisement in the local newspaper, just to make sure, because it was crunch time. We wanted the planning minister to withdraw the developer's marina proposal.

Another thing which was critical in all of this was our 600-page submission to the WA Planning Commission, put together by Ambrose with all the breaches of planning laws and policies identified and supported by expert evidence from a wide range of specialists. The submission was evidence based and unequivocal in its critique. I addressed the full board of the WA Planning Commission, and everything I said had been carefully researched and crafted. The evidence was so overwhelming, so compelling and substantial that by getting it all on the public record, it became something that the government couldn't ignore. The community knew exactly what was going on as well; nothing could be hidden away.

The day the proposal was thrown in the bin, I was on the freeway driving home, my phone was going off, and I'm thinking, "what's happened?" It's four o'clock, and the phone keeps going off. "Something's happened!" I got a call from the offices of Jeff Hutchinson from ABC Drive, the number-one ABC radio program when people are driving home from work in Perth. They told me the news. We had won! I wish I'd been on my own when I heard the news and not driving because I would love to have been able to have a cry. When you're on the freeway, you can't start crying.

It has been about 13 years now since I became aware of the issue, and we set up HOPP on social media about 10 years ago. It has been incredibly powerful, and we're still continuing to build it because it's not completely over yet, although it's looking pretty good now. They could come back again. It's not secure. It's never secure. Just ask Aboriginal communities. They resist inappropriate mining and pastoral activities, but the proponents keep coming back again and again to wear people down (see Chapter 5). We stopped this so-called development project, but the land needs to be given legal standing as an A-class reserve to give it substantial protection and for us to be absolutely sure they won't try again.

I'm telling you this story because . . .

My main reason for writing this for you is that it is important that other people get to hear about this story. I have learned so much valuable stuff:

> Firstly, you need to be determined and strategic; well networked; really big at getting information and making your own strategic decisions; and a critical thinker. You need to get all the information from different people, digest it and work out plans from there.

I would say that having a lawyer come on board the HOPP leadership group was crucial to the success of the campaign. Ambrose and I were on the same page. When people tried to confuse the issue, we worked together to unpack their messaging and challenge it. Further, having a lawyer whose job it is to critically evaluate and argue a case is amazing. We needed to push boundaries, but we also needed to be careful that we didn't go overboard because we could have ended up discrediting the campaign. We only say things based on facts; it's hard to argue with facts.

If enough people are made aware of the facts, the physical, scientific evidence and the detriments of such a development, there would be no way this could ever go ahead. It was bad from every angle: environmental, social, economic and planning. I believe that if you keep going, you can attract amazing, capable, clever people who know stuff – key people, passionate, committed, selfless people to add value to the power of the campaign. It is not just about one person; it's about a community.

It was important to keep going, no matter what. Over the years, when people saw what I was doing and that I was still going, they felt compelled to join in. In the end we had the Beeliar Wetlands people (see Chapter 6) come on board including professors for environmental responsibility from the city universities. It just keeps going. If you keep going, do enough and don't stop, people hear about it and get involved. It was so powerful in the end that the government had no choice. This is where social capital comes in. You need to have people who know about the importance of relationships, bringing people together and linking in with the right people inside and outside of your community.

This story is not about me; it is about the amazing people whom I worked with; we did it together. I was just the glue and the drive, the linchpin for harnessing all the stars. Other people have called me the driving force, and leadership is key without doubt. There is always something you can do to help, and I made sure everyone who wanted a job was doing a job, such as letterboxing and talking to their neighbours, because everyone can do something. Our big thing was people power. We had to get thousands of people to sign petitions, write and complain to their member of parliament and email local government councillors. Along the way, many people would say I was wasting my time, that I'd never to be able to stop the developers, and I would say, "No, I'm not going to stop". I thought if I didn't win, at least I would have done my best. It's a good story for other people who feel they are helpless and that they can't do anything; a group of committed people can achieve things. It is also all about the politics. The problem is that political parties rely on donations to fund their election campaigns to get re-elected, so the vested interests in the business sector generally donate to both the big parties. Property developers have the puppet strings of the politicians, and public land is a soft target. This public land is so amazing, and that's why they were after it. Whilst the proposal was being spruiked as much-needed infrastructure, it was always only about them getting their hands on prime public land, coastal real estate, for nothing. It was a public land grab. It was never about providing facilities at all.

I want to achieve more out of this other than winning the battle. I think it's important that we can empower ordinary people to do something about what they're faced with in their neighbourhoods. People say, "I can't do it, I'm not able". No. You've just got to keep going; you've got to make sure you've got the winning argument to start with. Don't just do stuff at random. Are the arguments there? Gradually go through and work out what your goal is at any one time. What are the best points to argue on? Make sure you mainstream your issues and aim to appeal to all sorts of people using common-sense arguments.

And finally

Despite the success of this project, it has come at a huge personal and health expense. I'm looking back, and I can see how I'm starting to reclaim my life now; it's wonderful. I gave 10 years of my life when I could've been doing other things, but I have no regrets. It's my son's 20th birthday tomorrow. I remember the time when he came to one of the rallies; he was about 12 years old at the time. He was a bit embarrassed about it, but now he's proud of it. His mates drop by, and they recognise me. People appreciate what I've done, not that I'm doing it for that, but people appreciate it. I'm off dancing this afternoon; it's what saved me and continues to do so.

Acknowledgements

I wish to acknowledge James, Debbie, George, Joan, Maryann and Rainer for their contribution to the success of HOPP!

Timeline including relevant history of the land

1955: The Stephenson Hepburn planning blueprint for the Perth metropolitan area earmarked all of Point (Cape) Peron as permanent public open space.

1964: The land at Point (Cape) Peron was transferred from the commonwealth to the state, subject to agreement that its future use would be "restricted to a reserve for recreation and/or park lands".

1968: The Australian government confirmed that the land must not be used "for private industrial, commercial or residential development".

1969: WA Premier Brand said that state government departments and the Rockingham Shire Council were being asked to prepare a master plan for the Development of Cape Peron as a park and recreational reserve and that the "amenities of the area would progressively become available to the general public".

1993: A proposal for boating facilities (offshore marina) in Mangles Bay without canals was rejected by the state government's EPA due to excessive seagrass loss.

2000: Much of the land at Cape Peron was classified by the WA government as "Bush Forever".

2003: To get around the previous EPA rejection due to excessive seagrass loss, the member for Rockingham supported the plan for an inland marina, which required canals from Mangles Bay to reach it inland.

2005 April: The Cape Peron Tourist Precinct Steering Committee was established to develop a marina-based tourist and residential precinct with Mangles Bay area of Cape Peron the focus for the development.

2005 November: Honourable Giz Watson, member for Legislative Council, tabled a petition in the Legislative Council [TP#1090] containing 2,145 signatures opposing the construction of a marina at Point Peron.

2006: Over the course of the year the following key events occurred:

A Parliamentary Petition into Marina at Point Peron was presented to the state government (Pratt, 2006).

The Development Plan for Cape Peron Tourist Precinct Project was submitted to the EPA by the developers.

The EPA Strategic Environmental Review report was published, outlining key issues and concerns with the project plans (Strategen, 2006).

2009: The Barnett government committed AU$3.7 million to fund the next phase of a proposed canal housing and inland marina project at Point Peron, known as the Cape Peron Tourist Precinct Project.

2010: During the year the following events occurred:

The federal environment minister decided to exclude the federally protected marine species Little Penguin from the federal assessment process.

The Barnett government announced that they had appointed a private sector development partner Cedar Woods to work on the next phase of the project.

The Rockingham Lakes regional parks management plan was released, which highlighted the outstanding conservation and recreational values of Cape Peron and set out a plan for its sustainable management as part of the Rockingham Lakes Regional Park (Overman, Dooley, Bowra & Strano, 2010).

2011: A HOPP rally at proposed development site attracted the biggest crowd to date (around 500). See the videos that on the HOPP website (HOPP, 2019), which are from the protest rally in January 2011:

- The rally begins – Hands Off Point Peron
- A poem by Janice
- Les Lowe discusses hydrology/water issues associated with canal developments

The environmental scoping document was released by Cedar Woods with proponents working to refine the 2006 development plan, which they had submitted to the EPA in 2006 (Strategen, 2011).

2012: The follow-up document by the developer – Mangles Bay marina-based tourist precinct: Public environmental review (Strategen, 2012) was submitted to government.

HOPP's 11,000-plus signature petition was tabled by Lynn McLaren, member Legislative Council, WA government.

Cape Peron coastal park vision was launched, followed later by a website with the same name.

2013: The petition no. 4 Mangles Bay tourist precinct submission was given to the standing committee on environment and public affairs (HOPP, 2013).

2014: The Federal Department of Environment issued environmental approval of the so-called Mangles Bay Marina (MBM) and Private Canal Housing Estate proposal on 2 October 2014.

In an open letter to the Australian government, Minister Greg Hunt (19 December 2014), concerns were raised by experts that the impacts on the Little Penguins were not considered due to a decision taken on 27 October 2010 to exclude this federally protected marine species from the federal assessment process. Twelve strong points were made as to why it was important to reconsider this decision (HOPP, 2014).

2015: The Western Australian Planning Commission (WAPC) sought public comment on its plan to rezone the land from Bush Forever and Regional Parklands to urban development/housing with submissions closing on 13 November 2015.

2016: On Wednesday, 8 June 2016, HOPP addressed the WAPC oral hearings committee to expand on their 600-page submission as to why rezoning Point Peron public land for an inland marina and housing estate would be a huge mistake from every angle.

2017: The WAPC met on 23 August 2017 to consider the proposal to rezone public land at Point Peron to private urban zoning under MRS Amendment 1280/41 – Mangles Bay Marina. HOPP founder Dawn Jecks attended this meeting and addressed the full committee of the WAPC on behalf of Hands Off Point Peron Inc.

2018: A major public meeting was held on 17 January 2018 at Rockingham's Gary Holland Centre with standing room only. In response Conservation Council WA joined in to assist the campaign.

People power won – finally. On 1 March 2018 WA Minister for Planning Rita Saffioti announced her decision that she had accepted the WAPC's recommendation to reject the proposed Mangles Bay Marina Metropolitan Region Scheme Major Amendment 1280/41 and withdrew the proposal. See WAPC (2018) report.

2019: one year on, in March 2019, HOPP wrote to the WA minister for planning reiterating the fact that successive governments over more than six decades have made promises to the people that align with this land becoming an A Class reserve under the conditions stipulated in the 1964 Point Peron Land Transfer agreement and expressing concern that to date there has been no apparent progress towards this.

References

Conde, M. (2016). Resistance to mining: A review. *Ecological Economics*, *132*, 80–90.

Crevani, L., Lindgren, M. & Packendorff, J. (2010). Leadership, not leaders: On the study of leadership as practices and interactions. *Scandinavian Journal of Management*, *26*, 77–86.

Hands Off Point Peron (HOPP). (2013). *Petition no. 4 Mangles Bay tourist precinct*. Retrieved from http://handsoffpointperon.com/wp-content/uploads/2016/06/HOPP-follow-up-to-standing-committee-re-petition.pdf

Hands Off Point Peron (HOPP). (2014). *Open letter to Minister Greg Hunt*. Retrieved from http://handsoffpointperon.com/wp-content/uploads/2016/06/Plight-of-the-Little-Penguin-An-Open-Letter-to-Minister-Greg-Hunt_BC_141210_Dec23.pdf

Hands Off Point Peron (HOPP). (2019). *Coastal tourist park, not canals*. Retrieved from http://handsoffpointperon.com/

Ife, J. (2016). *Community development in an uncertain world: Vision, analysis and practice* (2nd ed.). Cambridge, UK: Cambridge University Press.

Macetela, C. (2016). *Social media as a new mass media tool for environmental consciousness*. Retrieved from http://lup.lub.lu.se/luur/download?func=downloadFile&recordOId=8892053&fileOId=8892989

Organisation for Economic Co-operation and Development (OECD). (2019). *OECD insights: Human capital*. Retrieved from www.oecd.org/insights/37966934.pdf

O'Toole, J. (2013). The practical idealist: Gandhi's leadership lessons. In T. Sethia & A. Narayan (Eds.), *The living Gandhi: Lessons of our times* (pp. 141–163). New Delhi, India: Penguin.

Overman, J., Dooley, B., Bowra, T. & Strano, P. (2010). *Rockingham lakes regional park*. Retrieved from http://handsoffpointperon.com/wp-content/uploads/2016/06/DEC_rockingham-lakes-mgmt-plan_2010.pdf

Pratt, L. (2006). *A petition into the proposed marina at Point Peron*. Retrieved from http://handsoffpointperon.com/wp-content/uploads/2016/06/ParliamentaryEnquiry_2006_PointPeron_2.pdf

Pyles, L. (2009). *Progressive community organising: A critical approach for a globalising world*. New York, USA: Routledge.

Shields, C. (2011). Transformative leadership: An introduction. In P. Lang (Ed.). *Transformative leadership: A reader* (pp. 1–17). Retrieved from www.jstor.org/

Standing Committee on Environment and Public Affairs, Western Australian Legislative Council. (2006). *A report into the proposed marina at Peron Point*. Retrieved from www.

parliament.wa.gov.au/Parliament/commit.nsf/(Report+Lookup+by+Com+ID)/D8F3BF5C23AEB56648257831003E96D4/$file/ev.024.061206.rpf.007.xx.a.pdf

Strategen. (2006). *Strategic environmental review: Cape Peron tourist precinct project*. Retrieved from http://handsoffpointperon.com/wp-content/uploads/2016/06/Point_Peron_Strategic_Environmental_Review_2006.pdf

Strategen. (2011). *Manges Bay marina based tourist precinct: Scoping document*. Retrieved from http://handsoffpointperon.com/wp-content/uploads/2016/06/ManglesBay_Scoping_document_v91.pdf

Strategen. (2012). *Mangles Bay marina based tourist precinct: Public environmental review*. Retrieved from http://handsoffpointperon.com/wp-content/uploads/2016/06/CED10088.01-Mangles-Bay-PER-Rev-1.pdf

Western Australia Planning Commission. (2018). *Major amendment 1280/41: Mangles Bay marina*. Retrieved from www.planning.wa.gov.au/publications/7917.aspx

Wexler, M. (1996). A sociological framing of the nimby (not-in-my-backyard) syndrome. *International Review of Modern Sociology, 26*(1), 91–110.

Chapter 8

Species justice is for every body

Wallea Eaglehawk

Where love comes from

As a sociologist I feel it is my moral obligation to use my platform (be it social media or this chapter), research and knowledge to give a voice to the voiceless – which in this situation is nonhuman animals and the natural environment which we all inhabit. I must use my practice of writing as a space for activism and social change. I believe that species justice is for *every body* – every animal, both human and nonhuman, and every forest, every rock and mountain, every river and every ocean. I believe that to enact species justice is to live through an ethic of love which involves loving others as a radical act of disrupting the status quo, not just a hat one wears from nine to five. Rather, living through an ethic of love boils down to just one thing: seeing veganism as a moral baseline (Francione, 2016) from which everything else takes root. I strongly believe this because loving others involves a love for nonhuman animals, and you don't eat someone you love.

Veganism is a purist belief and practice that involves doing everything one can to ensure no harm comes to animals and the natural environment. Veganism maintains that there is no such thing as ethical slaughter and that all animal by-products are borne of exploitation and torture (Garlow, 2014). As such, veganism means: no consumption of animal products (meat, dairy, eggs and honey); no exploitative use of animals (circus performances, zoos, research and horse racing); and no purchasing of animal-derived goods such as wool or leather. Veganism is something achievable by anyone who buys their own groceries or who gets a say in what meals they consume. For example, through the act of eating a meat-free burger instead of a hamburger can come huge ripples of change, if enough people make this choice. This not only results in one less animal being slaughtered but saves 4,163 litres of water and 30 square feet of forest and creates a job for someone to manufacture and package a meat-free patty (The Vegan Calculator, 2019). Veganism is the most powerful form of activism *anyone* can take part in every single day and night.

The chapter explores species justice from the theory to what it looks like in action through internet activism using the example of live sheep export in WA.

Further, the complexities of species justice and veganism will be examined. Finally, a path towards species justice as the first step for social workers and activists everywhere will be detailed.

Species justice: love means no violence above all else

Social work continues to operate under the "assumption that anthropocentrism is a valid and non-negotiable given" (Ryan, 2011, p. 2). Anthropocentrism is also known as speciesism, which refers to the superiority of the human species and their control over nonhuman animals (Hanrahan, 2011). This means that through the hierarchical binary of human versus other, all that falls under the "other" category is treated as an object devoid of sentience (Borkfelt, 2011). According to Ross (2019) this then leads to a culture in which the mistreatment of animals is normalised and accepted. The complexity arises from humans' desire to derive sustenance, pleasure and entertainment from animals. Yet as Ross (2019) writes, the human population's ability to survive is intricately intertwined with nonhuman animals' ability to not only live but flourish.

Anthropocentrism is based on a hierarchical binary of human and animal, human and environment, or human and other. In the dualism, the first category of human is constructed as "superior to the excluded, subordinate, second category" (Derrida, 2016, p. 206). There is not only a hierarchy between human and everything deemed as other but also within the category of animal itself. There is a hierarchy of worth operating, with, for example, animals farmed for human consumption compared with the culling of feral pigs and camels. For social work and activists alike to take the next step towards a just world, the binary of human versus other needs to be removed entirely (Hanrahan, 2011).

A shift is needed from the personal to the global, from a human-centred practice of social justice to a species justice practice based on the intrinsic worth of all sentient beings including Mother Earth (Hanrahan, 2011). This can be understood as enacting an ethic of love. However, this is not to be taken as a passive act. Enacting an ethic of love means being resistive, holding tensions and working peacefully to bring about justice for all from a place of love (Ross, 2017). Eco-justice features an ethic of love (hooks, 2001), which means no violence to humans, nonhuman animals and the environment. This can look different depending on practitioners' areas of work or areas of protest. There is a feasible way to hold resistive tension to the status quo of speciesism and to ensure the least amount of harm to sentient beings and the environment. This is veganism, a word and practice that divides a nation but one that quite literally saves lives, ends suffering and reduces the destruction of natural environments on a global level (Francione & Charlton, 2015).

The legitimation of killing

The killing of some sentient beings is an institutionalised and cultural practice in Australia and around the world. Speciesism is legitimised through the media, education and training and laws and governance (Wewer, 2018). Industries based on use of animals continue to be granted a social licence to operate (Moffat & Zhang, 2014) by the broader Australian public. White (2018) explains how farm animals are close to the bottom of the nonhuman hierarchy with a significant amount of objectification due to their economic value. This process is institutionalised and legitimated through business structures as such Meat and Livestock Australia (2019) and is deeply rooted in the psyche of Australian everyday life (Bray & Ankeny, 2016). As farm animals serve a considerable purpose for almost all of the Australian population, the intrinsic value of their lives is barely acknowledged in the process of their rearing, exploitation and slaughter. For example, pigs are renamed as pork, cows are renamed beef, and "animal rights" organisations such as the Royal Society for the Prevention of Cruelty to Animals (RSPCA) endorse particular brands of animal products as humane and ethical (RSPCA, 2019). The RSPCA investigates harm to domesticated animals such as dogs and cats and often takes people to court over abuse of their pets which is deemed inhumane (Hook, 2019). However, the RSPCA does not extend the same level of investigation into the killing of farm animals as the process is legitimised, and the way in which it occurs is considered legal. The logic is that as long as the animal is killed in the correct way, there is no problem.

A species justice argument can be used here to challenge the nature and extent of harm experienced by farm animals. As White (2018, p. 239) writes, people and nonhuman animals who are victims of environmental harm are often not acknowledged as being victims of crime. There is little to no legal precedence for this, so irrespective of personal experiences, legally there is no crime and, therefore, no victim. White's idea of "green victimology" (2018, p. 239) when viewed with a species justice lens suggests that anyone being oppressed through any process, not just environmental harm, is the victim of a crime. This understanding allows for a repositioning from speciesism to species equality and legal rights (Bigould, 2014). White's (2018) concept of green victimology needs to be adapted to include not only environmental harm but social, species and economic harm. The new concept of "anthropocentric harm" is suggested, which encapsulates any harm caused by humans in an anthropocentric dominant society. Although there is no legal precedence to currently recognise such a complex issue, there is little standing in the way of a mass people movement reshaping the legal system. We are beginning to see this with the immense economic pull of a rapidly growing vegan market (Fox, 2018), where the law, much like the economy, has no choice but to meet consumer demand, if the people so demand it.

Anthropocentric harm argues that killing animals for human consumption cannot be justified on moral grounds or on grounds of logic as it has been shown that humans do not need to eat meat, eggs or dairy to survive and thrive. The old adage that humans need animal protein, or large amount of protein at all, has been disproven (Tello, 2018). However, dead cow, otherwise known as beef, is a common source of protein. This protein is derived from the muscle of the cow; which begs the question – where does the cow get its protein to build all that muscle? The answer to which is soy, corn and other grains. Soy crops used for animal agriculture account for 75% of soy crops globally, with 50% of habitable land around the world being used for the rearing of animals (One Green Planet, 2017). The crops are often grown by workers not able to use the beans or grain for themselves, nor are they able to afford the meat they raise (Latham, 2000). Further to this, the crops are highly water intensive, with a considerable environmental impact (Woody, 2015). The amount of crops currently produced globally are enough to feed every starving human being (Latham, 2000).

According to Simon (2013), violence towards animals ranges from a condoning of animals being killed for consumption to the hunting, gutting, skinning and processing of animals. Within this spectrum comes abuse towards domesticated animals, which is not legitimated and is not condoned. Simon (2013) writes that these social practices perpetuate cruelty and normalise violence. Gallagher, Allen and Jones (2008) explore the link between animal abuse and domestic violence and found that these two acts often occur in the same households. The single biggest threat to women in Australia is a man (Fitz-Gibbon & Maher, 2018) who is violent, and statistically, this tends to also be a man who has condoned violence towards animals at some point in his life (Gallagher et al., 2008). Hand in hand with anthropocentrism comes patriarchy and toxic masculinity. Patriarchy refers to a male-dominant societal structure in which, similar to humans and anthropocentrism, patriarchy exists to uphold the dominant male-centred discourse (Lerner, 1986). DeLessio-Parson argues that in patriarchal societies, masculinity implies an imperative to eat meat and that this imperative reinforces toxic masculinity (Chiorando, 2017). Marlborough (2017) writes that the Australian male identity is toxic when viewed as predominantly the Australian macho, violent-bloke archetype. Roose writes that it is this kind of masculinity, entrenched in acts of violence that is born of an "ideological masculinity" (2018, n.p.), which is emerging as a form of violent extremism. I acknowledge that my line of argument here co-exists with a recognition of the diversity of ways of being a male even within a patriarchal society. Racism is inter-connected with speciesism and patriarchal values that reinforce violence as shown in Australia, where a high proportion of jobs in slaughterhouses are filled by asylum seekers and refugees (Nayate, 2019). Research shows this type of employment can compound peoples' trauma due to the highly emotional and violent nature of the work (Nagesh, 2017).

In Australia, the welfare of animals is governed at a state and territory level with no overarching national laws (RSPCA, 2019). There is some recognition of sentience, with it being broadly acknowledged that animals can feel pain

(World Animal Protection, 2019). However, legislation still exists that animals can be used for sport, entertainment and clothing and still be slaughtered for sustenance. For example, legislation was recently passed in Australia that effectively brings an end to cosmetic testing on animals (Steiber, 2019), although it does not ban the act of testing itself nor the sale of products that have been tested on animals. The legislation passed after pressure from the public and organisations such as The Body Shop, which had campaigned for 30 years (Steiber, 2019). This outcome demonstrates that if there is a public demand for it, the government will make it so but only in a way that best serves them and the multinational companies that sell into the Australian market. Although most commentators are saying this will bring an end to animal testing, the law does not apply to other forms of research such as medical research, and the law does not make it illegal to perform cosmetic tests – it is just illegal to use the data (Steiber, 2019).

Alive and kicking: a WA example

When it comes to animals, there is one area which is governed at a national level and that is the exporting of live animals overseas for slaughter (RSPCA, 2019). According to the Australian Livestock Exporters' Council (ALEC, 2019), the live export of cows, sheep and goats is worth AU$2 billion a year. Australia is among the top 10 exporting nations in the world with 1 million cattle and 2 million sheep exported annually (ALEC, 2019). According to ALEC (2019), Australia's animal welfare standards for livestock export are the best in the world, despite World Animal Protection (WAP) finding that there is legislation, but with only partial application, and they grade Australia's treatment of farm animals a "C" (WAP, 2019). Countries such as New Zealand, the United Kingdom, Austria and Switzerland receive an "A" overall, and an "A" for their treatment of farm animals; as such Australia is far from being the best in the world (WAP, 2019).

The ALEC website argues for the economic importance of live animal export based on the employment of 10,000 Australians (ALEC, 2019). This is a common argument for any provocative industry, be it live export or coal mining, as demonstrated by Adani in Northern Queensland, promising 1,800 new jobs (The New Daily, 2019). Despite the environmental impact of Adani potentially leading to the degradation of the Great Barrier Reef, which currently creates 64,000 jobs (Great Barrier Reef Foundation, 2019). This example is used to demonstrate that although the need for an industry or trade is argued in economic terms, it is not job creation that politicians vote for; it is not job creation that justifies an unethical industry. The reality of the situation is that 10,000 people create $2 billion revenue in live export (ALEC, 2019), yet the Great Barrier Reef tourism industry employs 64,000 and generates $6.4 billion (Great Barrier Reef Foundation, 2019). This disparity is indicative of the vested interests and exploitative nature of the live animal export industry, which creates wealth for the few at the expense of 3 million sentient beings per year.

In 2017 the live animal export trade was nearly brought to its knees in WA after footage showing distressed, dying and dead sheep bound for the Middle East was aired on the television current affairs program *60 Minutes* (Laurie, 2019). Nearly 2,400 sheep died during the August 2017 voyage, sparking outrage from the Australian public that brought into question the very nature of the live animal export industry (Laurie, 2019). Because of this footage, and four more voyages documented by a whistle-blower, exporting company Emanuel had its licence to export cancelled by Agricultural Minister David Littleproud, the industry regulator (Laurie, 2019). In this unique circumstance, the public withdrew its social licence to operate through protests, both in person and online, which resulted in the removal of Emanuel's legal licence to operate. As Emanuel exported 71% of all export sheep in Australia in 2017, their inability to continue to export came at a huge cost to the industry, nearly halting it completely (Laurie, 2019). On the basis of this incidence, and many other incidents of animal welfare violations due to the cruel nature of live animal export, a bill to ban live animal export entirely nearly passed through the Australian government in 2018 (Laurie, 2019).

Online activism is for every body

This particular example brings to light the effect of people power, both in person through rallying and online through organising, sharing information and pressuring government representatives. Within days of the footage of dying sheep on Emanuel's ship being aired on television, there were protestors occupying space outside of the company's headquarters (Laurie, 2019). Across the nation everyday Australian's voices were heard, prompting the agricultural minister to fly to WA to demand answers from Emanuel (Laurie, 2019). Although there were a number of people around the nation physically protesting live sheep export, in the main the public was rallying online. Groups such as Stop Live Exports, a Fremantle-based not-for-profit, have amassed 17,500 followers on Facebook (Facebook, 2019). Stop Live Exports regularly shares up-to-date information about legal proceedings and politics and provides its followers with imagery to share to their own feeds as an act of social media activism (Facebook, 2019). It is groups such as these that are responsible for the bulk of organising online activism (Marichal, 2013). Anytime, anyplace, online activism can be taken up by anyone with an internet connection. Messages can be sent and received instantaneously, and change can follow just as quickly. Whether it be snap protests, as seen with activists holding a climate change "die in" on a busy Melbourne street (Smith, 2019), or global hashtag movements such as #BlackLivesMatter which on average receive more than 17,000 mentions online each day (Anderson, Toor, Rainie & Smith, 2018).

Coupled with personal actions, the use of social media as a tool to enact political or social change is particularly important, and empowering, for people of colour (Anderson et al., 2018). Social media can enable the public to "bypass existing realms of politics, social movements and campaigning" (Karatzogiani, 2016). When it comes to online activism, it can be tailored to meet the needs and desires of the original poster. People can choose to: re-share an image of a dying sheep on an Emanuel ship; write a comment on a pro-dairy post from a local politician; or share a poem about global warming to their friends list. Social media activism is the easiest and increasingly most common way to hold resistive tension with a vast array of social and political concerns (Marichal, 2013). There are few rules and regulations, yet it appears that the process is democratic when left to be governed by the public (Karatzogiani, 2016). Although it isn't an either-or choice between in-person protesting and online activism, a particular advantage of online activism is that individuals can take action irrespective of where they are or whether they belong to a larger activist group.

People participating in activism who identify, or are positioned by the media, as being vegan may experience a backlash from close family, friends and the broader community. For example, in 2019 in Australia the media reported on activists occupying private farmland as part of pro-animal rights protests and branded the activists as "vegan terrorists" (Molloy & Graham, 2019). As a result of this the current Australian government is seeking to pass legislation that will see "vegan terrorists" heavily fined and potentially facing jail time for such acts (Molloy & Graham, 2019). The internet also creates a space for another form of activism wherein often named "militant vegans" occupy slaughterhouses and live-stream inhumane conditions inside (Yahoo 7 News, 2019). This is often classed as eco-terrorism as it has the ability to cause a reputation and profit loss to the animal agricultural industry. Online activism in politically hostile situations, such as the current political climate in Australia, could be more impactful and less dangerous for individuals. Further, it requires no affiliation with larger groups, and individuals can self-determine the nature of their own contribution.

This is the movement of our lifetime

Although much activism is about collectivising around a shared justice concern, I feel that it is important to begin social change with self-reflection. In 2015 as a young, bright-eyed university student, I was confronted by veganism and made a snap decision to change on the spot. I quite literally threw my cow's milk coffee in the bin the second someone explained to me the morality of being vegan. In that moment, I was shown that my own morals and ethics did not truly align with my actions, and I saw no threat in changing – I embraced it. The first step to social change is to change oneself (Pandya, 2017) and lead by example in a nonviolent, actively resistive manner (Gaston, 2016). My form of activism has morphed from owning an all-vegan delicatessen to using my platform and white privilege to speak up for those whose cloven hoof would otherwise mince a keyboard.

Veganism is species justice in practice; veganism intersects with highly complex issues. I suggest anthropocentric harm as a new conceptualisation of harm caused by humans in an anthropocentric-dominant society. Anthropocentric harm builds on White's (2018) environmental harm to include economic, social and political harm. Speciesism goes hand in hand with anthropocentrism, operating within a hierarchical binary of human versus other, which sees the continued objectification and exploitation of humans, nonhuman animals and environments globally. Speciesism is normalised through the institutionalisation of the way Western capitalist societies treat their animals, in particular farm animals who are close to the bottom of the other hierarchy. In Australia, consuming animal products is a cultural practice deeply engrained in everyday life, and because of this the animal agricultural industry is granted a social licence to operate.

Species justice calls for nonviolence towards all living beings. Adopting an ethic of love in personal and professional practice can involve choosing to be vegan. When using a species justice lens, the harm experienced by farm animals can be brought into question. A valuing of all living beings means that there is no such thing as ethical or humane slaughter (Reese, 2018). There is a ground swelling movement of Australians with growing concern for animal welfare, which sits alongside an outcry for the environment. The answer to anthropocentric harm and speciesism is species justice and eco-justice more broadly.

To begin to shift from an anthropocentric moral and economic paradigm, a sociological imagination (Mills, 1959) must be used to link the personal to the political. Therefore, what each person eats is highly politicised. To eat and be vegan is a radical act of political defiance of the status quo.

The more people bring the legitimised nature of killing sentient beings out from behind the neatly kept lawns of pastoral care companies and into the living rooms of people wanting to do good, the faster social change will happen. This is the power of the internet and social media platforms, and the speed information can be shared – and protest movements can be instigated. Change has already begun which transcends cultural, physical, political and social differences. Veganism, although a hotly contested topic, is the social movement of the millennial generation (Hancox, 2018).

As hooks writes "to be truly visionary we have to root our imagination in our concrete reality while simultaneously imagining possibilities beyond that reality" (2000, p. 110). Species justice involves an imagining of a just world for every body while working to hold tensions in the here and now. Species justice sits among a diverse range of concepts and theories that give voice and power to those without. Species justice is for every forest, every river, every ocean; species justice is for every human and every nonhuman animal; species justice is for every body.

References

Anderson, M., Toor, S., Rainie, L. & Smith, A. (2018). *Activism in the social media age*. Retrieved from www.pewinternet.org/2018/07/11/activism-in-the-social-media-age/

Australian Livestock Exporters' Council (ALEC). (2019). *Economic impact*. Retrieved from https://auslivestockexport.com/about-alec/economic-impact

Bigould, L. (2014). *It's time to re-evaluate our relationship with animals*. Retrieved from https://youtu.be/Fr26scqsIwk

Borkfelt, S. (2011). Nonhuman otherness: Animals as others and devices for othering. In S. Sencindiver, M. Beville & M. Lauritzen (Eds.), *Otherness: A multilateral perspective* (pp. 137–154). Frankfurt, Germany: Peter Lang.

Bray, H. & Ankeny, R. (2016). *It's complicated: Australia's relationship with eating meat*. Retrieved from https://theconversation.com/its-complicated-australias-relationship-with-eating-meat-67230

Chiorando, M. (2017). *'Eating meat reinforces toxic masculinity' according to academic on Fox News*. Retrieved from www.plantbasednews.org/post/eating-meat-reinforces-toxic-masculinity

Derrida, J. (2016). *Of grammatology*. Baltimore, USA: John Hopkins University Press.

Facebook. (2019). *Stop live exports*. Retrieved from www.facebook.com/StopLiveExports.org/

Fitz-Gibbon, K. & Maher, J. (2018). *Men's violence against women: The leading threat to women's safety and wellbeing*. Retrieved from https://lens.monash.edu/2018/10/17/1362647/the-number-one-threat-to-womens-safety-and-well-being

Fox, K. (2018). *Here's why you should turn your business vegan in 2018*. Retrieved from www.forbes.com/sites/katrinafox/2017/12/27/heres-why-you-should-turn-your-business-vegan-in-2018/#69a32612144d

Francione, G. (2016). *Veganism as a moral imperative*. Retrieved from www.abolitionistapproach.com/veganism-moral-imperative/

Francione, G. & Charlton, A. (2015). *Animal rights: The abolitionist approach*. Utah, USA: Exempla Press.

Gallagher, B., Allen, M. & Jones, B. (2008). Animal abuse and intimate partner violence: Researching the link and its significance in Ireland: A veterinary perspective. *Irish Veterinary Journal, 61*(10), 658–667.

Garlow, A. (2014). *5 types of animal exploitation considered 'normal' in the US*. Retrieved from www.onegreenplanet.org/animalsandnature/5-types-of-animal-exploitation-considered-normal-in-the-usa/

Gaston, H. (2016). *The influence of active resistance on social change*. Retrieved from www.huffpost.com/entry/the-influence-of-active-resistance-on-social-change_b_583eea02e4b08347769c05d2?guc

Great Barrier Reef Foundation. (2019). *The value*. Retrieved from www.barrierreef.org/the-reef/the-value

Hancox, D. (2018). *The unstoppable rise of veganism: How a fringe movement went mainstream*. Retrieved from www.theguardian.com/lifeandstyle/2018/apr/01/vegans-are-coming-millennials-health-climate-change-animal-welfare

Hanrahan, C. (2011). Challenging anthropocentrism in social work through ethics and spirituality. *Journal of Religion & Spirituality in Social Work, 30*(3), 272–293.

Hook, C. (2019). *Animal cruelty case: Petting zoo owner jailed for stabbing dog with pitchfork*. Retrieved from https://7news.com.au/news/animals/petting-zoo-owner-jailed-for-repeatedly-stabbing-dog-with-pitchfork-c-187482

hooks, b. (2000). *Feminism is for everybody: Passionate politics.* Cambridge, UK: South End Press.
hooks, b. (2001). *Salvation: Black people and love.* New York, USA: William Morrow.
Karatzogiani, A. (2016). *Beyond hashtags: How a new wave of digital activists is changing society.* Retrieved from https://theconversation.com/beyond-hashtags-how-a-new-wave-of-digital-activists-is-changing-society-57502
Latham, J. (2000). There's enough food for everyone, but the poor can't afford to buy it. *Nature: International Journal of Science, 404*(202), 222.
Laurie, V. (2019, 4–5 May). Alive & kicking. *The Weekend Australian Magazine*, pp. 30–33.
Lerner, G. (1986). *The creation of patriarchy.* Oxford, UK: Oxford University Press.
Marichal, J. (2013). *Political Facebook groups: Micro-activism and the digital front stage.* Retrieved from https://firstmonday.org/ojs/index.php/fm/article/view/4653/3800
Marlborough, P. (2017). *How the Aussie bloke stereotype destroys Australian men.* Retrieved from www.vice.com/en_au/article/qv4m95/how-the-aussie-bloke-stereotype-destroys-australian-men
Meat and Livestock Australia. (2019). *Lamb campaigns.* Retrieved from www.mla.com.au/marketing-beef-and-lamb/domestic-marketing/lamb-campaigns/
Mills, C. (1959). *The sociological imagination.* Oxford, UK: Oxford University Press.
Moffat, K. & Zhang, A. (2014). The paths to social licence to operate: An integrative model explaining community acceptance of mining. *Resources Policy, 39*, 61–70.
Molloy, F. & Graham, B. (2019). *The drastic call to jail vegan 'terrorists' who target farmers with intimidation on their properties.* Retrieved from www.news.com.au/technology/environment/the-drastic-call-to-jail-vegan-terrorists-who-target-farmers-with-intimidation-on-their-properties/news-story/a792b3fe6a12a35d78e9694120a2cff8
Nagesh, A. (2017). *The harrowing psychological toll of slaughterhouse work.* Retrieved from https://metro.co.uk/2017/12/31/how-killing-animals-everyday-leaves-slaughterhouse-workers-traumatised-7175087/
Nayate, A. (2019). Slaughterhouses result in negative impact on surrounding community. Retrieved from www.weeklytimesnow.com.au/news/opinion/slaughterhouses-result-in-negative-impact-on-surrounding-community/news-story/8f7522ad75a2e1f3685b694c9cf9c1b2
The New Daily. (2019). *ADANI coal mine jobs start date.* Retrieved from https://thenewdaily.com.au/news/state/qld/2019/06/14/adani-coal-mine-jobs-start-date/
One Green Planet. (2017). *How planting crops used to feed livestock is contributing to habitat destruction.* Retrieved from www.onegreenplanet.org/environment/livestock-feed-and-habitat-destruction/
Pandya, B. (2017). *Change yourself, change the world.* Retrieved from www.huffpost.com/entry/change-yourself-change-th_b_803690
Reese, J. (2018). *There's no such thing as humane meat or eggs: Stop kidding yourself.* Retrieved from www.theguardian.com/food/2018/nov/16/theres-no-such-thing-as-humane-meat-or-eggs-stop-kidding-yourself
Roose, J. (2018). *'Ideological masculinity' that drives violence against women is a form of violent extremism.* Retrieved from https://theconversation.com/ideological-masculinity-that-drives-violence-against-women-is-a-form-of-violent-extremism-99603
Ross, D. (2017). A research-based model for corporate social responsibility: Towards accountability to impacted stakeholders. *Journal of Corporate Social Responsibility, 2*(8), 1–11.
Ross, D. (2019). Speciesism. In S. Idowu & R. Schmidpeter (Eds.), *International encyclopedia of sustainable management.* New York, USA: Springer Reference. [In publication].

Royal Society for the Prevention of Cruelty to Animals (RSPCA). (2019). *What is the Australian legislation governing animal welfare?* Retrieved from https://kb.rspca.org.au/knowledge-base/what-is-the-australian-legislation-governing-animal-welfare/

Ryan, T. (2011). *Animals and social work: A moral introduction.* New York, USA: Palgrave MacMillan.

Simon, K. (2013). *Hunting perpetuates cruelty, teaches violence.* Retrieved from www.dailynebraskan.com/opinion/simon-hunting-perpetuates-cruelty-teaches-violence/article_ba32788c-5583-11e3-8816-001a4bcf6878.html

Smith, R. (2019). *Snap 'climate emergency' rally to disrupt parts of Melbourne CBD at midday.* Retrieved from www.news.com.au/technology/environment/climate-change/snap-climate-emergency-rally-to-disrupt-parts-of-melbourne-cbd-at-midday/news-story/9a7b7772590f73917d91fd1dd7a3842b

Steiber, M. (2019). *Australia makes moves to ban animal testing in the cosmetics industry.* Retrieved from www.finder.com.au/australia-makes-moves-to-ban-animal-testing-in-the-cosmetics-industry

Tello, M. (2018). *Eat more plants, fewer animals.* Retrieved from www.health.harvard.edu/blog/eat-more-plants-fewer-animals-2018112915198

The Vegan Calculator. (2019). *How much have you saved?* Retrieved from https://thevegancalculator.com/

Wewer, E. (2018). *Man, animal, other: The intersections of racism, speciesism and problematic recognition within Indigenous Australia.* Retrieved from https://epress.lib.uts.edu.au/student-journals/index.php/NESAIS/article/view/1469/1582

White, R. (2018). Green victimology and nonhuman victims. *International Review of Victimology, 24*(2), 239–255.

Woody, T. (2015). *Holy cow! Crops that use even more water than almonds.* Retrieved from www.takepart.com/article/2015/05/11/cows-not-almonds-are-biggest-water-users

World Animal Protection. (2019). *Australia.* Retrieved from https://api.worldanimalprotection.org/country/australia

Yahoo 7 News. (2019). *Vegan protestors live-stream confronting scenes after breaking into piggery.* Retrieved from https://au.news.yahoo.com/vegan-protestors-live-stream-confronting-scenes-breaking-piggery-112821321.html

Chapter 9

International experiences with social licence contestations

Martin Brueckner & Lian Sinclair

Introduction

The stories told so far have shed light on social licence contestations in WA, where both legal and political licence interplays were shown to have stymied community efforts to assert social licence claims. In light of both the legal and political challenges, community activists needed to devise strategies to counteract or circumvent these structural constraints. In this chapter, attention is directed towards examples from further afield, each giving detail on how communities and activists have responded to structural licence constraints.

The examples are offered with a view to give guidance to communities and eco-activists who may see parallels between the cases detailed here and their own lived experience. The strategies employed by the groups from the chosen examples may thus inform the development of eco-activist strategies in other conflict areas. In what follows, cases are presented from Queensland, Mongolia and Indonesia, detailing the nature of political, legal and social licence interactions and how these have been navigated by local activists.

Adani Carmichael mine – Queensland

The first example, chosen because of its highly contentious social licence, focuses on the Adani Carmichael coal mine located in Queensland, Australia. Analogous to WA, Queensland is also considered a developmentalist state (Kellow & Niemeyer, 1999) that "still reflects a philosophy that extracting minerals are part of the human species' God ordained role to have dominion over the earth" (Keim QC, cited in Ritter, 2018, p. 76) while only "imposing some controls [on industry] to mitigate some of the very worst environmental impacts of mining projects" (Ritter, 2018, p. 76).

In 2011, Adani Mining Pty Ltd, a wholly owned subsidiary of India's Adani Group, purchased the lease of the Carmichael mine in the north of the Galilee Basin in Central Queensland with a view to operate six open-cut and five underground coal mines with an expected yield of 2.3 billion tons of thermal coal over the life of the mine (Slezak, 2017a). Part of the project was a

189-kilometre railway line connecting the mine to Moranbah from where coal would be forwarded on the Goonyella rail system to the coal terminals of the sea ports at Hay Point and Abbot Point (Queensland Government, 2018). For years, the proposed project has received political support at state and federal level (Ludlow, 2018; Bradley, 2019), and as such a political licence can be said to exist (Brueckner & Eabrasu, 2018). Further, in 2019, the project received federal government approval under the Environment Protection and Biodiversity Conservation Act 1999 (Coorey & Ludlow, 2019) as well as approval by the Queensland Department of Environment and Science (Cox, 2019a), helping Adani secure its actuarial (legal) licences for the mine. In social licence terms, the spectre of regional employment growth in Queensland's structurally weak, rural regions (Australian Government, 2018) has also translated into considerable community support for the mine (Bulloch, 2017). Nonetheless, the proposed Carmichael coal mine has long proved highly controversial on environmental, economic and socio-cultural grounds, with public opinion polls showing growing opposition to the project (Slezak, 2017b; Massola, 2018); overall, the project's social licence has been drawn into question.

Stated briefly, environmentally the mine is deemed unacceptable by critics, inter alia, on climate change grounds due to expected annual emissions of 77 million tons of CO_2-e (Meinshausen, 2015) as well as in terms of Adani's predicted groundwater use of 12 billion litres annually (Hannam, 2017). The mine is also seen to pose a risk to the Great Barrier Reef owing to its impact in coral bleaching due to rising ocean temperatures consequent to climate change (Hughes et al., 2017; Sparrow, 2017) as well as due to direct impacts such as the export of coal via ship from coal terminals adjacent to the reef, the dispersion of coal dust and increased risks of collisions and spills. The required expansion of existing coal terminals also requires dredging, proving problematic for local marine health (Climate Council, 2017a; Sparrow, 2017). Adani's poor track record on environmental stewardship (Environmental Justice Australia, 2015, 2017) serves to further fuel these concerns. In economic terms, the mine promised to create 10,000 jobs (Robertson, 2017), yet the real figure has been revealed to be closer to 1,464 jobs (Fahrer, 2015). Further, the Carmichael mine poses a threat to coal production in the neighbouring state of New South Wales (NSW), potentially undermining the viability of 10 other new projects (Long, 2017). Job losses are feared in the tourism sector due to concerns about the mine's impact on Great Barrier Reef-based tourism (Pearce, 2017). The economic case for the mine is considered weak with independent analyses regarding the project as being "unbankable" (Cox, 2015; Institute for Energy Economics and Financial Analysis, 2017; Quiggin, 2018). The mine is being opposed on cultural grounds, for it is to be built on the land of the Wangan and Jagalingou People, who resist the project in a bid to protect their ancestral lands and cultural heritage (Wangan and Jagalingou Family Council, 2018) including by challenging Adani in court.

Given the actuarial and political licence situation in Queensland, activists have largely focused on causing delays to project commencement, beyond seeking to galvanise public opposition to the project. There is a growing recognition of the long-term decline in demand for thermal coal (International Energy Agency, 2017), and this is the Achilles heel of the Carmichael project, as targeted export markets such as India, for example, have already indicated their desire to stop overseas coal imports altogether (Safi, 2017). Thus, the focus of activism has been the targeting of banks, many of whom are signatories to The Equator Principles projects (The Equator Principles Association, 2019), and thus banks are reputationally vulnerable when seen to be underwriting projects considered environmentally destructive. Worldwide more than 19 major banks have refrained from underwriting the Carmichael mine in part owing to concerns about environmental impacts and the associated reputational harm potential combined with the mine's lack of economic viability (Climate Council, 2017b). As a result, Adani not only needed to scale down the original proposal but also had to self-fund the project, for which the company requires extra time (Quiggin, 2019), seeking to raise more than $1 billion in debt on global markets. Compoundingly, as reported by Long (2019), the financial position of Adani's Australian subsidiary is precarious as its "current assets of less than $30 million are swamped by current liabilities, due over the next 12 months, of more than $1.8 billion . . . effectively on paper [Adani] are insolvent".

In a similar way, ongoing court proceedings instigated by traditional land owners and conservation groups are slowing down the project. These include the action by the Australian Conservation Foundation against the government's assessment of Adani's north Galilee water scheme (Cox, 2019b). Further, the actions taken by Wangan and Jagalingou People against the ILUA Adani registered with the National Native Title Tribunal have challenged the ILUA's legitimacy on grounds that it was reached through duress by Adani and bribery payments to tribunal members (Anon, 2017).

Protracted industry–community conflicts commonly tend to favour corporate actors in the face of community burnout and costly legal proceedings. In this case, however, time is on the side of activists, an issue recognised increasingly in the resource sector, which is sensitive to cost blowouts owing to project delays (Davis & Franks, 2014). Although it needs to be noted that legal avenues have not always been successful, as in the case of the Wangan and Jagalingou People, nor that delaying tactics have been the explicit goal of activists (they first and foremost opposed the approval and development of the mine), it bears noting that the project delays incurred thus far could prove decisive for the fate of the Carmichael mine, which still has many hurdles to take before becoming operational.

Rio Tinto Oyu Tolgo mine – Mongolia

Mongolia, whilst a resource-rich nation, is critically dependent on foreign direct investment for the development of its mineral resources (United Nations Conference on Trade and Development, 2018). The Mongolian government, which came to power in a landslide victory on a strong pro-mining platform during the 2016 election (Bittner, 2016), is hoping to gain significant economic, social and political benefits from the expansion of the mining sector. Its strong emphasis on economic development over environmental and social concerns combined with a lack of capacity to enforce – albeit gradually tightened – environmental laws (Stern, 2014; Rhodes, 2018) speak to the strength of the political licence and relative weakness of the actuarial licence in the country. At the same time, the government's focus on economic growth and support for mining development as well as the sector's significance to Mongolian GDP (Edwards, 2016) has rendered the government somewhat beholden to mine operators (Hume, 2019; World Bank, 2019). This is particularly the case for large mining projects such as the Rio Tinto-led Oyu Tolgoi joint venture, which by 2021 is expected to contribute close to 30% of the country's GDP and is thus seen as a symbol of Mongolia's economic rise (Wen, 2015). Given the country's recent economic downturn due to falling commodity prices, the success of the Oyu Tolgoi project is a priority for the Mongolian government (Edwards, 2019).

The Oyu Tolgoi copper–gold mine is placed in the arid environment of the South Gobi province, which has an average annual rainfall of 80 millimetres. The arrival of the mega project triggered concerns among nomadic herders about the loss or contamination of precious water resources. Nomadic pastoralism has for centuries been Mongolia's prevailing form of land use and a significant contributor to national GDP (Lkhagvadorj, Hauck, Dulamsuren & Tsogtbaatar, 2013). With the onset of the mining boom a decade ago, however, pastural lands have increasingly become fragmented due to the presence of open pit mines, heavy equipment accoutrements and safety exclusion, which has resulted in herders in mining regions losing access to their pastures (Cane et al., 2015). As in the case of the Oyu Tolgoi mine, Mongolia's nomadic herders, "who identify themselves as indigenous to the area with historical claim to traditional pasture rights and other protections", found their way of life threatened by the mining project, being forced to resettle and experiencing devastating herd losses (Mines and Communities, 2012). They were forced to move to inferior locations and were provided with insufficient assistance in the process. Although a number of displaced herders have found employment in the mine, the traditional way of life, their culture and livelihood for many herders have been disrupted. However, neither Rio Tinto, the Mongolian government nor the World Bank, as guarantor of the mine, accepted the herders as "land-based mobile peoples" to be protected under international conventions on Indigenous People's rights and dismissed calls for just compensation for the herders' livelihood and cultural losses (Snow, 2014).

A group of aggrieved herders organised and filed a series of complaints to the Compliance Advisor Ombudsman (CAO), claiming that the development of the mine was threatening their livelihoods, health and culture. The CAO is tasked with resolving disputes with local communities affected by investments made by the World Bank's International Finance Corporation (IFC), which provided US$400 million in direct financing to the Oyu Tolgoi project (Edwards, 2019). Over four years of CAO mediation, independent experts were appointed jointly by the herders and the owners of Oyu Tolgoi to investigate the herders' claims. The experts broadly supported the herders' claims and criticised the company's compensation processes and environmental assessment and monitoring practices. In the end, an agreement was reached among the herders, the mining company and also the government, which included commitments to improved environmental monitoring and management, compensation as well as a number of initiatives to boost the economic sustainability of the herders' traditional livelihood; the agreement rates as being largely unprecedented and historic (Austin, 2019; Edwards, 2019).

The herders' success was largely a function of having turned to the CAO instead of opting for litigation, direct negotiation without a mediator, and media campaigns or protests. The fortuitous timing of the complaints proved advantageous in light of the IFC's own social licence concerns at the time. Over the last decade, the IFC increasingly found itself the target of non-government organisations' (NGOs') complaints to be funding projects responsible for human rights abuses, displacement, loss of livelihoods, fear, violence, criminalisation and repression (Anderson, 2015). Arguably the CAO was set up in 2009 after a number of highly controversial IFC-funded infrastructure projects in an attempt by the World Bank and IFC to become more socially and environmentally conscious (Edwards, 2019). Yet, even the work of the CAO received criticism in light of public perceptions of having a poor track record on conflict resolution (Altholz & Sullivan, 2017). The situation was compounded further by much international attention focused on the Oyu Tolgoi conflict (e.g., Neate, 2013; Bale, 2014; Snow, 2014) as well as growing internal pressure within the World Bank. This was due to the United States refusing to vote on World Bank funding to expand the Oyu Tolgoi mine, citing inter alia concerns about the project's environmental impacts as well as the complaints from local herder communities before the CAO (Els, 2013).

Although the herders' concerns were largely overridden by the Mongolian government intent on seeing the Oyu Tolgoi mine assume full production and by a mine operator claiming to be working within existing rules and guidelines, they were able to make inroads with a project underwriter who was vulnerable to further reputational damage. Similar to Adani protestors turning to banks to block project financing, the IFC was targeted given its own undertakings to support socially and environmentally responsible projects. In this regard, the tainted image of the CAO may well have assisted in bringing about a positive outcome for herders in light of the public attention on the ombudsman's office.

Rio Tinto's ex-Kelian gold mine – Indonesia

Rio Tinto's ex-Kelian gold mine in East Kalimantan, Indonesia, presents a rare chance to study the interrelationship among social, actuarial and political licences before and after wide-ranging political change. In 1985, after a decade of exploration and testing, PT Kelian Equatorial Mining (KEM), 90% majority owned by Rio Tinto, signed a Contract of Work (CoW) with the Indonesian government to exploit the primary gold deposit on the Kelian river (Bachriadi, 1998, p. 161). Production began in 1992 and finished in 2005 (Kemp et al., 2013; Everingham et al., 2016). As this time span coincides with the democratisation and decentralisation of Indonesian politics following the resignation of President Suharto in May 1998, an examination is possible of how the political strategies of both the mining corporation and people affected by mining evolved under autocratic and democratic political contexts.

More than 444 families (4,000 people) living within the mining concession area were evicted and relocated between 1982 and 1992 by the company and local regency government (Mangkoedilaga, Widjojo & Nainggolan, 2000). Residents who refused to move were arrested, their houses and gardens burnt, or they were shot by police, military or company security (Bachriad, 1998, p. 181). Evictees staged hundreds of protests and blockades to demand what they considered fair compensation between 1991 and 1996. However, under the authoritarian politics of the Indonesian New Order regime, protected by security forces, Rio Tinto had little incentive to address their social licence to operate. Constraints of space mean that this article considers only the relationship between *evictees* and Rio Tinto; other groups affected by mining and other aspects of this case are considered elsewhere (Sinclair, Forthcoming).

The situation began to change when local organisers collaborated with national and international NGOs including *Jaringan Advokasi Tambang*; Mining Advocacy Network (JATAM), *Wahana Lingkungan Hidup Indonesia*, Friends of the Earth Indonesia (WALHI) and Community Aid Abroad (CAA; now Oxfam Australia) (Atkinson, 1998; Atkinson, Brown & Ensor, 2001; Macdonald & Ross, 2002). In 1997, CAA activists visited the Kelian area, produced a short documentary film and began publicising the case in the English language and in Australia. In January 1998, CAA funded a month-long Australian tour of five Indonesian mining advocates, including Pak Pius Nyompe, founder of local organisation *Lembaga Kesejahteraan Masyarakat Tambang dan Lingkungan* (LKMTL) (Atkinson et al., 2001, pp. 13–14; McSorley & Fowler, 2001). The tour culminated on 30 January in Melbourne, when Rio Tinto executives met Pak Pius and received a list of grievances (Kelian Activist, interview with second author, 10 October 2016). Then in May 1998, supported by CAA and London NGO Down to Earth, Pak Pius attended Rio Tinto's annual general meeting in London and again met with Rio Tinto executives.

These visits coincided with CAA's campaign in Australia to create a Mining Ombudsman, which would hold Australian-based mining companies operating abroad to the same standards that apply in Australia. Furthermore, the tour followed the successful action in the Victorian Supreme Court against mining company BHP by OK Tedi landowners over environmental pollution in 1996 (Kirsch, 2014, p. 102). Rio Tinto global executives, concerned about their international reputation, risk of litigation and risk of further regulation, ordered their subsidiary to negotiate with LKMTL (the mining community and environment welfare council) as the representative of evictees for compensation. These negotiations resulted in KEM paying 10 million Indonesian Rupiah ($AU1,632 at 30 June 1999 exchange rates) compensation to each of 444 evicted families.

Following the *reformasi* movement and fall of Indonesia's authoritarian New Order regime in 1998, the democratisation and decentralisation of Indonesian politics resulted in a smaller role for the military and an opening of spaces for communities and NGOs to express grievances (Hadiz, 2010, p. 144; Aspinall, 2013; Erb, 2016). Emboldened by the changing political climate, in 1998 and 1999, LKMTL demonstrations blocked the access road to the mine more than 10 times (Community relations manager, KEM, interview with second author, 8 August 2017). Then in July 1999, LKMTL members blocked the access road for 40 consecutive days. Desperately wanting to avoid violence and associated publicity, KEM resumed negotiations (KEM Consultant, interview with second author, 7 August 2017).

A report by Komnas HAM (National Commission on Human Rights) released in early 2000 found evidence supporting claims of human rights violations, including unlawful detentions, deaths in custody, destruction of houses and property and sexual violence. The report recommended further investigation and prosecution by Indonesian courts (Mangkoedilaga et al., 2000). Although Rio Tinto has since admitted its complicity in human rights abuses (Kemp et al., 2013, p. 82), no accusations ever proceeded to the court system. Instead KEM re-entered negotiations with LKMTL and in March 2001 announced a 60 billion Indonesian Rupiah compensation package (AU$11.1 million) for victims without admitting guilt or liability (Macdonald & Ross, 2003, p. 51; Nurcahyana et al., 2008).

This case of conflict among evictees, their allies and Rio Tinto shows how the strategies of groups to affect social licence to operate changed with differing political and legal contexts. Before 1998, the political and legal contexts in Indonesia were extremely favourable for mining corporations, even when compared to WA, Queensland and Mongolia, and Rio Tinto needed to have little concern for its social licence. However, similar to the Oyu Tolgo case, by "jumping-scales" local activists were able to access alliances, resources and media attention not available within East Kalimantan or Indonesia and challenge the legitimacy of Rio Tinto globally. The change to a more open legal and political climate in Indonesia, although still in favour of mining capital, meant that the lack of local social licence – manifesting in protests and blockades – could no longer be ignored. As demonstrated by the Komnas HAM report (Mangkoedilaga et al., 2000), in a more open political climate, the lack of a social licence could spill over into legal action against the company, underscoring the inherent slippage and even co-determination of the social, actuarial and political risks and licences.

Conclusion

These cases illustrate the impact of legal and political contexts on social, actuarial and political risk and licence dynamics. The legal and political environments of Queensland, Mongolia and Indonesia were all found, albeit to varying degrees, to have been restrictive concerning activists' ability to assert their social licence concerns given the dominance of the political licence and relative weakness of the actuarial licence. In contexts such as Indonesia, vocal opposition could indeed cost lives during the Suharto regime, whereas years later public protest proved effective.

Unsurprisingly, therefore, activists often look outside the system. For one, this may occur with a view to increase social licence risks for organisations related to the local industry–community conflict further afield. Carmichael and Oyu Tolgoi mine protesters, for example, targeted project underwriters, who themselves were protective of their social licence, or the parent company in the case of Kelian, which proved to be more responsive to activist demands when confronted with community concerns at company headquarters. Their actions made explicit perceived corporate double-standards concerning operations at home and abroad and gave visibility to a problem otherwise at risk of being deemed remote. Reaching out beyond the local context has also enabled the building of alliances and partnerships to increase size, voice and reach as well as overall capacity of grassroots movements. Collective action was central to all three cases, enabling court challenges and complaints to ombudsmen or representations to company senior management. Reaching out also equipped activists with tools previously unavailable to them, such as filmmaking, enabling them to more effectively tell their stories and reaching larger audiences internationally.

Overall, an awareness of risk and licence interplays brings the underlying dynamics of industry–community conflicts into sharper relief and assists with strategy making based on an understanding of structural constraints facing activists. The examples presented here illustrate how the effectiveness of activism can be judged in context, which in turn can inform future strategy making. In light of the rising number of extractive conflicts globally (Andrews et al., 2017), good strategy making will be vital for communities in their social licence struggles.

References

Altholz, R. & Sullivan, C. (2017). *Accountability & international financial institutions: Community perspectives on the World Bank's office of the compliance advisor ombudsman*. Berkeley, USA: University of California.

Anderson, M. (2015, 2 April). *World Bank funding 'shrouded in darkness and riddled with abuse'*. Retrieved from www.theguardian.com/global-development/2015/apr/02/world-bank-funding-darkness-abuse-ngo-report

Andrews, T., Elizalde, B., Le Billon, P., Oh, C. H., Reyes, D. & Thomson, I. (2017). *The rise in conflict associated with mining operations: What lies beneath* (pp. 1–127). Washington, USA: Canadian International Resources and Development Institute (CIRDI).

Anon. (2017, 4 December). *Traditional owners file Adani injunction*. Retrieved from www.sunshinecoastdaily.com.au/news/traditional-owners-file-adani-injunction/3281604/

Aspinall, E. (2013). A nation in fragments. *Critical Asian Studies, 45*(1), 27–54.

Atkinson, J. (1998). *Undermined: The impact of Australian mining companies in developing countries*. Melbourne, Australia: Community Aid Abroad.

Atkinson, J., Brown, A. & Ensor, J. (2001). *Mining ombudsman annual report 2000–2001*. Melbourne, Australia: NSW Ombudsman.

Austin, R. (2019). *Herders successfully reach tripartite settlement to remain on heritage land following lawsuit over impact of Oyu Tolgoi mine*. Retrieved from www.business-humanrights.org/en/mongolia-herders-successfully-reach-tripartite-settlement-to-remain-on-heritage-land-following-lawsuit-over-impact-of-oyu-tolgoi-mine

Australian Government. (2018). *Unemployment rate by state and territory*. Retrieved from http://lmip.gov.au/default.aspx?LMIP/LFR_SAFOUR/LFR_UnemploymentRate

Bachriadi, D. (1998). *Merana Di Tengah Kelimpahan, Pelanggaran-pelanggaran HAM Pada Industri Pertambangan di Indonesia*. Jakarta, Indonesia: ELSAM.

Bale, R. (2014). *Massive Mongolian mine endangers nomads' water and way of life*. Retrieved from www.pri.org/stories/2014-10-01/massive-mongolian-mine-endangers-nomads-water-and-way-life

Bittner, P. (2016, 1 July). *Mongolian people's party routs democratic party in parliamentary elections*. Retrieved from https://thediplomat.com/2016/07/mongolian-peoples-party-routs-democratic-party-in-parliamentary-elections/

Bradley, J. (2019, April). *How Australia's coal madness led to Adani*. Retrieved from www.themonthly.com.au/issue/2019/april/1554037200/james-bradley/how-australia-s-coal-madness-led-adani

Brueckner, M. & Eabrasu, M. (2018). Pinning down the social license to operate (SLO): The problem of normative complexity. *Resources Policy, 59*, 217–226.

Bulloch, S. (2017, 10 October). *Hundreds rush to apply for rocky Adani jobs*. Retrieved from www.themorningbulletin.com.au/news/hundreds-apply-for-rockys-adani-jobs/3232539/

Cane, I., Schleger, A., Ali, S., Kemp, D., McIntyre, N., Lechner, A., . . . Lahiri-Dutt, K. (2015). *Responsible mining in Mongolia: Enhancing positive engagement*. St Lucia, Australia: Sustainable Minerals Institute.

Climate Council. (2017a). *New report: Adani monster mine could damage climate, health, tourism*. Retrieved from www.climatecouncil.org.au/carmichaelmediarelease

Climate Council. (2017b). *Risky business: Health, climate and economic risks of the Carmichael coalmine*. Potts Point, Australia: Climate Council of Australia.

Coorey, P. & Ludlow, M. (2019, 9 April). *Adani approved by Morrison government*. Retrieved from www.afr.com/news/politics/national/morrison-government-approves-adani-ends-internal-war-20190409-p51c9k

Cox, L. (2015, 30 June). *Adani's Carmichael mine is unbankable says Queensland Treasury*. Retrieved from www.smh.com.au/business/companies/adanis-carmichael-mine-is-unbankable-says-queensland-treasury-20150630-gi1l37.html

Cox, L. (2019a, 13 June). *Adani cleared to start Carmichael coalmine work as groundwater plans approved*. Retrieved from www.theguardian.com/business/2019/jun/13/adani-cleared-to-start-carmichael-coalmine-work-as-groundwater-plans-approved

Cox, L. (2019b, 12 June). *Adani coalmine: Minister loses legal challenge on water pipeline assessment.* Retrieved from www.theguardian.com/environment/2019/jun/12/adani-coalmine-federal-government-loses-legal-challenge-on-water-assessment

Davis, R. & Franks, D. (2014). Costs of company-community conflict in the extractive sector. In *Corporate social responsibility initiative report.* Cambridge, USA: Harvard Kennedy School.

Edwards, S. (2019, 9 August). *How a group of Mongolian herders took on a mining giant: And won.* Retrieved from www.devex.com/news/how-a-group-of-mongolian-herders-took-on-a-mining-giant-and-won-90765

Edwards, T. (2016, 30 June). *Rio Tinto's Oyu Tolgoi rocks on as Mongolian opposition wins landslide.* Retrieved from www.afr.com/business/mining/copper/rio-tintos-oyu-tolgoi-rocks-on-as-mongolian-opposition-wins-landslide-20160630-gpvutz

Els, F. (2013, 9 March). *US raises serious concerns over Oyu Tolgoi's environmental, social impact.* Retrieved from www.mining.com/us-raises-serious-concerns-over-oyu-tolgois-environ mental-social-impact-21812/

Environmental Justice Australia. (2015). *A review of the Adani group's environmental history in the context of the Carmichael coal mine approval.* Carlton, Australia: Environmental Justice Australia.

Environmental Justice Australia. (2017). *The Adani brief: What governments and financiers need to know about the Adani Group's record overseas.* Carlton, Australia: Environmental Justice Australia.

The Equator Principles Association. (2019). *The equator principles.* Retrieved from https://equator-principles.com/about/

Erb, M. (2016). Mining and the conflict over values in Nusa Tenggara Timur Province, Eastern Indonesia. *The Extractive Industries and Society, 3*(2), 370–382.

Everingham, J., Kemp, D., Ali, S., Cornish, G., Langton, M. & Harvey, B. (2016). *Why agreements matter: A resource guide for integrating agreements into communities and social performance work at Rio Tinto.* Melbourne, Australia: Centre for Social Responsibility in Mining.

Fahrer, J. (2015). *Individual report to the Land Court of Queensland.* Melbourne, Australia: Australian-German College of Climate & Energy Transitions.

Hadiz, V. (2010). *Localising power in post-authoritarian Indonesia: A southeast Asia perspective.* Stanford, USA: Stanford University Press.

Hannam, P. (2017, 4 April). *'Barbaric': Farmers rattled as Adani coal mine granted unlimited water access.* Retrieved from www.smh.com.au/environment/barbaric-farmers-rattled-as-adani-coal-mine-granted-unlimited-water-access-20170404-gvdk5v.html

Hughes, T., Kerry, J., Álvarez-Noriega, M., Álvarez-Romero, J., Anderson, K., Baird, A., . . . Berkelmans, R. (2017). Global warming and recurrent mass bleaching of corals. *Nature, 543*(7645), 373.

Hume, N. (2019, 10 April). *Mongolia mining minister rules out Oyu Tolgoi deal changes.* Retrieved from www.ft.com/content/b7efbaec-5ae3-11e9-939a-341f5ada9d40

Institute for Energy Economics and Financial Analysis. (2017). *IEEFA update: An increasingly cursed Australian coal project.* Ohio, USA: Institute for Energy Economics and Financial Analysis.

International Energy Agency. (2017). *Market report series: Coal 2017.* Paris, France: International Energy Agency.

Kellow, A. & Niemeyer, S. (1999). The development of environmental administration in Queensland and Western Australia: Why are they different? *Australian Journal of Political Science, 34*(2), 205–222.

Kemp, D., Gronow, J., Zimmerman, V., Kim, J., Jørgensen, A. & Götzmann, N. (2013). *Why human rights matter*. London, UK: Rio Tinto.

Kirsch, S. (2014). *Mining capitalism: The relationship between corporations and their critics*. Oakland, USA: University of California Press.

Lkhagvadorj, D., Hauck, M., Dulamsuren, C. & Tsogtbaatar, J. (2013). Pastoral nomadism in the forest-steppe of the Mongolian Altai under a changing economy and a warming climate. *Journal of Arid Environments*, 88, 82–89.

Long, S. (2017, 6 July). *Galilee Basin mines will slash coal output, jobs elsewhere, Wood Mackenzie says*. Retrieved from www.abc.net.au/news/2017-07-06/galilee-basin-mining-project-will-reduce-coal-output:-research/8682164

Long, S. (2019, 24 July). *Adani's Carmichael coal mine surviving on lifeline from Indian parent company*. Retrieved from www.abc.net.au/news/2019-07-24/adani-carmichael-subsidiary-surviving-on-lifeline-from-parent/11338926

Ludlow, M. (2018, 14 February). *Adani to still receive special royalty deal from the Queensland government*. Retrieved from www.afr.com/news/politics/adani-to-still-receive-special-royalty-deal-from-the-qld-government-20180214-h0w29k#ixzz58wAiBHMf

Macdonald, I. & Ross, B. (2002). *Mining ombudsman annual report 2001–2002*. Sydney, Australia: Mining Ombudsman.

Macdonald, I. & Ross, B. (2003). *Mining ombudsman annual report 2003*. Sydney, Australia: Mining Ombudsman.

Mangkoedilaga, B., Widjojo, M. & Nainggolan, A. (2000). *Laporan Hasil Investigasi Masalah Hak Asasi Manusia di Sekitar Wilayah Pertambangan PT Kelian Equatorial Mining, Kabupaten Kutai Barat, Kalimantan Timur, Indonesia*. Jakarta, Indonesia: Komisi Nasional Hak Asasi Manusia.

Massola, J. (2018, 1 February). *Big surge in opposition to Adani, new polling reveals*. Retrieved from www.smh.com.au/politics/federal/big-surge-in-opposition-to-adani-new-polling-reveals-20180131-p4yz4o.html

McSorley, J. & Fowler, R. (2001). Mineworkers on the offensive. In G. Evans, J. Goodman & N. Lansbury (Eds.), *Moving mountains: Communities confront mining and globalization* (pp. 165–180). Otford, NSW, Australia: Mineral Policy Institute and Otford Press.

Meinshausen, M. (2015). *Individual report to the Land Court of Queensland on 'climate change – emissions'*. Melbourne, Australia: Australian German College of Climate & Energy Transitions.

Mines and Communities. (2012, 23 October). *Mongolian herders complain against Rio Tinto over Oyu Tolgoi mines*. Retrieved from www.minesandcommunities.org/article.php?a=11967

Neate, R. (2013, 19 April). *Rio Tinto accused of environmental and human rights breaches*. Retrieved from www.theguardian.com/business/2013/apr/18/rio-tinto-environmental-human-rights-breaches

Nurcahyana, Y., Nyompe, P., Tingang, V., Dullah, Y., Oktavianus, G., Rusulan, S. & Wibobo, S. (2008). *Status Penyelesaian Tuntutan Ganti Rugi Masyarakat oleh PT KEM: PT Kelian Equatorial Mining*. Samarinda, Indonesia: GVMachine.

Pearce, L. (2017, 26 June). *The Great Barrier Reef is worth $56 billion to our economy: Here's the proof*. Retrieved from www.huffingtonpost.com.au/2017/06/26/the-great-barrier-reef-is-worth-56-billion-to-our-economy-here_a_23001277/).

Queensland Government. (2018). *Carmichael coal mine and rail project*. Brisbane, Australia: Queensland Government.

Quiggin, J. (2018). The economic (non)viability of coal mining in the Galilee Basin. In D. Ritter (Ed.), *The coal truth* (pp. 121–136). Perth, Australia: University of Western Australia Publishing.

Quiggin, J. (2019, 3 June). *Opinion: Why would a billionaire persist with the Adani mine that will probably lose money?* Retrieved from www.sbs.com.au/news/opinion-why-would-a-billionaire-persist-with-the-adani-mine-that-will-probably-lose-money

Rhodes, L. (2018). Environmental crime and civilization: Identification; impacts; threats and rapid response – June 2018. *Comparative Civilizations Review*, 79(79), 3.

Ritter, D. (Ed.). (2018). *The coal truth*. Perth, Australia: University of Western Australia Publishing.

Robertson, J. (2017, 6 June). *Adani gives 'green light' to $16bn Carmichael coal mine.* Retrieved from www.theguardian.com/environment/2017/jun/06/adani-gives-green-light-to-16bn-carmichael-coal-mine

Safi, M. (2017, 13 June). *India has enough coal without Adani mine, yet must keep importing, minister says.* Retrieved from www.theguardian.com/environment/2017/jun/13/india-enough-coal-without-adani-mine-must-keep-importing-piyush-goyal

Sinclair, L. (Forthcoming). The power of multinational mining corporations, global governance and social conflict. In J. Mikler & K. Ronit (Eds.), *MNCs in global politics: Pathways of influence*. Cheltenham, UK: Edward Elgar Publishing.

Slezak, M. (2017a, 16 August). *Why Adani's planned Carmichael coalmine matters to Australia: And the world.* Retrieved from www.theguardian.com/business/2017/aug/16/why-adanis-planned-carmichael-coalmine-matters-to-australia-and-the-world

Slezak, M. (2017b, 7 October). *Most Australians oppose Adani mine, poll shows, amid national protests.* Retrieved from www.theguardian.com/environment/2017/oct/07/most-australians-oppose-adani-mine-poll-shows-amid-national-protests

Snow, K. (2014, 8 February). *Foreign mining, state corruption and human rights in Mongolia.* Retrieved from www.globalresearch.ca/foreign-mining-state-corruption-and-human-rights-in-mongolia/5367622

Sparrow, J. (2017, 7 April). *It's either Adani or the Great Barrier Reef: Are we willing to fight for a wonder of the world?* Retrieved from www.theguardian.com/commentisfree/2017/apr/07/its-either-adani-or-the-great-barrier-reef-are-we-willing-to-fight-for-a-wonder-of-the-world

Stern, R. (2014, 1 April). *Mongolia's mining boom raises environment concerns.* Retrieved from www.dw.com/en/mongolias-mining-boom-raises-environment-concerns/a-17534285

United Nations Conference on Trade and Development. (2018). *World investment report 2018*. New York, USA: United Nations Conference on Trade and Development.

Wangan and Jagalingou Family Council. (2018). *Our fight*. Retrieved from http://wanganjagalingou.com.au/our-fight/

Wen, P. (2015, 19 September). *Oyu Tolgoi is symbol on Mongolia's rise.* Retrieved from www.smh.com.au/business/companies/oyu-tolgoi-is-symbol-on-mongolias-rise-20150918-gjpl3z.html

World Bank. (2019). *Doing business 2019: Training for reform*. Washington, USA: World Bank.

Part 2

Clarion call for social work

Part 2 of the book builds on the eco-activist stories presented in Part 1 to distil and extend the authors' practice wisdom and insights into a guide for activist practice in situations of ecological conflict and injustice. Part 2 can be read as a comprehensive and adaptive model and related resources for practitioners seeking tools and guidance in their eco-activist work.

Chapter 10

The love ethic model

Dyann Ross

Overview of Part 2

Chapter 10 outlines the love ethic model, drawing on relevant literature and theories, and is inspired by the eco-activist stories highlighted in Part 1. The chapter commences with a consideration of eco-activism and inequality to establish the societal context of unequal power dynamics that compound inequality deriving from developmentalism (see Chapter 1). The chapter then proceeds to present the inter-connected components of the love ethic model, which includes the Eight Principles Schema and the Eco-activism Process Eight-Step Schema for engaging interest groups in supported dialogues as equals. The model is relevant for justice work that engages members of the social structures which are the bases of power for society's elite groups (Mills, 1953). The social structures are governments, social institutions (e.g., human service organisations, churches and schools), the military and business entities. The focus in the book is on community-based justice efforts in which there is a failure of two key social structures – business entities and government – to uphold their relevant social responsibility towards people, places and animals (see Brueckner & Ross, 2010). The major power inequities between business entities and government and the public indicate persisting vested interests and dominant influences that can adversely affect the quality of life and life chances of people (Thompson, 2018), animals and ecosystems (White, 2017, 2018). The love ethic model is also relevant for justice work within social structures such as universities and human service organisations to address organisational violence that can include neglect, bullying and scapegoating (Palmer & Ross, 2014). Although this is not the focus of the book, the model can be responsive to the presenting issues and available resources in any situation where power dynamics involving violence sit as the root cause of injustice and unsustainability.

The strength of the love ethic model is that it enables eco-activists to engage with, challenge and transform the unjust use of power and privilege of structurally advantaged groups (Pease, 2010) for the benefit of impacted groups' rights and interests (Ross, 2017a). This ethical stance of accountability to impacted groups' rights and interests in addressing matters of injustice is the core dimension of what comprises the public interest.

In Chapter 11, Dyann Ross and Marilyn Palmer build upon and further develop the eco-activist insights presented in Part 1 by explaining how to enact the love ethic model using a transformational change leadership approach (adapted from Pettit, 2018; Shields, 2011). The leadership approach is explored by working through the 8 Step Schema process of the model. Particular attention is given to how transformational change leadership enables ongoing civic participation in nonviolent direct action (NVDA) campaigns and the strategic use of dialogical group work (adapted from Nagda, 2017) between interest groups. The aim in all eco-activism approaches is to negotiate substantive justice outcomes for adversely impacted interest groups (Ross, 2013, 2017a). This aim is particularly challenging in situations when there are significant levels of power disparity. In these situations, powerful groups and entities (e.g., industries and political parties beholden to them) have a vested interest in maintaining the current unequal and unsustainable social and economic systems. The chapter presents context- and power-sensitive guidelines and tools which will resonate with eco-activists to support, and possibly extend, their eco-activist practice in a range of unjust and unsustainable situations.

In Chapter 12, the editors for this volume draw together the themes and insights of the book to establish the new directions for social work. The "Resources for practice" section can be accessed as needed in practice.

Eco-activism, inequality and power

The stories in Part 1 focused on the influence of eco-activism in relation to specific business entities, namely: the extractive resources mining industry (Chapters 2, 3, 4, 5 & 9); a large-scale public infrastructure project (Chapter 6); a private land development (Chapter 7); and live sheep exports in the farming sector (Chapter 8). The examples from WA involved the state government in a number of capacities including: giving legal approval, concessions and access to natural resources for industry to operate; attempting to implement a highly contested infrastructure project; failing to stop a land development proposal in a sensitive ecosystem on public land; and opting to ignore violations of licence agreements designed to protect the well-being of sheep during transit. A context- and power-sensitive approach to eco-activism requires a developed appreciation of how the specific issues of ecological injustice and harm are compounded by the pre-existing inequalities in society. Chapter 1 introduced this theme of pre-existing inequalities (Brueckner, Durey, Mayes & Pforr, 2014; Ross, 2017b) with the focus on the pro-development agenda of successive WA governments and their close relationship with big business. It was argued that there has been a persisting bias over many decades towards big business, a soft touch to industry regulation and a disdain for community activism against businesses that are regarded as the economic basis of the state. The logic of developmentalism (Thurbon, 2012) underpins the eco-activist stories and draws attention to the impacts of the dominant capitalist economic structure of Western societies that is typified by resistance to both the limits on growth and the taxing of wealth of the elites. Watts and Hodgson (2019) explain that capitalism is a mode of production of goods and services which values private property and the profit motive. Yet the assumption that capitalism can meet the complexity of human needs has to be questioned.

Capitalism is enabled by the political ideology of neo-liberalism which favours small government, individual responsibility and a largely free market of competing private interests (Baum, 2016). Further, capitalism is inter-related with colonialism, which refers to the domination of First Nation People, their lands and ways of being by, usually, white invaders which Seidman describes as involving "the ruthless psychic, cultural and social violence of the very souls of the colonised" (2016, p. 257). Both these systems disadvantage non-dominant groups and the environment and non-dominant nation-states and thereby have a significant bearing on the causes and nature of eco-injustice within and between nation-states. For example, capitalism creates economic inequality as shown by international research (Wilkinson, 2011) and in Australia, one of the most unequal countries in the world; this is evident in the extent of poverty and the gap between the richest and poorest social groups (Australian Council of Social Services (ACOSS), 2018). In turn, colonialism is indicated by the persistence of racism, both interpersonal and systemic, which creates a major racial divide in Australia that denies First Nation People sovereignty, economic independence, health and well-being. As Lindblom explains:

> In all the political systems of the world, much of politics is economics and most of economics is also politics . . . [and as a result] . . . politics and economics have to be held together in the analysis of basic social mechanisms and systems.
>
> (1977, p. 8)

The ideas and resources provided in this part of the book are context- and power-sensitive to respond to the wicked problems of eco-injustice. Wicked problems refer to "concerns emerging from the uncertain and complex interactions between economic, social, [political] and environmental systems" (Palmer, 2015, p. 578). As suggested by systems and complexity theories (Sanger & Giddings, 2012), there are no obvious, quick-fix or final solutions to wicked problems, but leverage points may be possible in these interconnecting systems. Palmer (2015) argues that ways forward can be found if the differences in worldviews, values and power of the interest groups in the wicked problem are made explicit and form the basis for dialogues. Therefore, justice work needs to be sensitive to, critically aware of and responsive to how contextual and power factors shape and are shaped by the positionalities of interest groups and their membership.

The love ethic model is explicit about power as the source of authority of interest group members and how they exercise both their personal power and any authority sourced in social structures beyond the individual in what Smith calls "the extra-local ruling relations" (1990, p. 42). Representatives of industry have legal, economic (and thereby) political and reputational power, and governments have constitutional, legal, political and regulatory (e.g., licencing of industry and ensuring public health) types of power. Impacted stakeholders potentially have social power (through collectivising) and can claim human rights and land rights (anti-discrimination and land rights legislation) and voting power at election time but typically are not speaking from an institutionalised power base. The book adapts Hyde's terms of "high power" and "low power" (2018, p. 53) to emphasise the interest groups' positionality in terms of persisting patterns of the structural and institutional bases of power. It is acknowledged that such terms are dualistic and simplistically describe complexities of power and, therefore, have only a limited utility in describing groups and situations if the analysis of power stops here.

Pullen-Sansfacon and Cowden explain that "the material power of one class over another [as argued by Marx] or powerful assumptions about who is capable of reason [as argued by Foucault] mean that the reality for less powerful groups in society is that their voices are rarely heard" (2012, p. 66). Hindess adds that power is not a generalised capacity but is rather related to the willingness of the less powerful groups of society to consent to being dominated (cited in Pullen-Sansfacon & Cowden, 2012, p. 66). The idea of consenting to conditions that do not serve people's needs is unsettling as it is too simplistic to regard it as a one-way transaction of power (see Palmer & Ross, 2014). At the same time, the dialogic approach in the love ethic model interlinks this persisting nature of structural power with an understanding of power as able to be negotiated, to some extent, in these unequal social relationships (Smith, 1990). The aim of dialogue is to create a third space (Bhabha, 1994) where members of low-power and high-power interest groups meet as equals and experience empowerment without being dominated or dominating (Ross, 2017a).

Although power is not only the preserve of dominant groups, there are largely predictable patterns of how privilege such as extreme wealth and ownership of large businesses continue to serve the elites at the expense of non-dominant groups. These persisting patterns of privilege can cohere to create a seemingly intractable or monolithic state of affairs (Leonard, 1997), where it is not readily apparent how a successful challenge can be undertaken. When the non-dominant groups are: animals and, within the category of animals, farm animals with economic value (Chapter 8); non-dominant social groups, in particular, First Nation People (Chapter 5); and the natural environment and, in this category, environmental issues in remote (Chapter 5) or rural locations (Chapters 2, 3 & 4) which are out of sight of city dwellers, there is a different order of complexity of power involved and inequality experienced. The intersectionality (Watts, 2015) between inequalities caused by developmentalism are compounded by inequality on the basis of social characteristics such as class, gender, age, race and disability (Thompson, 2018).

Nevertheless, well-conceptualised and implemented eco-activism can provide significant resistance to eco-injustice issues (Chapters 2, 3, 5 & 8) and, in some cases, can succeed in challenging and changing the unequal advantage of elite groups (Chapters 6, 7 & 9). The upholding of the rights, civil liberties and interests of citizens and through their representations, the upholding of the rights and interests of animals and the environment, are dependent on an active and informed citizenry who raise their voices in ways that can hold traction with the seemingly all-pervasive dominant interests and ideas. Members of the public are drawn to activism in different groupings, using a range of strategies over long periods of time to achieve some degree of eco-justice (see Chapter 2). These groups represent civil society, are non-dominant in terms of the power hierarchies of social structures but still can leverage power through collectivising, strategising and persisting with their justice goals.

The next section in the chapter presents an outline of the ethico-analytical-practice model that builds upon the eco-activist stories in Part 1 in the rich tradition of loving, nonviolent community activism and social movements (Burgmann, 2003).

The love ethic model

The love ethic model (Model) comprises three components set within a dynamic societal context. The first chapter of the book introduced the Eco-values and Responsibilities diagram that establishes the ethical sensibility and goals of the Model. Further, the SAP method (Bice, Brueckner & Pforr, 2017) was introduced and is adapted as an analytical method to show how to think critically about the contextual and power factors. The love ethic practice method interlinks with these two components to form the third dimension of the overall Model for responding to ecological injustice. An overview of the Model components is presented in figure 10.1.

The Model anchors the key values and ideas of the book and groups them in three inter-related components. A model is necessarily a simplification of relationships, power, processes and principles. Its utility is dependent on the citizens who seek to implement it, bringing the richness of their lived experiences, knowledge and values to the justice concern. The eco-activist stories in Part 1 show how diverse, passionate, resourceful, insightful and multiskilled citizens can be when they step into leadership roles relating to an issue that matters to them. The Model does a poor job at trying to explain the great work of these citizens-cum-eco-activists. They were in circumstances not of their choosing, but the circumstances were not beyond their ability to influence in positive and substantial ways. Figure 10.1 shows the "Eco-values and Responsibilities", the "SAP Analysis Method" and the "Love Ethic Practice Method". The three components exist in a dynamic context in which the Model will

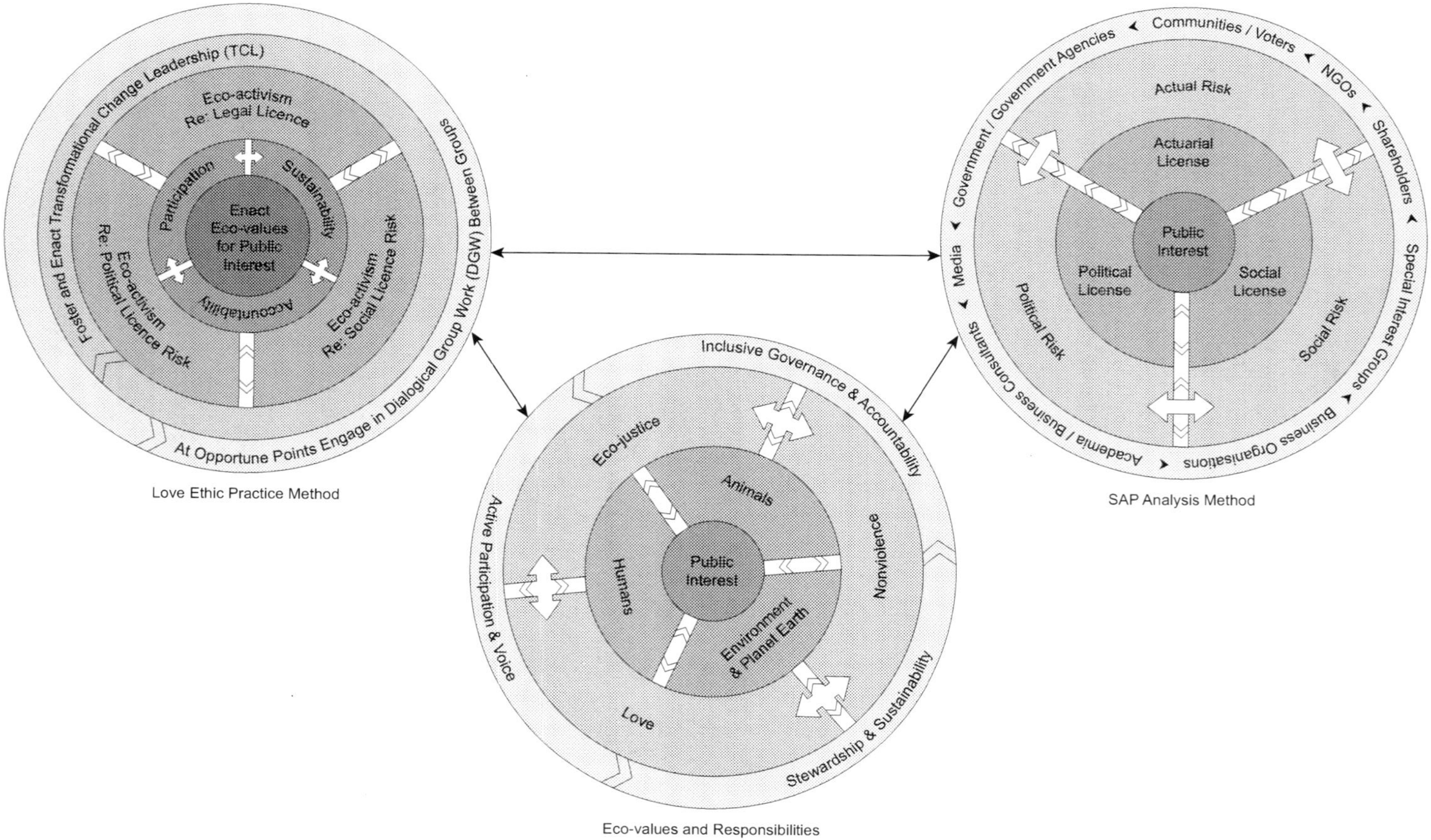

Figure 10.1 Overview of components of the love ethic model

be implemented. Thus, dynamics of history, law, social structures, culture, the environment, economics and politics affecting the justice concern will influence how eco-activists implement the Model.

The three components of the Model each cohere and intersect around the overarching principle of public interest. Justice work is about maximising the public interest in the specific situation based on the best possible interpretation of public interest and outcome, given the interest groups' rights, claims and responsibilities. It should be emphasised from the outset that some interest groups, such as government and industry representatives, have a higher order and different type of responsibility to address the justice concern. Chapter 11 elaborates further on the challenges of engaging the dominant interests in the justice work.

Eco-values and responsibilities

The Eco-values and Responsibilities component was introduced in the first chapter (see Figure 1.1) to establish the ethical sensibility of the book and of eco-activism. These values inform the justice work undertaken by eco-activists with interest groups or their representatives for social, environmental and species justice. There will typically be unequal power relationships among interest groups where the dominant interest groups, for our purposes, the government and industry, can strongly defend their interests because of their relatively high power, status and access to financial resources. Eco-activists will usually be acting in the public sphere of society with relatively low-power interest groups (including impacted communities, landscapes and animals) to challenge these dominant interest groups. This is an oversimplification for the moment; suffice it to say that the Model requires a non-combative, non-dualistic "us versus them", non-demonising approach to high-power interest groups. Therefore, eco-activism needs to engage the high-power interest groups and invite them to uphold their appropriate responsibilities. The impacted interest groups also need to be engaged and enabled to uphold their appropriate responsibilities which relate to active participation and voice, that is, speaking up and endeavouring to be heard about justice matters. What constitutes each interest group's appropriate responsibilities will depend on the nature of the issue and their positionality in it. In broad terms, the main responsibilities to be upheld for eco-justice to be realised are: stewardship and sustainability; inclusive governance and accountability; and civic participation and voice.

SAP Analysis Method

The SAP Analysis Method (Bice et al., 2017) was presented and explained in the first chapter (see Chapter 1, Figure 1.2), and examples of its utility are presented in Chapter 9. The purpose of the conceptual tool is to provide a framework for understanding the nature of the context- and power-sensitive relationships in contested ecological situations. The SAP Analysis Method is centred upon the idea of social licence to operate where businesses highly prize public acceptance and perceive any threat to this social approval as a direct risk to their business interests. The SAP Analysis Method goes further to identify the inter-related legal and political approvals or authorities needed for businesses and governments to operate without risk from public protest and disapproval. The idea of licences is useful; it draws attention to where the sources of authority lie for a business, government departments or the elected members of parliament and how these entities might therefore be engaged and, if necessary, challenged. In simplistic terms, eco-activism can come to represent a risk for the high-power entities which in turn can manifest as confrontation, denials and other tactics by the entities to avoid their appropriate responsibility for the specific justice concern (Burrell, 2013). Any specific situation is much more complicated than this, and the SAP Analysis Method encourages critical thinking and research before undertaking eco-activism.

Love Ethic Practice Method

The central circle in the Love Ethic Practice Method (Practice Method) diagram (see Figure 10.2) shows that implementing all components of the Model is needed to uphold the public interest. The eco-values of love, eco-justice and nonviolence are explicitly linked to the public interest at the centre of the Practice Method. This is encircled by a summary of the responsibilities to enact the eco-values, namely, the responsibilities of sustainability, participation, and accountability. The SAP Analysis Method is described in the third circle as: eco-activism in relation to legal licence and risk; eco-activism in relation to social licence and risk; and eco-activism in relation to political licence and risk. The outer two circles show the two main eco-activist strategies to address the justice implications arising from the SAP analysis. The two key strategies are, (a) transformational change leadership (TCL) to both foster and to enable ongoing use of NVDA campaigns, education and tactics and (b) dialogical group work (DGW) to engage high-power interest groups at opportune points in the campaigns in facilitated dialogues with the impacted interest groups.

The Practice Method is thus the way eco-justice values are enacted to uphold appropriate responsibilities in response to a critical understanding of the justice concern. The critical understanding is provided by the SAP analysis, using two main approaches of transformational change leadership and dialogical group work. These approaches are explained in Chapter 11 as part of showing how the Model is implemented. The following sections of the chapter discuss ethics in relation to eco-activism and provide an outline of the key schemas and processes of eco-activism.

Eco-activism: capacities, processes and a caution

The type of activism required in justice work is praxis where action is tied to reflection in context- and power-sensitive relationships with the relevant interest groups. Freire explains that actions without reflection are "actions for

The love ethic model 133

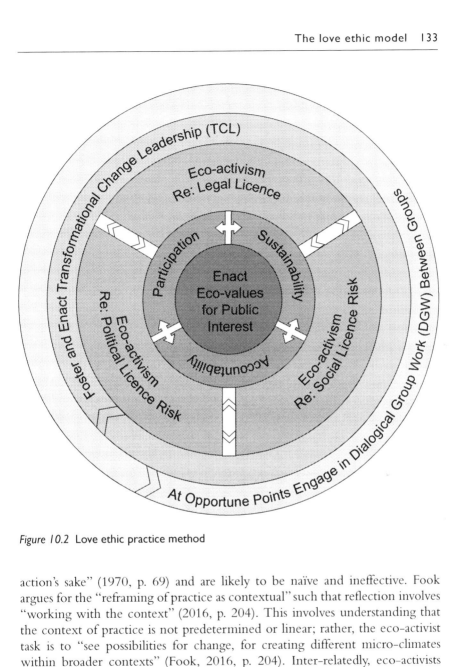

Figure 10.2 Love ethic practice method

action's sake" (1970, p. 69) and are likely to be naïve and ineffective. Fook argues for the "reframing of practice as contextual" such that reflection involves "working with the context" (2016, p. 204). This involves understanding that the context of practice is not predetermined or linear; rather, the eco-activist task is to "see possibilities for change, for creating different micro-climates within broader contexts" (Fook, 2016, p. 204). Inter-relatedly, eco-activists need to cultivate an awareness of their standpoint or positionality (Ortega, 2017) in relation to the justice concern by recognising their own values, interests, authority and capacities to make a constructive contribution. The Model assumes eco-activists are committed to the self-education required to be able to provide leadership guided by eco-justice values. The Model emphasises a critical awareness of ethics and the capacity to practice in alignment with cherished eco-values. Eco-values are placed in the centre of the Model precisely because they hold a power critique and loving, nonviolent challenge to dominant values and interest groups.

Further, the idea of "communitarianism" ethics (McAuliffe, 2014, p. 43) aims to avoid eco-activism as individualism which can result in too narrow a view of ethics and its potential in complex situations. The book locates its ethical stance in a sense of community as a political space that is inclusive of the low-power and high-power interest groups involved in the justice concern with a loving and critical understanding of power as integral to matters of ethics. This is different to conventional understandings of community building as locality-based development by non-dominant groups but is compatible with community development principles (Ife, 2016). Additionally, contemporary ethics literature (summarised by McAuliffe, 2014) has perhaps not sufficiently identified the embodied and material nature of ethics such that people and their cherished values are not separable from their bodies, relationships, social identities and the material effects of holding these values (Smith, 1990). Eco-activists can experience considerable personal burden and costs in challenging dominant interests and the status quo (see Chapters 2 & 7).

This section concludes with a caution regarding the use of the word *activism* because it aggravates an unintended dualism. It is used here with acknowledgement to the two social work activists who raised this as a concern (Palmer & Collard, personal communication, 26 July 2019). The primary purpose of activism is to be kind and to minimise the suffering of human and nonhuman species in the face of almost inevitable ecological overshoot and collapse (Bendell, 2018; Meadows, Randers & Meadows, 2005). The contributors to this volume understand that the word *activism* (and its companion activist) can be problematic because they imply standing out as a change agent, separate from the community, which is the antithesis of the goal of eco-activism. The word also (unintentionally) establishes an unhelpful binary, that is, activist or non-activist. This, again, is the antithesis of the intentions and desired outcomes of activist practice. The word so easily fits into the playbook of the loyalists of powerful interest groups who want to dismiss and demonise people who won't tolerate the abuse of animals, ecosystems, cultures and citizens. However, for now, there doesn't seem to be other words which will do to describe the people and the practices explored in the book.

Key schemas and processes – to enable NVDA strategies and facilitate inter-interest group dialogues

The Practice Method component of the overall Model has two inter-connected schemas called the Eight Principles Schema (8P Schema) and the Eco-Activism Process Eight-Step Schema (8 Step Schema). These schemas help eco-activists provide leadership in two main ways: firstly, in an ongoing capacity using long-haul NDVA strategies with impacted interest groups to influence government or industry to address perceived justice concerns. Secondly, eco-activists can provide a strategic contribution at opportune points in the justice concern by inviting all parties to an inter-interest group dialogue. This is where the Model comes into its own as the aim is to facilitate parties to meet as equals, without fear and exploitation, to listen, learn and find ways forward together. The theory is appealing, but the practice is enormously complex as international peace negotiations show (Ury, 2014).

The Eight Principles Schema

The Model's eco-values belong in a broader paradigm of worldviews, values, understandings and ways of being. The book's paradigm can be explained as supportive of, and in deference to, First Nation Peoples' perspectives (Poelina, this volume; Poelina, 2019; Woodley, this volume; Bennett, Green, Gilbert & Bessarab, 2013) alongside Western anti-oppressive approaches. These perspectives are sympathetic to the critical paradigm (Fook, 2016), which acknowledges the conflictual nature of society due to violence and inequality. Further, deference is also given to other non-dominant standpoint perspectives and related theories (see contributions in Harding, 2004). Deference in this context refers to deep respect for, and the willingness of members of dominant groups to learn from, the knowledge and views of members of non-dominant groups. This is an interpretation of hooks's (2000) love ethic as being about the willingness to extend oneself, that is, a willingness to learn from and with people and other beings constructed as "the other" (Seidman, 2016, p. 309) for the highest good in the situation. The 8P Schema provides a ready-to-hand way in practice to refer to the main dimensions of the Model. The 8P Schema takes the form of statements of principles that describe the finer level of detail of how the Model suggests the eco-values are enacted, close to action. The 8P Schema is compatible with and extends upon Boetto's (2019) idea of transformative eco-social change and her related (2018) principles and Ife's (2016) ecological justice principles for community development.

> **People–Animals–Planet Earth:** recognizing the intrinsic value of all beings and nature as a living being
> **Places & Spaces:** fostering nonviolent organisations, communities, ecosystems, localities, governments, businesses and other social structures
> **Public Interest:** upholding of nonviolence, love and eco-justice through sustainability, stewardship, inclusive governance and responsibility, and civic participation and voice
> **Power & Privilege:** addressing unfair advantage which causes injustice, lovelessness and inequality at structural, cultural and interpersonal dimensions of experience (hooks, 2000)
> **Political Analysis**: cultivating context and power literacy, for example, by employing the SAP Analysis Method, and learning from: First

> Nation Peoples' experiences and worldviews; other non-dominant groups' experiences and standpoint theories, and; anti-oppressive ideas
> **Process**: undertaking transformational change leadership to: enable responsibility via NVDA; facilitate inter-interest group-based dialogues, and; provide ongoing public and corporate education on nonviolence, love and justice
> **Principles**: upholding ideas that support eco-justice values, ethical literacy, integrity and communitarianism ethics
> **Products**: ensuring substantive justice is experienced by impacted interest groups – seeking evidence and indicators of equality, sustainability, well-being and accountability in addition to restoration, compensation and negotiated trade-offs

Eco-activism which employs the 8P Schema seeks to activate a vision of upholding the public interest on behalf of, and with, people–animals–planet earth in a range of places and spaces. The eco-activists' positionality in turn will intricately influence the political analysis they develop about the nature of power and privilege and how interest groups are thereby themselves positioned in the justice concern. Eco-activists understand that their practice needs to embrace and demonstrate the principles and a developed ethical literacy as they ask the same of interest group members. This creates a heartfelt and relationship-valuing emphasis to the justice work alongside the collaborative efforts to enable products which are consistent with justice outcomes. Eco-activism involves a broad range of power-sharing and power-equalising processes through which these strategies can support negotiations between interest groups for the enacting of their appropriate responsibilities.

Eco-activism Process 8 Step Schema

The 8 Step Schema is a set of eight steps for engaging members of the relevant interest groups in dialogue to name, understand and respond to the justice concern in an equal, collaborative and nonviolent manner. The 8 Step Schema is premised on the importance of including people involved in the justice issue, both the impacted interest groups and the perceived dominant interest groups who are gaining from the injustice. The inter-interest group dialogue, described in Chapter 11 as dialogical group work between groups to emphasise the group-based nature of the dialogue, is implemented using this schema. It can also be used by eco-activist groups to guide their NVDA strategies to get the issue on the public agenda. This orientation makes the 8 Step Schema a tool for responding to justice concerns arising from wicked problems in which dialogue increases the possibility of elegant, inclusive and substantive justice outcomes due to activating the collective wisdom and knowledge of the interest groups.

As Figure 10.3 shows, the initial action involves community members with the lived experience of the impact of the injustice (and their supporters) naming

The love ethic model 137

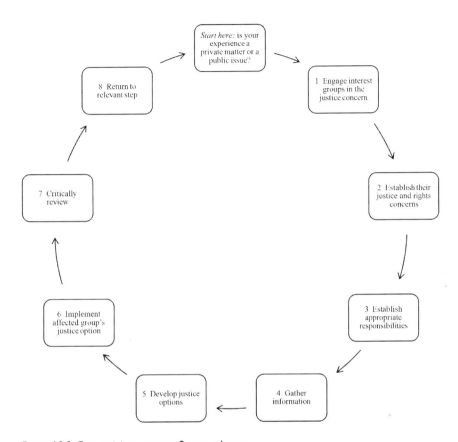

Figure 10.3 Eco-activism process 8 step schema

their private troubles as a justice concern that constitutes a public issue (Mills, 1959). The impacted community will usually have an accurate view of both the nature of the justice concern and who needs to be engaged to address it. This is about the generative power of lived experience, local knowledge and a community's social capital (Ife, 2016) that combine to create standpoint, bottom-up and inductive theories for practice.

Step 1 in the 8 Step Schema assumes all relevant interest groups are engaged and are willing to begin a dialogical process of "courageous conversations" (Sebaly, 2016) about how each group understands the matter of concern.

In Step 2 all points of view are to be placed on the dialogue table to ensure the diversity and complexity of views and experiences are generated.

Step 3 involves establishing who is responsible for what aspect of the identified justice concern where this may already be evident from how members of interest groups at the dialogue table are interacting and the substance of what they are contributing. The step is not as simple as asking the question – are you willing to be responsible for this aspect of the issue? But this is what needs to be clarified as far as possible while maintaining relationships across differences of power, agendas and rights.

Step 4 involves gathering information; this is also a complex undertaking as there still may be no agreement on the causes of the justice concern. Additionally, what counts as valid knowledge and evidence will possibly already be fraught and contested. A cursory viewing of the community activist group CAPS's website will show the extensive range and amount of information they have needed to access and use in their ongoing conflict with Alcoa (see Chapter 2; CAPS, 2019). Over the life of the process, obtaining new information from sources that are respected by all parties at the dialogue table can be crucial as well as likely to intensify the claims and counter-claims (see Chapter 7).

Step 5 involves developing action options to address the justice concern. As an exercise on paper, it might be possible to collaboratively generate as many options as possible in the manner of a facilitated ideas-generating exercise. In practice, what counts as justice will be contested, and if this is the case, the deference needs to be given to the preferred option of the impacted interest group. This deference is implied by a justice ethic (Ross, 2017a) and is likely to be strongly contested or ignored, with the dialogue breaking at this point. It can't be the prerogative of the high-power interest groups to say what justice is and when justice is done. Complexities relating to this step are further explored in Chapter 11.

Step 6 is about implementing the justice option, and as might be expected, this can be complex even when there is a clear action, and the low-power interest group has the authority to act and acts in the public's interest (see Chapter 6). Further, a success may be short-lived and cannot always be guaranteed as shown by Jecks's comment that the Point Peron resolution in favour of protecting the ecosystem has yet to be ratified by the WA Planning Commission (see Chapter 7).

Step 7 involves undertaking a critical review and is important as it can guide eco-activists in what worked, what didn't work and how there may be a need to loop back to earlier steps and re-negotiate by building understanding, good will and collaboration across the contested differences. This reviewing can occur at any step in the process in the manner of participatory action research (MacDonald, 2012), which employs rolling sequences and layers of acting and then reflecting and acting on the substance of this reflecting.

Step 8 involves a weighing up of the critical review outcome to decide which step in the schema should be revisited for further consideration. When considering Step 8 it may be far from clear which step in the schema needs to be revisited. Chapter 11 explores what the likely nature of dialogue processes using this schema may involve and how to work with the arising challenges and complexities.

The 8 Step Schema identifies a process similar to the conventional problem-solving model but with the recognition that it is too simplistic to assume that justice concerns are problems to be solved through a rational, linear, a-contextual process. Further, an assumption that eco-activism is about conflict resolution methods which typically follow a problem-solving approach is also too simplistic for the wicked problems where justice outcomes are sought. At the same time at the micro-level of practice in direct relationships, including between eco-activists as one of the interest groups, some problem-solving and conflict resolving will be appropriate (Coleman, Deutsch & Marcus, 2014). The 8 Step Schema embraces micro-level skills and group-based models (see Ortega, 2017) and extends these for present purposes for upward-to-power invitations to dialogue to assume their responsibility for fostering justice for impacted interest groups. This upward-to-power focus in social action is encapsulated in the idea of "conflict sensitivity", which involves "gaining a sound understanding of the two-way [or multiple-way] interactions, activities and context and acting to minimise negative impacts and maximise positive impacts of intervention on conflict" (Global Conflict Sensitivity Community Hub, 2019, n.p.).

One of the keys to the Model working is that the inter-interest groups' dialogue process is voluntary where the parties are invited and not coerced to attend and contribute. Yet as Freire (1970) notes, it can be expected that the high-power interest groups, whom he calls oppressors, will not want to dialogue. He explains it in this way:

> Dialogue is the encounter between . . . [people] . . . mediated by the world, in order to name the world. Hence dialogue cannot occur between those who want to name the world and those who do not wish this naming – between those who deny others the right to speak their word and those whose right to speak has been denied them.
>
> (Freire, 1970, p. 69)

The way to peace and justice is by peace and justice (Tich Nhat Hahn, 1993). In an unequal society this potentiality pivots on the voice of impacted interest groups being heard and influencing the justice agenda. Gandhi's commitment to the power of soul force (Gandhi, 2013), that is, the power of appealing to dominant interest groups' moral integrity, is the first aim of nonviolent eco-activism. The need for long-haul NVDA to gain dominant groups' attention as shown in the eco-activist stories in Part 1 suggests this is difficult for, without a willingness to engage as equals, dialogue is not possible. The promise of the Love Ethic Model is a big promise and often not witnessed or experienced by people struggling for their rights and interests. Therefore, Chapter 11 works with the dynamic, contested and complex nature of reality and relationships as part of accenting the context- and power-sensitive considerations of justice work. It acknowledges that reality and relationships are socially constructed where inequality and violence intricately shape who is valued, listened to and able to influence dominant constructions of reality.

References

Australian Council of Social Services (ACOSS). (2018). *2018 poverty in Australia*. Retrieved from www.acoss.org.au/poverty/

Baum, F. (2016). *The new public health* (4th ed.). South Melbourne, Australia: Oxford University Press.

Bendell, J. (2018). *Deep adaptation: A map for navigating climate tragedy*. Retrieved from www.lifeworth.com/deepadaptation.pdf

Bennett, B., Green, S., Gilbert, S. & Bessarab, D. (2013). *Our voices: Aboriginal and Torres Strait Islander social work*. South Yarra, Australia: Palgrave Macmillan.

Bhabha, H. (1994). *The location of culture*. Abington, UK: Routledge.

Bice, S., Brueckner, M. & Pforr, C. (2017). Putting social license to operate on the map: A social, actuarial and political risk and licensing model (SAP Model). *Resources Policy*, 53, 46–55.

Boetto, H. (2018). Transformative eco-social work: Incorporating being, thinking and doing in practice. In M. Pawar, W. Bowles & K. Bell (Eds.), *Social work: Innovations and insights* (pp. 79–93). North Melbourne, Australia: Australian Scholarly Publishing.

Boetto, H. (2019). Advancing transformative eco-social change: Shifting from modernist to holistic foundations. *Australian Social Work*, 72(2), 139–152.

Brueckner, M., Durey, A., Mayes, R. & Pforr, C. (Eds.). (2014). *Resource curse or cure? On the sustainability of development in Western Australia*. Heidelberg, Germany: Springer.

Brueckner, M. & Ross, D. (2010). *Under corporate skies: A struggle between people, place and profit*. Fremantle, Australia: Fremantle Press.

Burgmann, V. (2003). *Power, profit and protest: Australian social movements and globalisation*. St. Leonards, Australia: Allen & Unwin.

Burrell, A. (2013). *BHP talked up Ravensthorpe mine even after it decided to close it down*. Retrieved from www.theaustralian.com.au/business/mining-energy/bhp-talked-up-ravensthorpe-mine-even-after-it-decided-to-close-it-down/story-e6frg9df-1226567056943

Coleman, P., Deutsch, M. & Marcus, E. (Eds.). (2014). *The handbook of conflict resolution: Theory and practice* (3rd ed.). San Francisco, USA: Jossey Bass.

Community Alliance for Positive Solutions Inc. (CAPS). (2019). *The Yarloop story*. Retrieved from https://caps6218.org.au/bucket-brigade/

Fook, J. (2016). *Social work: A critical approach to practice*. Thousand Oaks, CA, USA: Sage Publications.

Freire, P. (1970). *Pedagogy of the oppressed*. London, UK: Penguin.

Gandhi, R. (2013). Gandhi's journey to ahimsa. In J. Sethia & A. Narayan (Eds.), *The living Gandhi: Lessons for our times* (pp. 101–117). New Delhi, India: Penguin Books.

Global Conflict Sensitivity Community Hub (CSC-Hub). (2019). *Conflict sensitivity*. Retrieved from http://conflictsensitivity.org/

Harding, S. (2004). *The feminist standpoint theory reader: Intellectual and political controversies*. London, UK: Routledge.

hooks, b. (2000). *All about love*. UK: New Visions.

Hyde, C. (2018). Leading from below: Low power actors as organisational change agents. *Human Service Organisations: Management, Leadership & Governance*, 42(1), 53–67.

Ife, J. (2016). *Community development in an uncertain world* (2nd ed.). Port Melbourne, Australia: Cambridge University Press.

Leonard, P. (1997). *Postmodern welfare: Reconstructing an emancipatory project*. London, UK: Sage Publications.

Lindblom, C. (1977). *Politics and markets: The world's political-economic systems*. New York, USA: Basic Books.

MacDonald, C. (2012). *Understanding participatory action research*. Retrieved from https://pdfs.semanticscholar.org/3b78/ecfe0b4a0a7591d2ea068c71e8ea320ff451.pdf

McAuliffe, D. (2014). *Interprofessional ethics: Collaboration in the social, health & human services*. Port Melbourne, Australia: Cambridge University Press.

Meadows, D., Randers, J. & Meadows, D. (2005). *Limits to growth: The 30-year update*. London, UK: Earthscan.

Mills, C. (1953). *The power elite*. Oxford, UK: Oxford University Press.

Mills, C. (1959). *The sociological imagination*. Oxford, UK: Oxford University Press.

Nagda, B. (2017). Intergroup dialogue: Engaging difference for social connectedness and social change. In C. Garvin, L. Gutierrez & M. Galinsky (Eds.), *Handbook of social work with groups* (pp. 384–416). New York, USA: The Guilford Press.

Ortega, R. (2017). Group work and socially just practice. In C. Garvin, L. Gutierrez & M. Galinsky (Eds.). *Handbook of social work with groups* (2nd ed., pp. 93–110). New York, USA: The Guilford Press.

Palmer, M. (2015). Wicked problems. In S. Idowu (Ed.), *International dictionary of corporate social responsibility* (pp. 578–579). Hamburg, Germany: Springer.

Palmer, M. & Ross, D. (2014). Tracing the maddening effects of abuses of authority: Rationalities gone violence in mental health services and universities. *Social Alternatives*, 33(3), 28–36.

Pease, B. (2010). *Undoing privilege: Unearned advantage in a divided world*. New York, USA: Zed Books.

Pettit, J. (2018). *Unpacking the "black box" of social movement leadership*. Retrieved from https://tcleadership.org/introduction/#_unpacking-the-black-box-of-social-movement-leadership

Poelina, A. (2019). *Economies of nature*. Retrieved from https://greataustralianstory.com.au/story/economies-nature

Pullen-Sansfacon, A. & Cowden, S. (2012). *The ethical foundations of social work*. Essex, UK: Pearson Education.

Ross, D. (2013). Social work and the struggle for corporate social responsibility. In M. Gray, J. Coates & T. Hetherington (Eds.), *Environmental social work* (pp. 193–210). London, UK: Routledge.

Ross, D. (2017a). A research-based model for corporate social responsibility: Towards accountability to impacted stakeholders. *Journal of Corporate Social Responsibility*, 2(8), 1–11.

Ross, D. (2017b). Dynamics of corporate social responsibility in Australia's mining sector: A critical sociological analysis. In M. Aluchna & S. Idowu (Eds.). *The dynamics of corporate social responsibility: A critical approach to theory and practice* (pp. 187–222). Germany: Springer.

Sanger, M. & Giddings, M. (2012). Teaching note: A simple approach to complexity theory. *Journal of Social Work Education*, 48(2), 369–376.

Sebaly, A. (2016). *Personify leadership: Courageous conversations*. Retrieved from www.youtube.com/watch?v=FQibPslmN0I

Seidman, S. (2016). *Contested knowledge: Social theory today* (5th ed.). West Sussex, UK: Wiley-Blackwell.

Shields, C. (2011). *Transformative leadership: An introduction.* Retrieved from https://eric.ed.gov/?id=ED527955

Smith, D. (1990). *The conceptual practices of power: A feminist sociology of knowledge.* Boston, USA: Northeastern University Press.

Tich Nhat Hahn. (1993). *Love in action: Writings on nonviolent social change.* Berkeley, USA: Parallax Press.

Thompson, N. (2018). *Promoting equality: Working with diversity and difference.* London, UK: Palgrave Macmillan.

Thurbon, E. (2012). From developmentalism to neoliberalism and back again? Governing the market in Australia from the 1980s to the present. In C. Kyung-Sup, B. Fine & L. Weiss (Eds.), *Developmental politics in transition: The neoliberal era and beyond* (pp. 274–295). London, UK: Palgrave Macmillan.

Ury, W. (2014). *The walk from no to yes.* [video] Retrieved from www.ted.com/talks/william_ury?language=en

Watts, J. (2015). *Gender, health and healthcare.* Surrey, UK: Ashgate.

Watts, L. & Hodgson, D. (2019). *Social justice theory and practice for social work: Critical and philosophical perspectives.* Gateway East, Singapore: Springer.

White, R. (2017). Corruption and the securitisation of nature. *International Journal for Crime, Justice and Social Democracy, 6*(4), 55–70.

White, R. (2018). Ecocentrism and criminal justice. *Theoretical Criminology, 22*(3), 342–362.

Wilkinson, R. (2011). *How economic inequality harms societies.* Retrieved from www.youtube.com/watch?v=cZ7LzE3u7Bw

Chapter 11

Transformational change leadership and dialogue between groups

Dyann Ross & Marilyn Palmer

Introduction

The chapter outlines how to implement the Love Ethic Model by focusing on insights gained from the leadership and strategies evident in the stories in this volume of eco-activists' justice work. The Love Ethic Model adopts a leadership approach with a values-for-practice emphasis to guide NVDA and to encourage dialogue between interest groups in situations of eco-injustice. As such, there is a focus on ecological values, principles, processes and strategies for action. The analysis part of the Model (as per the SAP Analysis Method, see Chapters 1, 9 & 10) is informed by a range of theories in addition to the strong ethical sensibility and action focus of the overall Love Ethic Model. The key informing theories can be broadly captured within a post-structural eco-feminist worldview and include: anti-oppressive theories, including anti-racism, post-modernism, post-structuralism, post-colonialism, anti-capitalism (see Seidman, 2016; Kelly & Westoby, 2018); eco-feminism (Mies & Shiva, 1993; Shiva, 2014), green social work and environmentalism (Dominelli, 2012, 2018; White, 2013); and post-humanism and post-anthropocentrism (Braidotti, 2013). Further, social work theories informed by critical theory are relevant (e.g., Bennett, Green, Gilbert & Bessarab, 2013; Thompson, 2018; Fook, 2016; Payne, 2014; Morley, Ablett & Macfarlane, 2019).

Transformational change leadership for eco-justice

The ability to organise people power to safeguard the public interest, and to sustain the momentum for long-haul multifaceted campaigns, is encapsulated in the idea of transformational change leadership (TCL) (Pettit, 2018). Pettit's construct extends the idea of transformative leadership, which is contrasted in the literature with laissez-faire and transactional leadership approaches. Transactional leadership reflects most people's experiences and expectations of leadership; it generally operates within an overt or covert hierarchy between leaders and followers engaged in an exchange relationship involving rewards and punishments for doing what is required or expected (Northouse, 2010, p. 172). Dubrin, Dalglish and Miller (2006) note that transactional leadership "tends to be transitory as there is no enduring purpose to keep the parties together once the transaction is complete" (2006, p. 105). Laissez-faire leadership (which implies everyone is free to do as they wish) can be a misnomer for transformational leadership, belying the (often invisible or difficult to see) discipline and structure required for a vibrant, relationship-based transformational leadership approach.

Transformational leadership requires leaders who can establish credibility by engaging with others and demonstrating vision and a strategic focus. According to Dubrin et al. "transformational leaders articulate the problems in the current system and have a compelling vision of what a new society or organisation could be. This new vision is linked to both the leader's and the followers' values" (2006, p. 105). The authors identify five components of a transformational leadership approach when it is used to drive change at a strategic level:

- Facilitating higher-level thinking
- Gathering inputs from diverse sources
- Anticipating and creating the desirable future
- Encouraging and supporting radical thinking
- Creating a vision for the future.

(Dubrin et al., 2006, p. 402)

A key element of transformational leadership is the extent to which relationships and relationship-building are central to its success. Chen, Zheng, Yang and Bai (2016) relate transformational leadership to social capital, noting that it is social capital which provides the relational resources needed to achieve the desired change. Transformational leadership has been developed and used with success in public- and private-sector organisations including grassroots community development organisations (Fisher, 2013), human service organisations (Mary, 2005), New York City public schools (Sun & Henderson, 2017), and emergency management response agencies (Valero, Jung & Andrew, 2015).

Pettit's (2018) idea of TCL describes leadership specifically in the context of radical social change and social change movements. This compares with transformational leadership within a business-as-usual industry or organisation where the aim is to make things more efficient or profitable. For our purposes, context- and power-sensitive practice to address injustice is all-important. Thus, the concept of change in transformational leadership needs specifying, as suggested by Pettit, who describes TLC as "a process through which an individual, organisation, or collective guides large, fundamental, radical transitions from one existing state to a more positive, desired state. . . . Those who practice transformational change leadership embody it fully in the way they live their lives, carry out their work, and communicate their philosophies" (2018, p. 20). TCL is characterised by vision, empathy, perseverance, community, risk, collaboration and mobilisation (Pettit, 2018, p. 21).

The distinctiveness of TCL can be understood on the basis of the values, motives and assumptions which describe the context in which the leadership practices take place (Kanungo, 2009). TCL, if it is ethical and authentic, will be underpinned by an explicit, declared moral foundation. Shields's (2011) idea of "transformative leadership" is similar to Pettit's (2018) TCL, and she explains that it refers to "the critique and disruption of the status quo" (cited in Hewitt, Davis & Lashley, 2014, p. 229). Whereas Hewitt et al. (2014) and Shields (2011) use the language of transformative leadership, this book merges their understandings into Pettit's (2018) idea of TCL and adapt it for present purposes. The significant point is that Pettit's (2018) idea of TCL needs to be extended upon to encompass eco-values and eco-justice goals. Thus, TCL for eco-activist practice is leadership located within an explicit commitment to inter- and intra-species justice in tandem with environmental sustainability and stewardship. TCL is considered as the main characteristic of eco-activist practice which transforms the eco-values and responsibilities that are congruent with the Love Ethic Model into action and outcomes. A TCL team has two key tasks: enabling the use of NVDA in justice work and bringing interest groups together in a dialogue with equal voice to negotiate sustainable and fair outcomes.

Group-based dialogues between interest groups

The Love Ethic Model provides a way to engage and facilitate members of interest groups in a justice concern to meet as equals, to engage in dialogue and to negotiate just outcomes. Therefore, the TCL team needs a broad range of skills, particularly the ability to facilitate groups and meetings. The facilitative and educative roles required for successful collectivist practice identified by Ife (2016) provide an indicator of what is required, such as active listening, managing group dynamics, group facilitation, conflict resolution, consciousness raising and enabling consensus- and decision-making processes.

The main focus in the social justice group work literature relates to group facilitation where there are differences within a group comprised of members who share a similar life experience or social identity where intragroup facilitation is required (Shapiro, 2003; Brubaker, Garrett, Rivera & Tate, 2011). Ortega (2017) explains how even small groups can reflect and intensify broader social patterns of inequality such as discrimination on the basis of age, gender, race, socio-economic status and disability. This can present in small group dynamics as "micro-aggression, the imposition of unearned privilege and other means of oppression that endure in society" (Ortega, 2017, p. 93). Thus, the focus in literature on group work practice tends to relate to personal and social empowerment goals (Sullivan, Mesbur, Lang, Goodman & Mitchell, 2003) for members of social groups experiencing discrimination and disadvantage (e.g., Dylan, 2003; Singh & Salazaar, 2011).

Irrespective of the membership of groups, it is important that the TCL team is reflexive in relation to their own power (Meihls & Moffatt, 2000) and that they give careful consideration to how group meetings are conducted. The emancipatory communitarianism approach articulated by Brubaker et al. (2011) illustrates what this might involve. When done well, participants can experience the intrinsic value in being involved in a public campaign. This kind of group work "promotes critical consciousness, a strengths orientation, self-determination, communal responsibility and advocacy [where] power dynamics are levelled" (Brubaker et al., 2011, p. 35).

This intragroup focus of social justice group work practice in the literature can also be the basis for a between-groups or an intergroup approach, which involves an additional layer relating to the complexity between interest groups in an ecological justice conflict. Bargal writes that "intergroup relations" (2017, p. 332) involve situations where members of each group tend to act in unison around their respective group identification in the group situation. Tajfel explains that intergroup relations of this type are "one of the most difficult and complex knots of problems we confront in our times" (cited in Bargal, 2017, p. 332). This dynamic is one that will demand the attention of transformational change leaders as it goes to the heart of who is speaking, for whom and who is able to influence the justice concern.

Nagda's "critical-dialogic intergroup dialogue" (2017, p. 393) fills in many of the direct practice gaps in Freire's (1970, 1997) description of his approach to dialogue as conscientisation of oppressed people. Nagda uses the term "intergroup dialogue" to describe "a group-based approach to engage issues of diversity and . . . justice through relationship building" (2017, p. 387). The task is to engage group members with explicit regard for the differences between them (usually tied to their association with their specific interest group) with the aims of social connectedness and social change (Nagda, 2017). We use the term *dialogical group work (DGW) between interest groups* here to refer to DGW with members from government, industry and civil society where there are competing interests. Nevertheless, Nagda's four-stage practice model can be used for the micro-details of how to facilitate an inter-interest group dialogue. The stages of this process include the following:

- Group beginnings, forming and building relationships – including identifying the context
- Exploring differences and commonalities in experiences – including mapping individual impact and structural causes of differences
- Dialoguing about hot topics – for example, exploring the issues, examining different views and experiences and mapping the historical, personal and political dimensions
- Action planning and collaboration – by exploring individual and social actions and strengthening relationships for this action.

(Nagda, 2017, p. 398)

Further to the dialogical approaches of Freire (1970) and Nagda (2017), the literature on social justice group work contains a range of useful micro-skills and processes for facilitating collaborative, culturally appropriate, empowering and social goals-focused interactions (e.g., Zastrow, 2015; Benjamin, Bessat & Watts, 1997; Hogan, 2007; Garvin, Gutierrez & Galinsky, 2017). Power differentials within and between interest groups can be addressed in direct practice, to an extent, by inlaying micro-skills in working with conflict, both overt and covert forms, elegantly challenging unfair behaviour (Thompson, 2018) and using group processes to enable the equalising of power relations (e.g., Barksy, 2017; Claremont & Davies, 2005; Coleman, Deutsch & Marcus, 2014; Conflict Resolution Network, 2019). Additionally, other relevant ideas and skills can be found in the literature on community development (Ife, 2016; Ingamells, Lathouras, Wiseman, Westoby & Caniglia, 2010; Westoby, 2016; Westoby & Dowling, 2013; Kelly & Westoby, 2018) and community cultural development (Sonn, Drew & Kasat, 2002; Ayala & Zaal, 2016).

Implementing the love ethic model

There is no blueprint for implementing the Love Ethic Model, and therefore, practice-oriented resources relevant and adaptable to a wide range of circumstances are important. The resources in this chapter build on the eco-activist stories from Part 1 to illustrate processes adapted from Freire's (1970) problem-posing method that he developed to enable conscientisation in poor and illiterate communities in Brazil. Conscientisation refers to "learning to perceive social, political and economic contradictions, and to take action against oppressive elements of reality" (Freire, 1970, p. 17). Freire's (1970, 1997) method is conveyed here as a questioning technique which is illustrated by asking a range of power-, context- and relationship-sensitive questions. The questions are asked by the TCL team of the interest groups in specific contexts and about specific justice concerns where conflict is occurring. To be effective the question-posing technique needs to be an integral part of engaging and collaborating with members of the interest groups. Young (1990) explains that social justice is the absence of oppression and is demonstrated by the inclusion of people affected by the oppression with the implication that their voices will be heard. This means that members of relevant interest groups need to be regarded as equal moral individuals with an equal voice in the justice negotiations (Fraser, 2009).

The first section on practical resources, inspired by the eco-activists' stories, are useful in a range of NVDA contexts and will possibly be needed to bring dominant groups to the dialogue table. The mapping tools are organised around Kelly and Sewell's (1994) head, heart and hand trialectic, which is a metaphor that conveys to eco-activists the ethical imperative of personal and professional integrity by aligning theories (head) with values (heart) and actions (hand). The subsequent section on implementing the Love Ethic Model focuses on the inter-interest group dialogue approach. It shows how the TCL team can employ the question-posing approach with the 8 Step Schema (see Chapter 10, Figure 10.3) to engage interest groups as equals and to collaboratively gather relevant information and co-create the ways forward.

Contextualised tools for NVDA

Eco-activism is a summary term for a broad range of NVDA strategies for an equally broad range of justice concerns. A set of linked tools are presented here which can assist in guiding practice in diverse contexts. These tools comprise a set of overview questions about the justice concern and an example of a tool for mapping a specific issue or task related to addressing the concern. The techniques can be used in the initial planning phase or a reflection and regrouping phase after an action has taken place. They can also be used with interest groups for their respective preparatory work prior to engaging in dialogue with interest groups with whom they are in a conflict.

Practice overview mapping tool

These main practice-oriented questions act as a guide and checklist for eco-activists:

Head (ideas and analysis)

1. What is the eco-justice issue?

    - What are the social and animal sustainability dimensions?
    - What are the economic sustainability dimensions?
    - What are the environmental sustainability dimensions?
    - What are the legal and political sustainability dimensions?

2. How do other stakeholders see the issue?
3. What evidence do you have of the causes of the issue?
4. What information is available in the public domain?
5. What are the lived experiences of impacted communities, groups, animals and ecosystems?
6. What can you learn from similar situations elsewhere about how to understand the issue?

Heart (values and principles)

The heart component is where values and principles are identified and used to guide the head and hand aspects of the justice work. The list that follows is not in order of priority and is illustrative rather than exhaustive. It is recommended that eco-activists add to and adapt this list (see Boetto, 2018; Ife, 2016). It can be used to highlight which particular values are most important at any point in time and which values to be aware of that may be in tension for members of the eco-activist group.

Values

Do no harm and nonviolence
Love, care and respect for all beings and ecosystems
Social justice
Environmental justice
Animal justice
Accountability for harm
Relevant social responsibility of business, government and citizenry
Effectiveness of government in upholding legislation and industry licencing conditions
Citizenship and legal rights of people and animals
Inclusive and participatory democracy
Sustainability – all dimensions, present time and for future generations
Dialogue and collaborative problem-solving

Pointers for practice: It may be that all interest groups can agree to these values as being important to them. If not, remember that people can't be argued out of their values. Also, it is preferable to change out the formal language in the list and to use your own language, or that of the impacted interest group, with whom you are working. For example, "citizenship" may change to "belonging" and "justice" may change to "fairness". Also, it is important to appreciate that a word such as "injustice" is possibly a confronting and even provocative word for big businesses who see themselves as good corporate citizens.

The principles that follow bring explicit challenges to the interest groups most advantaged by the status quo. It will be the case that some of the principles are already not being upheld by the responsible entity.

Principles

Supporting all sectors of society in nonviolence, love and justice education
Upholding the environmental precautionary principle
Upholding a social precautionary principle
Upholding all forms of justice
Strengthening government's regulatory effectiveness
Strengthening social responsibility of industry
Increasing transparency of government and industry relations and communications
Increasing sustainability – all dimensions
Ensuring accountability and redress of harm

Pointers for practice: Both lists can enable an ethical literacy by the interest groups, and this begins with a shared language of cherished ideas. Exploring what the values and principles mean to the interest groups in itself would be illuminating and if facilitated well could provide a basis for building goodwill and trust between the interest groups.

It is important that members of interests group can see that their values and principles are respected and are accepted as part of the justice work. There are some no-go values and principles that may become apparent. For example, in the Yarloop story at the height of community upheaval due to intrusions by Alcoa, some residents talked about wanting to blow up the alumina trains that passed through the town. This was not agreed to by other community members or the university research team.

As noted with values, aim to use language that is relevant to the interest groups, and further to this, craft the principles to be action ready. Thus, "upholding all forms of justice" can change to "all actions need to be fair", and as part of this fairness, the follow-on language might be "have the people who are responsible acted fairly?"

Hand (strategies and resources)

The hand component takes shape out of the head questions in the form of action steps, for example:

1. Gather ongoing evidence about the causes of the justice concern
2. Gather information available on the public domain
3. Gather ongoing information about the lived experiences of impacted communities, groups, animals and ecosystems
4. Organise and maintain an accessible and well-promoted website for the materials
5. Engage interest groups
6. Undertake relevant nonviolent actions, using repeating action–reflection–action cycles
7. Build a network of supporters and resource experts.

Specific issue or task mapping tool

This tool also involves a series of head, heart and hand questions, but this time the questions relate to a specific issue within the justice concern. The example draws from the Yarloop controversy (see Chapter 2) during which Alcoa took control of measuring the air quality of the refinery and handing the results to the government. The residents didn't trust the results, and the measurement process was contested by many of the residents.

The questions for the specific aspect of this issue follow:

Transformational change leadership 151

Head (ideas and analysis)

1. What are the options for obtaining independent emission samples for the industrial site?
2. What is both feasible and likely to be effective?
3. What knowledge, precedents and case studies are there about this?
4. Who needs to be engaged, and what is needed to make it happen?
5. Who might be interested in or threatened by the sampling results?
6. What are other stakeholders' strengths that can be utilised to address the issue?
7. What are the risks of backlash, and how might this look and be responded to?
8. What is the specific strategy?
9. What is the backup plan?
10. How are the public kept informed and supporters mobilised?

Heart (values and principles)

Please refer to the material in the heart segment in the main practice-oriented questions section. The prioritising of values to act upon and principles to guide these actions may change in specific micro-situations. Alternatively, engage the interest groups in a round-the-circle process through which members can identify the values they think are important and what their bottom-line no-go countering values of a backlash would be. Thus, if a dominant interest group is not open to engaging, and they threaten violence or otherwise try to intimidate the eco-activist leadership group, or low-power interest groups, this is a serious issue. It needs to be part of the pre-planning phase to have a fall-back, safe position if the situation becomes threatening or chaotic where people feel unsafe.

Hand (strategies and resources)

This part of the mapping tool follows through to include the strategies related to the specific aspect of the justice concern, for example:

1. List pros and cons of all the options for independent air sampling
2. Choose one of the options, and develop an action plan
3. Prepare a backup plan, and identify the circumstances when it may be needed
4. Implement the action plan
5. Keep the public informed and supporters mobilised through an up-to-date website and local media releases.

In relation to this real-life example, CAPS, the Yarloop eco-activist organisation, initiated an independent bucket brigade strategy which was so successful that the government negotiated with them to take over the responsibility (see the Yarloop bucket brigade, CAPS, 2019).

Inter-interest group dialogue: 8 Step Schema

In specific practice situations, especially where there are extreme power differences between interest groups and where conflict is covert and yet intensely impacting a community, animals or landscape, it can be unclear how to interpret the group work and community processes in the resources noted here. The eco-activism 8 Step Schema (introduced in Chapter 10, Figure 10.3) aims to meet the challenge of what to do when interest groups in a controversy meet about the justice concern. At such times the power complexities are increased by bringing parties who have different views, interests, status and rights in the conflict to the "dialogue table" (Ross, 2017, p. 7). This gives a whole new layer of complexity to group work and leadership.

The overall 8 Step Schema contextualises the practice situation through an adaptation of the Freirian (1970) question-posing process. The facilitated group-based activity is dialogical when members at the dialogue table feel respected, heard and able to contribute without threats or exploitation. The 8 Step Schema (which is preceded by a reconnaissance phase) is outlined as follows, and key challenges related to implementing the inter-interest group dialogical process are discussed in the last section of the chapter.

Reconnaissance: It is important to approach and take guidance from First Nation People of the area in addressing ecological conflict. This needs to be done according to the cultural protocols of the respective Nations' elders.

These are some questions for the reconnaissance of the justice concern to be considered by the initiating group of eco-activists prior to engaging the interest groups:

- Is this a justice concern for humans? Which social group is it a concern for? Who is speaking for them, and what are their vested interests in the concern? What is the impacted social group's view or views?
- Is this a justice concern for animals? Who is speaking for the animals, and what are their vested interests in the concern? What are the competing or alternative views?
- Is this a justice concern for the natural environment? Who is speaking for the environment, and what are their vested interests in the concern? What are the competing or alternative views?
- How does the justice concern intersect with other types of justice claims?
- Are any of the types of justice concern claims more valued than others and if so by whom?
- What is being done to equalise the value of each type of justice claim?
- How do each of these views relate to the impact on the following:
    - Social sustainability?
    - Species sustainability?
    - Environmental sustainability?
    - Economic sustainability?

- Are any of these types of sustainability more valued than others and if so by whom?
- What is being done to equalise the value of each type of sustainability?

Pointers for practice: It is not about having the answers or presuming to know what other parties think as there may be no clear answer or enough information at this stage. The questions are premised on the idea that all justice concerns involve intersections between human, animal and environmental factors to some extent. A failure to achieve sustainability is indicated by inequality and violence (social and species), irretrievable bio-diversity loss (environmental) and unfair or extreme accumulation of wealth and profits (economic).

By the time the decision is taken to proceed with NVDA and as part of this, to undertake a dialogical group work approach with the interest groups, the TCL team needs to be established. It is preferable to enlist an independent person to lead the dialogue meetings supported by the TCL team using the 8 Step Schema as explained here:

1 Engage interest groups involved in or impacted by the justice concern:

   1.1 Who are all the interest groups involved in, or impacted by, the justice concern? Who is speaking for them, and what are their vested interests in the concern? What are the impacted social, species or environmental representative group's views?
   1.2 Which of these interest groups are low power in relation to the justice concern?
   1.3 What factors affect this low power status?
   1.4 Which of these interest groups are high power in relation to the justice concern?
   1.5 What factors affect this high power status?

2 Establish their positioning – that is, their interests and rights in the justice concern:

   2.1 What is the main strongly held position of each interest group?
   2.2 Is there any common ground among the interest groups?
   2.3 Are there irreconcilable differences among the interest groups?

3 Clarify the social responsibility of interest groups:

   3.1 What is the nature of each interest group's –

   - Social responsibility?
   - Species responsibility?
   - Environmental responsibility?

   3.2 Does the relevant interest group accept this social, species or environmental responsibility?

3.3 If not, what do they accept as their social, species or environmental responsibility?

3.4 Are there unaddressed justice concerns not being represented in the dialogue group or being neglected by an entity with responsibility for it?

Pointers for practice: If there are unaddressed concerns with no one taking responsibility for them, consider the ability to influence through legal, political and social licences and avenues. In some instances, it will be difficult to progress beyond this step without agreement about the dominant interest group's social, species or environmental responsibility towards the issue. It may transpire that subsequent steps of the schema need to be progressed without the participation of some parties in the process.

4   Gather relevant information:

4.1 Whose ideas and what knowledge is valued?

4.2 With what consequences?

4.3 What is best practice research saying?

4.4 Does the information gathered hold a power analysis and give equal regard to divergent views?

4.5 Has the lived experience of impacted interest groups been included as important information?

4.6 What are the gaps and not-known aspects of the justice concern?

4.7 What knowledge is being generated by the inter-interest group dialogue meetings?

Pointers for practice: The aim is to gather the range and depth of relevant information in a transparent and collaborative manner which may involve inviting experts to the dialogue meetings to share specialist knowledge and to answer members' questions. In contested circumstances or where the science is unclear or insubstantial, the dialogue group can be supported to call on government to enact the social precautionary principle (usually embedded in public health legislation and policies) and environmental precautionary principle (see later section – "When dialogue is not enough").

5   Develop justice action options:

5.1 What are all the possible solutions or partial solutions to the justice concern?

5.2 Are all members putting their ideas forward?

5.3 Are there any barriers to all ideas being placed on the dialogue table for consideration by the group?

5.4 Has research been done to see how other communities with similar issues have addressed them?

5.5 What are feasible, short-term steps that can be taken towards bigger justice goals?

Pointers for practice: The facilitator from the TCL group can act to place contentious ideas on the table if some members feel unsafe to raise them. There can be a range of barriers to participation, including subtle ones such as Ortega's idea of "epistemic privilege" (2017, p. 94), which relates to low-power members feeling disempowered in the presence of high-power members. For this part of the process to work, it is important that all members are be able to put forward ideas without feeling they are committing to them right then and there and for members to be able to let ideas they don't agree with to come forward. The one proviso is any idea that is against the key eco-justice values of nonviolence, justice and love will need an intensive, separate discussion.

6 Implement justice option preferred by the low-power or most impacted interest group:
   6.1 How is the decision to be made about the way forward in addressing the justice concern?
   6.2 Do all members of the dialogue group support the plan?
   6.3 What is possible if there is not unanimous agreement?
   6.4 Is there a gap between what the plan is and the willingness of the responsible entity to put it into action?
   6.5 Of all the options on the dialogue table, which is the one preferred by the impacted interest groups?
   6.6 What are the barriers, if any, to upholding the impacted interest groups' justice option?
   6.7 What if anything can the dialogue group agree on at this time?
   6.8 What would enable a forward step?

Pointers for practice: The TCL group enables members of interest groups to uphold their appropriate responsibilities. They understand the power complexities and work to engage high-power interest groups in the justice concern. They also understand how to progress towards a resolution even if high-power groups do not engage voluntarily in the justice work.

7 Critically review:
   7.1 How is power showing and being used in the dialogue group?
   7.2 What are the effects of power dynamics in the meeting space?
   7.3 What is happening after the meetings that may be influencing who participates and how?
   7.4 Do the high-power members at the dialogue table have the authority to make decisions on behalf of their organisation?

7.5 Have issues of representation arisen, and if so how is this affecting the authority of low-power members at the table?

7.6 Is there an agreement in place regarding how the group will make decisions and what they will do if they can't agree on a forward plan?

Pointers for practice: At this stage in the 8 Step Schema, the task is to take a "balcony view" (Ury, 2014) of the justice work and weigh up how power is being used and with what effect. The role of the eco-activist leaders also needs to be considered in this activity as it can be complicated trying to be on all sides and respecting all views simultaneously in a conflict situation yet ultimately to be only on the "side" of justice. The question that needs to be asked is: how does the positionality of the leadership team influence their authority to facilitate the dialogical process?

The review can use the SAP Analysis Method (Bice, Brueckner & Pforr, 2017) and can include a consideration of how far a communitarian (i.e., shared and informed) ethical literacy has been fostered within the dialogue group. An indicator of this shared capacity would be language that suggests there is some common ground among the parties on how to treat each other, what is fair and, thus, what would serve the public interest.

Reflection and review of the process, decisions and actions are ongoing activities for transformational change leaders. When this is undertaken with dialogue group members, either in the main dialogue group or within their respective interest groups, this can increase understanding of divergent views as well as spread the leadership through the whole group. The shared awareness of and, ideally, the shared responsibility for the dialogical process facilitates this, adding to a sense of buy-in which can be harder to achieve from the high-power interest groups.

8. Return to relevant activism dimensions as needed if justice concern persists:

8.1 Is there a willingness in the dialogue group membership to keep dedicating to the process?

8.2 What are the specific tasks and goals that the dialogue group can agree to?

8.3 Is there a need for more knowledge or information (return to Step 4)?

8.4 Does the dialogue process need to be augmented with other strategies?

8.5 If so, what NVDA strategies will maintain the political and moral pressure to address the justice concern?

When dialogue is not enough – towards Earth jurisprudence

The final section focuses on the challenge of how to ensure the high-power interest groups take responsibility for the harm and injustice they cause or have failed to address. This is about situations in which invitations to dialogue are declined by high-power interest groups and other avenues of voluntary engagement and nonviolent action to pressure for this engagement are not sufficient. A hard-won lesson from the engagement of Alcoa and the Yarloop community in dialogue, enabled by the authors and their research team in the early 2000s (Ross, 2003, 2009, 2013, 2017), is that dialogue is unlikely to succeed as the only strategy in a justice negotiation. After 18 months of public meetings between local Alcoa representatives and Yarloop residents, the dialogue, in the form of facilitated public meetings, stopped. The collaborative negotiations had focused on obtaining a fairer property purchase plan for the community (Brueckner & Ross, 2010). Although recognised as an issue in the state government's parliamentary inquiry (Sharp, 2004), Alcoa's senior management group failed to uphold some of the key recommendations developed by the inter-interest groups, which included, therefore, undermining local Alcoa managers. This usurping of local, collaborative negotiations, facilitated by the research team from ECU, also usurped the interest groups' confidence in dialogue as a method that could work despite major power differences between the parties.

In similar situations of significant power disparities between a community, the government and the industry entity, it is recommended that eco-activists consider negotiating, at the outset of attempts to dialogue, a set of warrants or agreements which are available for public scrutiny. The idea of warrants (adapted from Fox & Miller, 1995) is that a set of ground rules are developed so the way power is used in the dialogues can be monitored to gauge the parties' support for the justice work. The warrants that need to be upheld are: building sincere relationships; making substantial and relevant contributions to resolving the justice concern; being willing to focus on matters of significance to the impacted interest group; and limiting the adverse effects of government and industry power relations in both the process and outcomes (Ross, 2017, p. 9). When one or more of the warrants is transgressed, this is to be discussed with the interest groups. It may indicate that the process has become anti-dialogical, which Freire (1997) refers to as a monologue, or one-way flow of power, by the dominant parties.

Independent evidence can make a major contribution in justice work as Jecks demonstrated in the HOPP campaign (see Chapter 7). It is also the case that claims of evidence and scientific proof should be treated cautiously in contested contexts such as environmental harm and pollution from the mining industry or property developments on public land. The story of Hinkley in the United States, made famous by the Erin Brockovich film (Soderbergh, 2000), had its breakthrough on the basis of scientific evidence of the gas plant leaking toxins into the local waterways. However, it did not save the town of Hinkley, which has not been able to turn around the compounding losses of population and decline in property values (Pearl, 2015). At this time, although limited, there is research in the international literature that shows some aspects of the human and environmental harm arising from exposure to aluminium which is the end product from alumina refineries (Mercola, 2014). The funding of a comprehensive research program to establish the nature of pollutants from alumina refineries, coal mines, gas-fracking wells, iron-ore facilities and the extent of human, environmental and species harm is a missing piece of the justice struggle.

Warrants, in the form of good will agreements, are more effective if supported by legal requirements that can hold industry accountable. The environmental precautionary principle is a legal obligation on the part of government usually embedded in their Environmental Protection Act (WA Government, 1986). The principle requires the government to not proceed with a development or industry expansion if there is concern that it could cause irretrievable harm (Meyers, 2002). Depending on the nature of the justice concern, eco-activists may wish to consider NVDA to pressure the government to uphold this principle or the parallel social precautionary principle implied in protecting public health as required by the relevant state Public Health Act (WA Government, 2016). It is important to note that many of the eco-activists in this book worked closely with legal advisors and skilled NGOs, such as the Conservation Council of WA to argue their case, with the Yindjibarndi People's land rights claim being legally represented in the High Court of Australia (see Chapter 5). Shearman (2018) supports the call by a major alliance of leading environmental groups, legal and medical experts for an independent national environmental protection agency in Australia. This development would increase the scope for eco-activists to challenge the legal licence of unsustainable businesses and the political licence bestowed on those businesses by politicians, public servants and political party loyalists.

The global scale and complex nature of wicked problems where ecological injustice is occurring are of such importance to global citizens that another layer of checks and balances is needed. White offers an Earth Jurisprudence perspective that can be understood in terms of "wild law" which seeks to curtail human behaviour for the sake of the well-being and the "long-term preservation of all Earth's subjects" (2018, p. 346). Higgins (2010) believes this type of legal regulation, which limits, for example, the exploitative natural resource sector, is crucial to avoid *ecocide*, where there is an unwarranted and irretrievable level of loss and harm to Planet Earth. Significantly, Poelina calls for the upholding of the First Law of First Nation Peoples when she writes, "First Law is ancient, from the beginning of time. These natural laws continue to exist. First Law teaches us that the law is in the land and not in the human" (Foreword, in this volume).

Poelina is referring to the worldwide collective wisdom located in land, humans and nonhuman beings that exists in resistance to the excesses of human greed and domination. This active hope for a just, loving and sustainable world needs to become dominant to shift from the current era of the Anthropocene to the Symbiocene. Albret explains that human domination has caused climate change where the issue is:

The whole capitalist development paradigm that is at the dark heart of maldevelopment – that which undermines and destroys the very foundations of all life on earth.

(2016, p. 12)

Albret offers the term "Symbiocene" for the new era which is related to the "word 'symbiosis' [which] implies living together for mutual benefit . . . [and as] a core aspect of ecological thinking, symbiosis affirms the interconnectedness of life and all living things" (2016, p. 13).

Local, community-based activist groups linked directly, or by association due to shared justice concerns, with other activist groups are integral to the sustainability of Planet Earth. Eco-activism is a crucial resource and civic task. As a profession that is dedicated to social justice, social work has the potential to stand and be counted on the side of love, justice and nonviolence in publicly contested places and spaces. There is room for all citizens and professions to contribute small steps to the revolutionary change promise of TCL and the Love Ethic Model.

References

Albret, G. (2016). *Exiting the Anthropocene and entering the Symbiocene*. Retrieved from www.humansandnature.org/exiting-the-anthropocene-and-entering-the-symbiocene

Ayala, J. & Zaal, M. (2016). Poetics of justice: Using art as action and analysis in participatory action research. *Networks: An Online Journal for Teacher Research, 18*(1). https://dx.doi.org/10.4148/2470-6353.1019

Bargal, D. (2017). Groups for reducing intergroup conflicts. In C. Garvin, L. Gutierrez & M. Galinsky (Eds.), *Handbook of social work with groups* (2nd ed., pp. 331–343). New York, USA: The Guilford Press.

Barksy, A. (2017). *Conflict resolution for the helping professions* (3rd ed.). Belmont, USA: Thomson.

Benjamin, J., Bessat, J. & Watts, R. (1997). *Making groups work: Rethinking practice*. St Leonards, Australia: Allen & Unwin.

Bennett, B., Green, S., Gilbert, S. & Bessarab, D. (2013). *Our voices: Aboriginal and Torres Strait Islander social work*. South Yarra, Australia: Palgrave Macmillan.

Bice, S., Brueckner, M. & Pforr, C. (2017). Putting social license to operate on the map: A social, actuarial and political risk and licensing model (SAP Model). *Resources Policy, 53*, 46–55.

Boetto, H. (2018). Transformative eco-social work: Incorporating being, thinking and doing in practice. In M. Pawar, W. Bowles & K. Bell (Eds.), *Social work: Innovations and insights* (pp. 79–93). North Melbourne, Australia: Australian Scholarly Publishing.

Braidotti, R. (2013). *The posthuman*. Cambridge, UK: Polity Press.

Brubaker, M., Garrett, M., Rivera, E. & Tate, K. (2011). Justice making in groups for homeless adults: The emancipatory communitarianism way. In A. Singh & C. Salazaar (Eds.), *Social justice in group work* (pp. 34–43). London, UK: Routledge.

Brueckner, M. & Ross, D. (2010). *Under corporate skies: A struggle between people, place and profit*. Perth, Australia: Fremantle Arts Press.

Chen, L., Zheng, W., Yang, B. & Bai, S. (2016). Transformational leadership, social capital and organizational innovation. *Leadership & Organization Development Journal, 37*(7), 843–859.

Claremont, R. & Davies, R. (2005). *Collaborative conflict management.* Sydney, Australia: Lansdowne Publishing.

Coleman, P., Deutsch, M. & Marcus, E. (Eds.). (2014). *The handbook of conflict resolution: Theory and practice* (3rd ed.). San Francisco, USA: Jossey Bass.

Community Alliance for Positive Solutions Inc. (CAPS). (2019). *The Yarloop bucket brigade.* Retrieved from https://caps6218.org.au/bucket-brigade/

Conflict Resolution Network. (2019). *Our vision is to create a conflict resolving community in a culture of peace and social justice.* Retrieved from www.crnhq.org/

Dominelli, L. (2012). *Green social work: From environmental crises to environmental justice.* Cambridge, UK: Polity Press.

Dominelli, L. (Ed.). (2018). *The Routledge handbook of green social work.* New York, USA: Routledge.

Dubrin, A., Dalglish, C. & Miller, P. (2006). *Leadership* (2nd Asia-Pacific ed.). Milton, Australia: John Wiley & Sons.

Dylan, A. (2003). Talking circles: A traditional form of group work. In N. Sullivan, E. Mesbur, N. Lang, D. Goodman & L. Mitchell (Eds.), *Social work with groups: Social justice through personal, community and societal change* (pp. 119–134). New York, USA: Routledge.

Fisher, L. (2013). Transformational leadership among grassroots social service organizations. *Community Development, 44*(3), 292–304.

Fook, J. (2016). *Social work: A critical approach* (3rd ed.). Los Angeles, USA: Sage Publications.

Fox, C. & Miller, H. (1995). *Postmodern public administration: Towards discourse.* Thousand Oaks, USA: Sage Publications.

Fraser, N. (2009). Who counts? Dilemmas of justice in a post Westphalian world. *Antipode, 41*(1), 281–297.

Freire, P. (1970). *Pedagogy of the oppressed.* London, UK: Penguin.

Freire, P. (1997). *Pedagogy of the heart.* New York, USA: Continuum.

Garvin, C., Gutierrez, L. & Galinsky, M. (Eds.). (2017). *Handbook of social work with groups* (2nd ed.). London, UK: The Guilford Press.

Hewitt, K., Davis, A. & Lashley, C. (2014). Transformational leadership in a research-informed leadership program. *Journal of Research on Leadership Education, 9*(3), 22–253.

Higgins, P. (2010). *Eradicating ecocide.* London, UK: Shepheard-Walwyn.

Hogan, C. (2007). *Facilitating multicultural groups: A practical guide.* London, UK: Kogan Page Publishers.

Hyde, C. (2018). Leading from below: Low power actors as organisational change agents. *Human Service Organisations: Management, Leadership & Governance, 42*(1), 53–67.

Ife, J. (2016). *Community development in an uncertain world* (2nd ed.). Port Melbourne, Australia: Cambridge University Press.

Ingamells, A., Lathouras, A., Wiseman, R., Westoby, P. & Caniglia, F. (Eds.). (2010). *Community development practice: Stories, method and meaning.* Melbourne, Australia: Common Ground Publishing.

Kanungo, R. (2009). Ethical values of transactional and transformational leaders. *Canadian Journal of Administrative Sciences.* https://doi.org/10.1111/j.1936-4490.2001.tb00261.x

Kelly, A. & Sewell, S. (1994). *With head, heart and hand: Dimensions of community building* (3rd ed.). Bowen Hills, Australia: Boolarong Press.

Kelly, A. & Westoby, P. (2018). *Participatory development practice: Using traditional and contemporary frameworks.* Rugby, UK: Practical Action Publishing.

Mary, N. (2005). Transformational leadership in human service organizations. *Administration in Social Work, 29*(2), 105–118.

Meihls, D. & Moffatt, K. (2000). Constructing social work identity based on the reflective self. *British Journal of Social Work, 30*(3), 339–348.

Mercola. (2014). *First case study to show direct link between Alzheimers and aluminium toxicity.* Retrieved from https://articles.mercola.com/sites/articles/archive/2014/03/22/aluminum-toxicity-alzheimers.aspx

Meyers, N. (2002). *The precautionary principle puts values first.* Retrieved from http://rachel.org/files/document/The_Precautionary_Principle_Puts_Values_First.pdf

Mies, M. & Shiva, V. (1993). *Ecofeminism.* Winnipeg, USA: Fernwood Publications.

Morley, C., Ablett, P. & Macfarlane, S. (2019). *Engaging with social work: A critical introduction* (2nd ed.). Melbourne, Australia: Cambridge.

Nagda, B. (2017). Intergroup dialogue: Engaging difference for social connectedness and social change. In C. Garvin, L. Gutierrez & M. Galinsky (Eds.), *Handbook of social work with groups* (2nd ed., pp. 384–416). New York, USA: The Guilford Press.

Northouse, P. (2010). *Leadership: Theory and practice* (5th ed.). Thousand Oaks, USA: Sage Publications.

Ortega, R. (2017). Group work and socially just practice. In C. Garvin, L. Gutierrez & M. Galinsky (Eds.), *Handbook of social work with groups* (2nd ed., pp. 93–110). New York, USA: The Guilford Press.

Payne, M. (2014). *Modern social work theory* (4th ed.). London, UK: Palgrave Macmillan.

Pearl, M. (2015). *The town Erin Brockovich rescued is basically a ghost town now.* Retrieved from www.vice.com/en_au/article/xd7qvn/the-town-erin-brockovich-rescued-is-now-almost-a-ghost-town-992

Pettit, J. (2018). *Unpacking the 'black box' of social movement leadership.* Retrieved from https://tcleadership.org/introduction/#_unpacking-the-black-box-of-social-movement-leadership

Ross, D. (2003). *Reviewing the land management issues: Some common ground at a point in the process: A Report on the collaboration between Alcoa, Wagerup and Yarloop/Hamel Property Owners.* Bunbury, Australia: Centre for Regional Development & Research, Edith Cowan University.

Ross, D. (2009). Emphasizing the 'social' in corporate social responsibility: A social work perspective. In S. Idowu & W. Leal Filho (Eds.), *Professional perspectives of corporate social responsibility* (pp. 301–318). Frankfurt am Main, Germany: Peter Lang.

Ross, D. (2013). Social work and the struggle for corporate social responsibility. In M. Gray, J. Coates & T. Hetherington (Eds.). *Environmental social work* (pp. 193–210). London, UK: Routledge.

Ross, D. (2017). A research-based model for corporate social responsibility: Towards accountability to impacted stakeholders. *Journal of Corporate Social Responsibility, 2*(8), 1–11.

Seidman, S. (2016). *Contested knowledge: Social theory today* (5th ed.). West Sussex, UK: Wiley-Blackwell.

Shapiro, B. (2003). Social justice and social work with groups: Fragile – handle with care. In N. Sullivan, E. Mesbur, N. Lang, D. Goodman & L. Mitchell (Eds.), *Social work with groups: Social justice through personal, community and societal change* (pp. 7–24). New York, USA: Routledge.

Sharp, C. (2004). *Report for the standing committee on environment and public affairs in relation to the Alcoa refinery at Wagerup inquiry.* Perth, Australia: Government of Western Australia.

Shearman, D. (2018). *Why Australians need a national environmental protection agency to safeguard their health.* Retrieved from https://theconversation.com/why-australians-need-a-national-environment-protection-agency-to-safeguard-their-health-93861

Shields, C. (2011). *Transformative leadership: An introduction*. Retrieved from https://eric.ed.gov/?id=ED527955

Shiva, V. (2014). *The Vandana Shiva reader*. Kentucky, USA: University of Kentucky Press.

Singh, A. & Salazaar, C. (2011). *Social justice in group work: Practical interventions for change*. London, UK & New York, USA: Routledge.

Smith, D. (1990). *The conceptual practices of power: A feminist sociology of knowledge*. Boston, USA: Northeastern University Press.

Soderbergh, S. (2000). *Erin Brockovich* [film]. Retrieved from www.brockovich.com/the-movie/

Sonn, C., Drew, N. & Kasat, P. (2002). *Conceptualising community cultural development: The role of cultural planning in community change*. Perth, Western Australia, Australia: Community Arts Network WA Inc.

Sullivan, N., Mesbur, E., Lang, N., Goodman, D. & Mitchell, L. (Eds.). (2003). *Social work with groups: Social justice through personal, community and societal change*. New York, USA: Routledge.

Sun, R. & Henderson, A. (2017). Transformational leadership and organizational processes: Influencing public performance. *Public Administration Review, 77*(4), 554–565.

Thompson, N. (2018). *Promoting equality: Working with diversity & difference*. London, UK: Palgrave Macmillan.

Ury, W. (2014). *The walk from no to yes*. [video] Retrieved from www.ted.com/talks/william_ury?language=en

Valero, J., Jung, K. & Andrew, S. (2015). Does transformational leadership build resilient public and nonprofit organizations? *Disaster Prevention and Management, 24*(1), 4–20.

Western Australian Government. (1986). *Environmental Protection Act 1986*. Retrieved from www.legislation.wa.gov.au/legislation/statutes.nsf/main_mrtitle_304_homepage.html

Western Australian Government. (2016). *Public Health Act 2016*. Retrieved from www.legislation.wa.gov.au/legislation/statutes.nsf/main_mrtitle_13791_homepage.html

Westoby, P. (2016). *Soul, community and social change*. London, UK: Routledge.

Westoby, P. and Dowling, G. (2013). *Theory and practice of dialogical community development: International perspectives*. London, UK: Routledge.

White, R. (2013). *Environmental harm: An eco-justice perspective*. Chicago, USA: Bristol University Press.

White, R. (2018). Green victimology and nonhuman victims. *International Review of Victimology, 24*(2), 239–255.

Young, I. (1990). *Justice and the politics of difference*. Princeton, USA: Princeton University Press.

Zastrow, C. (2015). *Social work with groups: A comprehensive worktext* (8th ed.). Belmont, USA: Brooks Cole.

Chapter 12

Conclusion

New directions in leadership and group work

Dyann Ross, Marilyn Palmer, Wallea Eaglehawk & Martin Brueckner

Eco-activism as justice work with heart

The Love Ethic Model is presented as a way to do justice work using public campaigns, research, community arts practice and other NVDA strategies. The overarching aim is to place moral pressure on high-power entities such as governments and businesses to address eco-justice concerns. The Model is premised on an active and ongoing commitment to the eco-values of love, eco-justice and nonviolence for the purpose of upholding the public interest. The public interest involves the highest expression of eco-values possible in specific contexts of injustice and harm within the broader societal and global contexts of inequality and violence. Eco-activism is the uptake of these eco-values using a range of strategies to pressure high-power interest groups to assume their responsibility for the harm caused by their privilege, power and wealth-seeking behaviour. The book focuses on the social responsibility of governments and business entities that gain from the use of natural resources and the compounding of inequality for low-power social groups, nonhuman species and the environment. In turn, there is a different order of responsibility for citizens to raise justice concerns and to thereby pressure relevant parties to be accountable, in particular, in contexts of ecological conflict and harm. As West writes, "Justice is what love looks like in public" (2011, n.p.), and in private, as well as in forests and other homes of nonhuman species. Accountability has to be enacted towards adversely impacted interest groups and ecosystems for justice to be achieved.

The contributors' stories of eco-activism informed the Love Ethic Model, which distils the two key capacities of TCL and a particular form of DGW, namely, DGW between interest groups. TCL is a collaborative, relationship-centred approach of power sharing and power challenging that is loving, just and nonviolent and directed towards eco-justice. This necessarily includes relationships with nonhuman species and ecosystems as interest groups with equal intrinsic value and rights to be heard and treated in ways that are fair and sustainable. Eco-justice goals cannot be conflated with contradictory processes of dominating relationships, unfair processes and exploitation of people, animals and landscapes. Roy explains that dominant war and imperialist discourses gain by conflating peace and justice with their opposite such that "love is hate, north is south, peace is war" (2001, n.p.). Although the transformational aim of social change may not be assured, it is further from reach if contradictory language and dominating processes are employed by the leadership team undertaking the justice work.

DGW refers to the liberatory praxis of Freire (1970) based on his idea of conscientisation, which involves acting and reflecting on the world to change it and the idea of dialogue between the oppressors and oppressed. Dialogue is occurring when people meet as equals, without exploitation, to negotiate fair and substantive outcomes to a justice concern. DGW is the main method for the TCL team as it can create a third space for transformational change to occur in the relationships of the relevant parties to practice freedom (hooks, 1994). Further, dialogue within an eco-justice approach involves dialogue between humans, nonhuman species and landscapes. Buber's theory of dialogue centres on the ideal of "I-Thou" relationships (1970, p. 62) as a deep spiritual connection which can be reinterpreted to be inclusive of all beings and entities. This is about communion with "the other" as a mutual and loving exchange in comparison with "I-It" relationships, where the "I" is the subject and the "It" is the object and thereby objectified. Buber writes that when people engage in "I-You" relationships of subject to subject, the sacredness of all life can permeate "I-It" relationships and transform them towards "I-Thou" (1970, pp. 148–149). "I-Thou" is the between space in relationships where love, nonviolence and justice are present.

The two capacities of TCL and DGW between interest groups bring a focus to new directions in how leadership and group work can be understood and practiced in social work and related disciplines. The directions are new in seven ways, by:

1 Repositioning social work with eco-justice values, responsibilities and goals
2 Reconceptualising the taken-for-granted hierarchical relationships of worker–client, student–lecturer, human–animal, human–nature, researcher–researched, activist–non-activist and expert–lay citizen to ones of equal intrinsic value and mutual partnerships
3 Enabling an understanding of leadership as a group activity in which all parties in the practice situation are leaders and thus members of the TCL team
4 Adopting the context- and power-sensitive SAP Analysis Method that is able to extend on social work knowledge and theories in complex conflict situations that are inclusive of and, at the same time, reach beyond interpersonal and organisational contexts
5 Seeking opportunities to use DGW in intragroup contexts with members of impacted low-power groups to name, affirm and explore solutions to their lived experiences of injustice
6 Proactively initiating and facilitating DGW among the low-power group and relevant high-power interest groups using the Love Ethic Model

7   Committing to supporting each other within the TCL team to develop shared leadership skills, group processes and ethical literacy.

The first new direction relates to the capacities of TCL and DGW between interest groups being directed towards eco-justice goals across all the social work fields and domains of practice (Chenoweth & McAuliffe, 2012). Secondly, there is a need for social workers and others engaged in justice work to reconceptualise their role to co-partnering and co-creating solutions with citizens, animals and the environment.

This makes possible the third new direction in which TCL is an inclusive, collectivist approach to practice that comprises a local eco-activist group among a globally dispersed group or network of eco-activists. TCL is instigated whenever activists' partner as equals with citizens, animals and ecosystems to address matters of lovelessness (hooks, 2000), violence and injustice (Young, 1990) and environmental degradation (White, 2017). It includes a diverse cross section of people, not defined by direct relationship, locality, profession or social status but by their eco-activism.

The fourth new direction involves the adoption of the SAP Analysis Method (Bice, Brueckner & Pforr, 2017) to extend social work knowledge to understand how to engage with multiple interest groups and dominant social structures. The SAP Analysis Method shows how dominant interest groups can be engaged if they perceive a risk to their interests in situations of ecological conflict. The types of risks at play indicate to eco-activists the related type of licence or authority – social, actuarial (legal) or political – that needs activating to challenge the unfair use of power by dominant interests, typically government and industry.

The fifth new direction is where the TCL approach can enable dialogue in intragroup situations by involving individuals who share similar life experiences (Nagda, 2017). Impacted, low-power interest groups need to be empowered to sustain themselves for the long haul effort of justice work. The social justice group work literature contains valuable examples of group work utilising empowering and participatory democratic processes for social justice goals (Singh & Salazaar, 2011). It is the case though that low-power groups experiencing harm or injustice need access to high-power interest groups if the structural disadvantage they experience is to be addressed.

The fifth new direction links to the sixth new direction because the TCL approach places the issue of unequal power and conflict at the centre of group work practice. This involves fostering a group dialogue process between interest groups in situations of eco-injustice. The requirement of engaging high-power interest groups is crucial in justice work. It may include parallel, separate group-based processes with government and business entities to prepare them for dialogue with low-power groups impacted by their policies and decisions. This requirement of DGW to adopt an upwards-to-power-elites focus tends to be absent in group work and community development literature. That is, the Love Ethic Model requires substantial engagement with high-power interest groups at some stage in the low-power group's process for it to shift the responsibility for addressing the justice concern to the parties who cause it. Thus, TCL teams look for opportunities to engage and facilitate relevant members of high- and low-power interest groups in dialogue to address the justice concern.

The seventh new direction is that members of the TCL team dedicate to their own group processes and dynamics to foster congruence and ethical integrity between what they ask of others and how they act themselves. The TCL team members thereby develop eco-values literacy and practice in their own group through the sharing of ideas, skills and power for eco-justice work. Kelly and Westoby's "person-centred" (2018, p. 13) approach to participatory development practice has much to offer practitioners including many useful ideas in their chapter on the *implicate method*, which refers to being aware of one's own story and undertaking self-development work.

Clarion call to social work

The book is a clarion call to social work and other disciplines with a declared commitment to justice to join the social, animal rights and environmental movements of our times. Green (2018), echoing Poelina (in this volume), writes that Aboriginal culture is based on caring for each other and the land which is part of a holistic, collectivist world view that has sustained one of the oldest, continuing human societies in the world. Woodley, a Yindjibarndi elder, explains that is it is no longer only a responsibility of First Nation People to uphold this guardianship role (personal communication, 15 February 2019). The eco-justice framing of the book acknowledges and engages in collaboration with this wisdom and heritage.

Social work is a diverse and multifaceted profession which is strongly shaped by the history, discourses and social, economic and political systems of the host society in which it operates. As such social work is implicated in the "extralocal relations of ruling" of society (Smith, 1990, p. 17) due to its central role in the provision of state sponsored human services. This is discussed in the social work literature as a practice tension between the social change, social care and social control aspects of the social work role across all of the domains of practice: individual and family work, group and community work, policy, education, research and organisational leadership and management (Chenoweth & McAuliffe, 2012). For example, social work has acknowledged its part in creating the Stolen Generations in Australia, where Aboriginal children were removed and placed in homes away from their families (Australian Human Rights Commission (AHRC), 1997). This racist and colonialist practice constituted an attempt at genocide of First Nation People in Australia (AHRC, 1997). The Australian Association of Social Workers (2017) has subsequently apologised to First Nation People for the harm caused by the profession.

The book makes a contribution at the intersection of wicked problems, state-sponsored social work and the ethical integrity of social work as a profession. It takes as its starting position that social workers are already located in complex power relationships, and although implicated in maintaining the status quo, their practice context is also where the opportunities for justice work exist. The TCL ideas and the DGW between interest groups approaches are adaptable in any context where social workers may be working. For example, in the policy domain of practice, Palmer (2018) recommends that policy makers adopt a sustainable-participatory social policy approach, privileging the voices of those most impacted by policy decisions while recognising the indivisible bond between social justice and ecological care (Beresford, 2016; Pedersen, 1998). Palmer describes elements of the campaign to stop the WA state government's threatened closure of 150 remote Aboriginal communities where the campaign leaders illustrated all the components of TCL, including a commitment to nonviolence through a code of conduct for protesters (sosblakaustralia, 2015). She explains that examples abound of this kind of leadership and the possibilities for sustainable-participatory social policy, even though it is not in the interests of high-power groups and their loyalists to make these readily known or celebrated (Palmer, 2018).

In the social work research domain, as another example, Godden's (2018) research with East Timorese community members explicitly engages participants in naming their reality and understanding of love to draw out the relevance of love in their lives and communities. Godden (2016) included creative arts and narrative processes in her community-level research as part of meeting with people across cultural and language differences. The final example is provided by Seiver, a community artist, who has been involved with Yarloop since the research undertaken by ECU (2002–2004). Separate to the university research and her more recent art projects in the community after the major bush fire of 2016 (see Chapter 4), Seiver welded a metal frame in the shape of a leaf (as a traditional symbol of renewal and the logo of the local shire council) and invited people to write their hopes and visions for the future of Yarloop on strips of coloured cloth, and to then make the cloth into string and weave this onto the leaf shape. The leaf was installed in the town library (in the grounds of the Yarloop Primary School), when Seiver and Palmer (see Chapter 3) released a report into a research project about leadership and its findings.

Alongside their professional roles, social workers can make important contributions as citizens by joining or initiating public campaigns for eco-justice. The social workers who contribute to this volume have walked this parallel path which was afforded by the privilege of academic positions that support community engagement. Palmer and Ross have had a long-term connection with Yarloop where they have responded to requests and invitations to support the community. This is an example of the rich interplay between professional and civic responsibilities. Here the authors wish to acknowledge the crucial role played by lawyers who volunteer their time to justice causes such as the Yindjibarndi Peoples' struggle for fair compensation from a mining company (see Chapter 5) and the protection of a public ecosystem at Point Peron (see

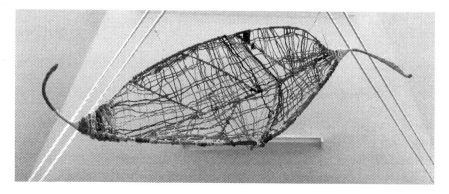

Figure 12.1 The leaf art installation, Yarloop
Source: Photograph: H. Seiver

Chapter 7). All the eco-activist stories in fact involved citizens who had other jobs but who stepped forward to be counted on an issue that mattered to them.

Social work has a commitment to social justice and human well-being (International Federation of Social Workers, 2018) which can be extended to embrace a more developed ethical capacity to include justice for animals (Hanrahan, 2011) and the environment as equally valued beings (Poelina, 2019; Boetto, 2019). There is a groundswell movement in social work towards an ecological understanding of social issues (Gray, Coates & Hetherington, 2013; Boetto, 2019), and the book has shown how the idea of eco-social work is an ethical and feasible way forward for the profession. Eaglehawk (in this volume, Chapter 8) suggests the term *anthropocentric harm* to refer to the injustice caused by the human-centric bias of dominant groups against low-power social groups, nonhuman species and the environment. Social workers understand the importance of self-reflective practice (Fook, 2016) and can include in their ongoing self-education the work of undoing their human privilege alongside, if appropriate, their other linked obligations of: undoing their white privilege that causes racial harm; class privilege that causes harm to people with low incomes (Pease, 2010): and professional privilege that causes harm to citizens receiving human services.

Conclusion

The book offers inspiration and hope to social workers and other justice workers with stories from eco-activists in WA. The predominant focus on WA is due to the pro-development government which has created a political context that is resistive to challenges to state authority and any threats to businesses' pursuit of profits. The WA politico-economic context is mirrored in Western capitalist countries around the world and is indicated by what Moore calls "the rise of cheap Nature" (2016, p. 78). Moore explains that "for capitalism, Nature is 'cheap' in a double sense: to make Nature's elements 'cheap' in price; and also to cheapen, to degrade or to render inferior in an ethico-political sense, the better to make Nature cheap in price" (2016, pp. 2–3). The stories are offered in support of the international network of eco-activists seeking to revalue nature and all sentient beings and to enable transformational change.

The clarion call to social work asks social workers to explicitly link love, eco-justice and nonviolence in their current practice and as well it asks social workers to activate their public practice as citizens. The inclusion of love as a defining value and practice in social work will give recognition to the heart of the profession that has always been part of social work but a largely denied and underappreciated part of its ethical premise. The Love Ethic Model can support and extend social workers' practice in any context and can open the doors to a new field of practice in situations of ecological conflict. Social workers can be part of the worldwide movement of eco-activism that is heralding in the new world order which Albret (2016) calls the "Symbiocene" to highlight the interconnectedness and intrinsic value of all life. This new order is a return to the deep wisdom of Planet Earth as reflected in Australia's First Nation Peoples' First Law, the ancient laws of nature where the law is in the land and not in humans (Poelina, this volume).

References

Albret, G. (2016). *Exiting the Anthropocene and entering the Symbiocene*. Retrieved from www.humansandnature.org/exiting-the-anthropocene-and-entering-the-symbiocene

Australian Association of Social Workers. (2017). *Ninth anniversary of the apology to the Stolen Generations*. Retrieved from www.aasw.asn.au/aasw-news/9th-anniversary-of-the-apology-to-the-stolen-generations

Australian Human Rights Commission. (1997). *Bringing them home report*. Retrieved from www.humanrights.gov.au/our-work/bringing-them-home-report-1997

Beresford, P. (2016). *All our welfare: Towards participatory social policy*. Bristol, UK; Chicago, USA: Policy Press.

Bice, S., Brueckner, M. & Pforr, C. (2017). Putting social license to operate on the map: A social, actuarial and political risk and licensing model (SAP Model). *Resources Policy*, 53, 46–55.

Boetto, H. (2019). Advancing transformative eco-social change: Shifting from modernist to holistic foundations. *Australian Social Work*, 72(2), 139–152.

Buber, M. (1970). *I and Thou* (W. Kaufmann, trans.). New York, USA: Simon & Schuster.

Chenoweth, L. & McAuliffe, D. (2012). *The road to social work and human service practice: An introductory text* (3rd ed.). South Melbourne, Australia: Cengage.

Fook, J. (2016). *Social work: A critical approach* (3rd ed.). Los Angeles, USA: Sage Publications.

Freire, P. (1970). *Pedagogy of the oppressed*. London, UK: Penguin.

Godden, N. (2016). A co-operative inquiry about love using narrative, performative and visual methods. *Qualitative Research*, 17(1), 3–19.

Godden, N. (2018). Love in community work in rural Timor-Leste: A co-operative inquiry for a participatory framework of practice. *Community Development Journal, 53*(1), 78–98. doi:10.1093/cdj/bsw022

Gray, M., Coates, J. & Hetherington, T. (Eds.). (2013). *Environmental social work*. London, UK & New York, USA: Routledge.

Green, S. (2018). Aboriginal People and caring within a colonised society. In B. Pease, A. Vreugdenhil and S. Stanford (Eds.), *Critical ethics of care in social work: Transforming the politics and practices of caring* (pp. 139–147). New York, USA: Routledge.

hooks, b. (1994). *Education as the practice of freedom*. New York, USA: Taylor & Francis.

hooks, b. (2000). *All about love*. New York, USA: New Visions.

Kelly, A. & Westoby, P. (2018). *Participatory development practice: Using traditional and contemporary frameworks*. Rugby, UK: Practical Action Publishing.

Hanrahan, C. (2011). Challenging anthropocentrism in social work through ethics and spirituality. *Journal of Religion & Spirituality in Social Work, 30*(3), 272–293.

International Federation of Social Workers (IFSW). (2018). *Global social work statement of ethical principles*. Retrieved from www.ifsw.org/global-social-work-statement-of-ethical-principles/

Moore, J. (2016). The rise of cheap nature. In J. Moore (Ed.). *Anthropocene or Capitalocene? Nature, history, and the crisis of capitalism* (pp. 78–116). Oakland, USA: PM Press.

Nagda, B. (2017). Intergroup dialogue: Engaging difference for social connectedness and social change. In C. Garvin, L. Gutierrez & M. Galinsky (Eds.), *Handbook of social work with groups* (2nd ed., pp. 384–416). New York, USA: The Guilford Press.

Palmer, M. (2018). Sustainable-participatory social policy. In P. Beresford & S. Carr (Eds.), *Social policy first hand: An international introduction to participatory social welfare* (pp. 262–276). Bristol, UK: Policy Press.

Pease, B. (2010). *Undoing privilege: Unearned advantage in a divided world*. New York, USA: Zed Books.

Pedersen, K. (1998). Environmental ethics in interreligious perspective: Comparative religious ethics and interreligious dialogue. In S. Twiss & B. Grelle (Eds.), *Explorations in global ethics* (pp. 253–290). Boulder, USA: Westview Press.

Poelina, A. (2019). *Economies of nature*. Retrieved from https://greataustralianstory.com.au/story/economies-nature

Roy, A. (2001). *War is peace*. Retrieved from www.wussu.com/current/roy.htm

Singh, A. & Salazaar, C. (2011). *Social justice in group work: Practical interventions for change*. London, UK & New York, USA: Routledge.

Smith, D. (1990). *The conceptual practices of power: A feminist sociology of knowledge*. Boston, USA: Northeastern University Press.

sosblakaustralia. (2015). *Information pack: 10 points to a cultural code of conduct*. Retrieved from www.sosblakaustralia.com/media

West, C. (2011). *Cornel West: Justice is what love looks like in public*. Retrieved from www.youtube.com/watch?v=nGqP7S_WO6o.

White, R. (2017). Corruption and the securitisation of nature. *International Journal for Crime, Justice and Social Democracy, 6*(4), 55–70.

Young, I. (1990). *Justice and the politics of difference*. Princeton, USA: Princeton University Press.

Resources for practice

Preamble

Transformational social change from the local to the global takes place in relationships, groups and communities including families, interest groups, neighbourhoods, public spaces and as well in and between social structures such as human service organisations, businesses and governments. The purpose of "Resources for practice" is to provide sources and links for material which will help the reader develop and sustain loving, just and nonviolent relationships and actions.

Social work educators have long framed their discipline as one which prepares workers for practice by addressing the relevant knowledge, values and skills most conducive to good practice outcomes. Kelly and Sewell (1988) developed a model for community practice based on the idea of head, heart and hand. Boetto (2018) refers to this trilectic as the thinking (epistemological), feeling (ontological) and doing (methodological) elements of practice. Kelly and Westoby (2018) offer a framework for understanding the intersecting contexts and tasks of practice that includes the implicate method (awareness of self and own story), micro practice method (fostering direct relationships), messo method (capacity building in group contexts), macro method (crafting organisational dimensions) and meta method (engaging the local-global nexus) for participatory development work. Activists will have their own preferences for how they construct their practice framework and what resources may be relevant for them. The "Resources for practice" section assumes an eco-justice ethical orientation to how activism is approached. This will ensure the resources are utilised in ways that serve the public interest because activists will maintain ethical integrity by aligning their heads, hearts and hands in complex situations of ecological conflict.

The book presents the values (or feeling) elements as the heart dimension of practice, where the activism has arisen due to unwelcome circumstances. People become sick at heart when their values of justice and love for one another, animals and the natural realm are trampled on or violated. The activist stories in Part 1 of the book drew on a broad range of knowledge (or thinking) elements to explain what people have done to protect the natural realm (including humans) from intrusion and violation and why they have done this. However, powerful vested interest groups hold competing values and knowledge claims which undermine the seriousness of the threats human face as a species and the threats humans pose to other species and ecosystems. Therefore, it is the responsibility of each person as a world citizen to develop his or her own ethical sensibility by acquiring the leadership skills and acting with others to bring the elements of his or her respective experience of the head, heart, hand trilectic together.

This coherence among the head, heart and hand is how ethical integrity can be maintained during the struggles to move beyond the Anthropocene era of human domination to create a Symbiocene legacy of mutuality and sustainability (Albrecht, 2016). Addams, one of the founders of social work, wrote that the moral task is one of committing to a "cosmic patriotism" where "peace is no longer an abstract dogma but . . . a rising tide of moral enthusiasm slowly engulfing all pride of conquest and making war impossible" (1907, p. 238).

The resources can contribute to interpersonal, inter-interest group and planetary peace and well-being. The contents are indicative of useful guidelines and actions rather than being exhaustive or the most salient for different regions, cultural groups and types of ecological conflicts and justice concerns. The heading at the start of each section indicates the theme for that set of resources.

Resources for nonviolent social change

At the macro level of planning a large-scale campaign, Moyer (1987), a founding member of Movement for a New Society, developed the Movement Action Plan for social change activists based on eight stages:

1. Existence of a critical social problem
2. Proven failure of official institutions
3. Ripening conditions
4. Take-off
5. Perception of failure
6. Majority public opinion
7. Success
8. Continuation.

Knowledge of these stages can assist activists to anticipate and plan the appropriate tactics and strategies for the specific context at hand:

Moyer, B. (1987). *Movement action plan*. Retrieved from www.historyisaweapon.com/defcon1/moyermap.html

In 2001 Moyer co-authored the book *Doing democracy*, which expanded on this movement action plan and identifies nonviolent training for activists:

Moyer, B., McAllister, J., Finley, M. & Soifer, S. (2001). *Doing democracy: The MAP model for organising social movements*. Canada: New Society Publishers.

This next resource shows how to use the internet to undertake activism, described as digital campaigning:

The Change Agency. (2019). *Online activism: Insights to guide social movement electronic communication*. Retrieved from www.thechangeagency.org/campaigners-toolkit/training-resources/social-action-skills/

(Scroll down the page, join up – it's free – then download the file with the name listed here.)

A resource that has stood the test of time is *Resource manual for a living revolution*. The book is a manual of specific skills in relation to visioning, nonviolent direct action, leadership and decision-making in groups:

Coover, V., Deacon, E., Essex, C. & Moore, C. (1981). *Resource manual for a living revolution: A handbook of skills & tools for social change activists*. Philadelphia, USA: New Society Publishers.

A contemporary resource for activist educators is the *People power manual: Campaign strategy*, which includes many key capacities and processes for nonviolent direct action, including the following:

1. Campaign strategy
2. Community organising
3. Civil resistance
4. Working with groups
5. Returning to strength: movement resilience in the face of repression
6. Educating the activist educator.

The resources are user friendly and have been developed by activists and educators. They can be purchased for a modest price. Other resources on this website are free:

Whelan, J. & McLeod, J. (2016). *People power manual: Campaign strategy*. Retrieved from www.thechangeagency.org/campaigners-toolkit/training-resources/people-power-manual/

The same authors wrote a second companion resource that covers topics related to community organising:

- Relational community organising
- Developing and supporting leaders
- Building strong teams
- Sharing stories – personal, public and campaign narratives.

The materials provided are user friendly and practical:

Whelan, J. & McLeod, J. (2016). *People power manual: Community organising*. Retrieved from www.thechangeagency.org/campaigners-toolkit/training-resources/people-power-manual/

There are numerous books providing nonviolent strategies for social justice; for example, Gandio and Nocella's edited collection covers topics such as pro-justice in the classroom, activist guidelines and peace as a political force:

Gandio, J. & Nocella, A. (2014). *Educating for action: Strategies to ignite social justice*. Gabriola Island, Canada: New Society Publishers.

The New Tactics in Human Rights website has some good practical tools for undertaking human rights work and is available in non-English language options. For example, go to the online tactical mapping tool, which can be used to identify and track power dynamics in key relationships:

New Tactics in Human Rights. (2019). *Tactical mapping tool*. Retrieved from https://tmt.newtactics.org/

Also go to their strategic effectiveness method in the Strategy Toolkit section, and listen to the video about a how to undertake human rights work:

New Tactics in Human Rights. (2019). *Strategy toolkit*. Retrieved from www.newtactics.org/toolkit/strategy-toolkit

---

Sharp's list of 198 methods of nonviolent action includes methods of protest and persuasion, economic non-co-operation (e.g., strikes and boycotts), political non-cooperation (e.g., civil disobedience in relation to unjust laws) sit-ins and protest theatre:

Albert Einstein Institute. (1973). *198 methods of nonviolent action*. Retrieved from www.aeinstein.org/nonviolentaction/198-methods-of-nonviolent-action/

His book expands on these tactics and strategies:

Sharp, G. (2005). *Waging nonviolent struggle: 20th century practice and 21st century potential*. Dexter, USA: Extending Horizons Books.

To varying degrees these actions can hold a resistance and challenge dominant groups in conflict situations but are more effective if part of a coordinated social movement or campaign if the conflict is part of a complexity of wicked problems.

Resources for education and activism for animal rights

Francione says veganism is the moral baseline of nonviolence and for a quick sense of his ideas of how the public can contribute to not harming animals, see the following:

The Radical Revolution. (2014). *Gary L Francione: How to get people to think about veganism*. Retrieved from https://youtu.be/OOixczB7qRg

---

This video eloquently puts the case for animals to have legal rights:

Bigould, L. (2014). It's time to re-evaluate our relationship with animals. *Ted-Talk*. Retrieved from https://youtu.be/Fr26scqsIwk

---

The Nonhuman Rights Project, which is part of an international nonhuman rights movement, has lobbied to gain legal rights for chimpanzees. For more details go to this blog:

Choplin, L. (2016). *Chimpanzese recognised as legal persons*. Retrieved from www.nonhumanrights.org/blog/cecilia-chimpanzee-legal-person/

A well-known animal rights group is People for the Ethical Treatment of Animals (PETA), with their website claiming "animals are not ours to experiment on, eat, wear, use for entertainment, or abuse in any other way". A current Bear Witness campaign is in support of vegan activists who are being targeted by state governments in Australia:

PETA. (2019). *PETA's take on new laws targeting vegan activists in Australia*. Retrieved from www.peta.org.au/news/vegan-activist-laws-australia/

This organisation offers online opportunities to join animal rights campaigns.

Voiceless is the website for The Animal Protection Institute that provides information about many animals' rights issues and articles such as animal sentience:

Voiceless (2019). *Animal sentience*. Retrieved from www.voiceless.org.au/hot-topics/animal-sentience

---

Resources for environmental protection and sustainability

The website Centre of Humans and Nature has the subtitle of "expanding our natural and civic imagination". This is an apt description for one of its contributors, Vandana Shiva whose internationally renowned book *Earth democracy* (2005) has been pivotal for understanding the interconnections among capitalism, lack of food and seed security, genetic food engineering and poverty of the mind of nation-states and multinational companies:

Centre of Humans and Nature. (2019). *Vandana Shiva*. Retrieved from www.humansandnature.org/vandana-shiva

Shiva, V. (2005). *Earth democracy: Justice, sustainability and peace.* Cambridge, MA, USA: South End Press.

The film about Shiva and her eco-activism contains a statement that "if you control food you control people and if you control seeds you control the world":

Becket Films. (n.d.). *The seeds of Vandana Shiva.* Retrieved from http://vandanashivamovie.com/

A resource for a regional approach to sustainable development in the Czech Republic shows how to develop and evaluate a sustainable development plan:

Hrebik, S., Trebicky, V. & Gremlica, T. (2006). *Manual for planning and evaluation of sustainable development at the regional level.* Retrieved from www.sd-network.eu/pdf/resources/SD_manual_CZ.pdf

---

The Australian government's *Working with Indigenous communities* is a resource for the mining industry on sustainable development. It includes ideas such as co-management of resources, and although it leaves unaddressed issues of inequality in negotiations over Indigenous land rights, it has useful material nonetheless:

Australian Government. (2016). *Working with indigenous communities.* Retrieved from https://industry.gov.au/resource/Documents/LPSDP/guideLPSD.pdf

---

This is a useful guide that covers planning, facilitating and enabling participation in grassroots sustainable development work in Kenya:

Lelo, F., Masika, A., Wasao, S., Gichere, S. & Shah, W. (2006). *A manual for trainers in participatory and sustainable development planning.* Retrieved from https://financiamentointernacional.files.wordpress.com/2013/12/manual-de-formac3a7c3a3o-de-formadores-em-gestc3a3o-de-projectos.pdf

---

Resources for fostering dialogue, hope and love

The bell hooks Institute gathers together the life and contributions of bell hooks, who's writing on love as the answer to oppression has been influential in social movements of the past and currently:

bell hooks Institute, Berea College. (2019). *bell hooks*. Retrieved from www.bellhooksinstitute.com/

The Dulwich Centre in Adelaide, Australia, is an education and resource sharing initiative based on narrative approaches. They produce the *International Journal of Narrative Therapy and Community Work*. See their "Friday afternoon videos" for practice inspiring work:

Dulwich Centre. (2019). *Friday afternoon videos*. Retrieved from https://dulwichcentre.com.au/category/friday-afternoons/?v=6cc98ba2045f

---

The Freire Institute provides information about Freire's legacy of transformational education to overcome oppression, resources for practitioners and fee-based online education modules on topics such as "Communities and conflict":

Freire Institute. (2019). *Paulo Freire*. Retrieved from https://freire.org/paulo-freire

---

The Albert Einstein Institution promotes freedom through nonviolent action and provides a range of resources including films and videos via their website: www.youtube.com/channel/UCZvhWKy2dYmv6Hh4nzBmRVA/playlists

In particular, see Sharp and the Institute's *How to start a revolution*:

Albert Einstein Institute. (2011). *How to start a revolution*. Retrieved from www.aeinstein.org/free-resources/video/

Joanna Macy's work based on deep ecology is inspirational and involves extensive publications that convey how to be in the world and how to make a difference without giving in to despair and inaction. See her book on active hope and resources on her website:

Macy, J. & Johnstone, C. (2012). *Active hope: How to face the mess we are in without going crazy*. Novato, USA: New World Books.

Joanna Macy. (2019). *Joanna Macy and her work*. Retrieved from www.joannamacy.net/main

---

The practice of dialogue often occurs in circumstances of complex conflicts in which the parties are fixed in their positions of how they want things to be resolved. The aim of nonviolent conflict resolution is to enable parties to identify with interests which may open up possibilities for co-created solutions.

For specific conflict response skills and processes, go to the Conflict Resolution Network website and note ideas such as fair fighting:

Conflict Resolution Network. (2015). *Resolve the conflict guide*. Retrieved from www.crnhq.org/

Barsky provides a good skills guide text that covers negotiation, mediation, advocacy, facilitation and restorative justice:

Barsky, A. (2017). *Conflict resolution for the helping professions* (2nd ed.). New York, USA: Thompson Cole.

The Global Conflict Sensitivity Community Hub provides resources pitched at national- and international-level development and humanitarian initiatives and show how to plan for and implement conflict impact assessments and peace-keeping strategies:

Gaigais, C. & Leonhardt, M. (n.d.). *Conflict sensitive approaches to development practice*. Retrieved from http://conflictsensitivity.org/wp-content/uploads/2015/05/Conflict-Sensitive_Approaches_to_Development.pdf

For specific group work skills and guidelines go to The Change Agency website which has a campaigner's toolkit and within that there are resources for working in groups, for example, decision-making and group process, tension within a group, alternative dispute resolution and meeting facilitation:

The Change Agency. (2019). *Campaigner's toolkit*. Retrieved from www.thechangeagency.org/campaigners-toolkit/training-resources/working-in-groups/

The edited book by Plant is interesting as an example of women's visioning, analysis and storying as eco-feminists and shows the ways woman and nature are treated as "the other":

Plant, J. (1989). *Healing the wounds: The promise of ecofeminism*. Philadelphia, USA: New Society Publishers.

Boyle writes about the catastrophic impact of dominant political and economic systems to establish the urgent need for new visions "to resist, revolt, rewild":

Boyle, M. (2015). *Drinking Molotov cocktails with Gandhi*. Gabriola Island, Canada: New Society Publishers.

Community arts and community care

This website shows how to undertake community development art-based projects:

Useful Community Development. (2019). *Asset-based community development focuses on the strengths*. Retrieved from www.useful-community-development.org/asset-based-community-development.html

---

This resource is a step-by-step guide to good community arts practice and includes some case studies:

Arts Victoria. (2014). *Making art with communities: A work guide*. Retrieved from https://creative.vic.gov.au/__data/assets/pdf_file/0005/57065/Community_Partnerships_Workguide_lores_2014edit.pdf

---

The WA Community Arts Network's "vision is towards a just, diverse and resilient society". Its website has a wealth of information regarding community development and the use of art in community visioning towards a creative future:

Community Arts Network. (2019). *Dream, Plan, Do: A comprehensive "how to" community arts publication and film resource*. Retrieved from www.canwa.com.au/

Their projects include inspirational, culture-building initiatives such as *Because of her, we can*, which honours First Nation women using portrait photography and storytelling:

Community Arts Network. (2019). *Because of her, we can*. Retrieved from www.canwa.com.au/project/because-of-her-we-can/

References

Addams, J. (1907). *Newer ideals of peace*. London, UK: Macmillan.
Albrecht, G. (2016). Exiting the Anthropocene and entering the Symbiocene. *Minding Nature, 9*(2), 12–16.
Boetto, H. (2018). Transformative eco-social work: Incorporating being, thinking and doing in practice. In M. Pawar, W. Bowles & K. Bell (Eds.), *Social work: Innovations and insights* (pp. 79–93). North Melbourne, Australia: Australian Scholarly Publishing.
Kelly, A. & Sewell, S. (1988). *With head, heart and hand*. Brisbane, Australia: Boolarong Press.
Kelly, A. & Westoby, P. (2018). *Participatory development practice*. Rugby, UK: Practical Action Publishing.

Index

Note: Numbers in italic indicate figures on the corresponding page.

Aboriginal People: Australia, as the first people of 49, 61; citizenship rights 17, 64, 66, 71, 83–84; forced relocation 62–63, 167; holistic care culture 166; on the value of life in all living beings 7, 17, 158
Adani Carmichael mine 111; *see* coal mining
Alcoa World Alumina (Alcoa): buffer zones, creating 27, 28, 29, 33, 41; social and economic impact created by 29, 30, 36, 40; Wagerup land management policy 37, 47
All about love (hooks) 6, 7, 21, 135, 165
Alston, M. 7, 42, 45, 47
animal exporting: abuse and cruelty, revealing 105; activism, power of social media on 106; animal rights activism 8, 175; argument for 104
animal rights 8, 102, 106, 175
animal rights groups: Our Planet. Theirs Too *23*; Royal Society for the Prevention of Cruelty to Animals 110; World Animal Protection *25, 110*

Bailey, S. 3, 19
Beeliar Wetlands: community activism and protection of 75–76, *77*, 79–80, 86; Indigenous bushland area 74, 83, 84
Bennett, B. 4, 19, 135, 143
Bennetts, S. 83, 86
Bessarab, D. 4, 19, 135, 143
Besthorn, F. 3, 7, 19
Bice, S. 11, 19, 26, 129, 156, 165
Boetto, H. 3, 8, 135, 148, 168, 171
Brady, D. 17
Brueckner, M. i, xiii, 3, 8, 10, 11, 14, 18, 19, 26–28, 31–33, 40, 56, 112, 125, 126

buffer zone property purchases 27–29, 33, 37, 41
Butler, P. 31–32, 37

Charlton, A. 8, 100, 175
Chenoweth, E. 6, 20
Chenoweth, L. 165–166
Cleary, P. 7, 20, 61, 62, 67, 72
climate change 7–8, 10, 112–113
coal mining: Adani Carmichael in Queensland 10, 111; economic ramifications on job creation 104; ecosystems as threatened by 18; environmental impacts of 111
Coates, J. 4, 21, 141
community activism: accountability and social responsibility, linked to 26–27; big business relationships and 126; nonviolent and social aspects of 6, 18, 74, 81, 106, 129; person-in-environment concept and 3, 57; Point Peron, campaign against 17, 89; short term goals, clear focus on 31; social capital, building through 42; social licence to operate concept and 9
Community Alliance for Positive Solutions (CAPS): as an accountability activist group 26, 27, 30–31, 151; fact-gathering advocates, skill level of 33–34; fire, members initiating inquiry regarding 36, 40
community art and cultural mapping 51, 53–54
Conde, M. 5, 20, 30, 31, 89, 98
Corporate Social Responsibility (CSR) 26; *see* social responsibility

Index

developmentalism 1, 3, 13, 14, 19, 27, 125, 126, 128
developmentalism as a government priority 13–15, 126
dialogue 4, 6, 40, 50–53, 57, 128, 135–139, 143, 145–149, 153–157, 164–166, 176–177
dialogical group work (DGW) i, 126, 130, 132, 133, 136, 146, 153
Dominelli, L. 3, 20, 143, 160

Eaglehawk, W. 18
eco-activism: conflict resolution, 8-step schema process for 139, 152; ecological injustice 126, 129; governmental influence against 15; justice for community 3, 18, 33, 129, *130*, 134, 139, 152; legal, social and political license relationship 132, 159; love ethic, combining with public service 1, 6–7, 125, 131, *133*, 136, 163; political voice of 9, 10, 132; public interest, serving 3, 9; resources for 173; social licence, difficulty in asserting 118; social media and 89
eco-justice: i, 4, 16, 129, 143, 145, 148, 155, 163–167, 169, 171; animal rights and 101, 107, *130*; leadership strategy on conflict resolution 1, 3, 5, 8; responsibilities of 131–133 135–136
eco-social work: compassion and dialogue in 6; disaster research and 45; human, nonhuman animals and country, inseparability of 4
eco-values, i, 4, 5, 129, *130*, 132–133, 135, 145, 163, 166; responsibilities of 5, 129, 131
economic development and decolonization x, 8, 14
economic growth, governmental focus of 11, 13, 114
Edith Cowan University (ECU) 27, 40, 50
environmental justice, linking with rights of nature 7–8, 149; *see also* eco-justice
ethic of love xiii, 51, 100, 101, 107

First Nation People ix, xii, 1, 4, 6; attempts to abolish and exploit 66–67, 68, 74, 127, 128, 135, 157; *see also* Aboriginal People
Fook, J. 43–45, 47, 133, 135, 168
Fortescue Metals Group (FMG): economic inequality, fight of indigenous peoples against 61, 66–67, 69–70; iron ore mining and 17, 67; splinter group support 68
Francione, G. 8, 21, 100, 101, 108, 175
Freire Institute 177
Freire, P. 6, 18, 21, 133, 139, 147, 157, 164

Gallagher, B. 103, 108
Gilbert, S. 4, 19, 135, 143
Global Social Work Statement of Ethical Principles (IFSW) 7, 22, 170
Godden, N. 7, 21, 39, 45, 47, 167, 169
Gray, M. 3, 21, 168
Green, S. 4, 7, 21, 166, 170
Greenslade, L. 3, 21
Group work 145–147, 152, 164–165, 178; *see* dialogical group work

Habibis, D. 4, 25
Haines, F. 9, 11, 21
Hands of Point Peron (HOPP) 90–93
Hanrahan, C. 3, 21, 101, 168
Hargraeaves, D. 42, 47
Harrison, A. 30, 38
Hazeleger, T. 42, 47
heart values and principles 148
Hollo, T. 7, 18, 21
hooks, b. 6, 7, 21, 107, 109, 135, 164, 165, 170
human rights 66, 114, 116

Indigenous Land Use Agreement (ILUA) 66
Indigenous people *see* Aboriginal People
International Federation of Social Workers 7, 22, 170

Jaysawal, N. 6, 22
Jecks, D. xv, 17–18, 89
Jones, P. 3, 22
Juluwarlu Group Aboriginal Corporation (JGAC) 71

Kellow, A. 13, 15, 22, 31, 111

Layman, L. 13, 14, 22
leadership *see* transformational change leadership
legal licence to operate: environmental protection conflicts 10–11, 16, 105, 158; as protection for the public and environment 9, 17
love i, x, xi, xii, 1, 4–8, 16, 37, 63, 69, 100–101, *130*, 132, 135–136, 149, 155, 159, 163–164, 167, 169, 171, 176

love ethic i, 3, 6, 7, 135
love ethic model i, xii, 4, 6, 16, 18, 125, 126, 128, 129, *130*
love ethic practice method 129, *130*, 132, *133*

Mardoowarra (Indigenous river) viii, xi
McAuliffe, D. 134, 141
Meihls, D. 146, 161
Mills, C. 4, 23, 107, 109, 125, 137, 141
mining operations: community impact of 7, 16, 27–28, 33, 65, 68, 116; environmental impacts, slowing due to 113; herders, complaining against 114
Moffat, K. 9, 23, 102, 109, 146
Molyneux, R. 3, 23
Mongolia, GDP of 114
Morrison, J. 9, 10, 12, 23
Murdoch University 27

Niemeyer, S. 13, 15, 31, 111
Nixon, R. 26, 34, 38
nonviolence i, 5, 6, 8, 81, 107, *130*, 132, 135–136, 149, 155, 159, 163–164, 167, 169, 175
nonviolent direction action (NVDA), protest conducted without physical violence 77, 79, 81, 82, 83, 86, 126, 132, 134, 136, 139, 143, 145, 147, 148, 153, 156, 158, 163
Noongar, Indigenous Peoples of Western Australia 49, 74, 83, 90
Norton, C. 3, 23
Nussbaum, M. 6, 23

O'Toole, J. 89, 98
Our Planet. Theirs Too (animal rights group) 23
Oyu Tolgoi copper mine 18, 114

Palmer, M. i, 3, 16, 18, 39, 44, 68, 125, 126, 127, 128, 134, 143, 163, 167
Payne, M. 9, 24, 143, 161
Pedagogy of the Heart (Freire) 146, 147, 157
Pedagogy of the Oppressed (Freire) 18, 21, 133, 139, 147, 164
Pedersen, A. 8, 24, 31, 38
Pedersen, K. 167, 170
Peeters, J. 3, 24
Pforr, C. 10, 11, 14, 19, 126, 129, 156, 165
Phillimore, J. 13, 14
Point Peron: community objections to development of 17–18, 89; HOPP campaign 90–93; strategic network for success 94
Poelina, A. xii, 4, 7, 24, 135, 158, 166, 168
political licence 10
Phillimore, J. 13, 14, 24
O'Toole, J. 89, 98
PT Kelian Equatorial Mining (KEM) 116
Puccio, V. 16, 27, 35, 36, 40

Registered Native Title Body Corporate (RNTBC) 69
responsibilities 4, 5, 6, 62, 81, 129, *130*, 131–132, 136, 145, 164, 167
Rio Tinto: ex-Kelian gold mine, Indonesia 115; Oyu Tolgoi mine, Mongolia 113; social licence to operate, protests against 116–117
Roe 8 Highway controversy 15, 74
Ross, D. i, xiii, 3, 7, 8, 16, 18, 26, 27, 28, 29, 31, 32, 33, 40, 51, 56, 101, 125, 126, 128, 138, 143, 152, 157, 163, 183
Royal Society for the Prevention of Cruelty to Animals (RSPCA) 102, 104, 110

Seiver, H. xv, 16, 41–43, 49, 167
Sharp, C. 40, 48, 157
Sharp, G. 6, 24, 77, 174
Sinclair, L. 18, 122
slow violence of mining operations 16, 26, 34
Social Actuarial Political Model (SAP) 11, *12*, 18, 129, *130*, 131, 132, 135, 143, 156, 164, 165; *see also* legal licence; political licence; social licence
social change: self-reflection and, 106; social media, power of, 107; species justice, fight for, 100; as transformational, 144, 171
social justice: defining, 7; environment and, 8; love ethic and, 51, 101, 145, 147; nonviolent mission of, 3–4, 159; as the voice of the people and the land, 167
social licence: approval and loss of, 9, 16, 26, 102, 105–107, 116–118; employment opportunities as generating support, 112; Indonesian New Order regime, as ineffective against, 116
social responsibility xiii, 7–8, 26–27, 125, 149, 153, 161, 163; *see* responsibilities
social work as a love ethic model: components of 129, *130*; nonviolent actions as promoting social justice 125, 135, 139, 163; power as authority 128,

166, 169; practice, method of 132, *133* 143, 147
social work: environment reconstruction 45; environmental change, leadership strategy for 3, *5*, 9, 39, 126; love ethic 6, 16, 134, 143, 169; whiteness theory 4
Sonn, C. 51, 52, 147
species justice: in equality and legal rights theory 102, 103; First People, holistic perspective of 7–8; live animal export and 104–105; veganism, nonviolence and 101, 107; voice for the voiceless 100, 106
Stephan, M. 6, 20
sustainability: environmental stewardship and 4, *5*, 18, 145; social responsibility and 7, 45

Taylor, S. 4, 25
Tischler, A. 3, 24
traditional ownership 15, 61, 66, 90; *see also* Aboriginal People
Transformational Change Leadership (TCL): eco-activism and *130*, 132, *133*, 143; leadership and social work, new direction of 164–166; love ethic model 145–146, 148, 153

Under Corporate Skies (Brueckner) 3, 8, 10, 14, 18, 19, 27, 31
United Nations (U. N.) 6, 25, 113, 122
Universal Declaration of Human Rights 6, 25

Walter, M. 4, 25
Walters, R. 4, 9, 25

West, C. 6, 25, 163
Western Australia, government of *viii*, 11, 13, 14
Wheeler, C. 4, 25
White, R. 7, 8, 25, 68, 102, 107, 125, 143, 158, 165, 170
Wirlumurra Yindjibarndi Aboriginal Corporation (WMYAC) 68, 69
Woodley, M. xv, 4, 17, 61, 135, 166
World Animal Protection (WAP) 104; *see also* animal rights groups

Yarloop: activism of residents 27–30, 33; art, hope and healing in 167, *168*; brush fires, community involvement after 36, 57–59; community art, on the role of 50–51; devastation of fire, residents recalling 35–36; mining operations, slow violence from 16, 26; photographs, cultural and community development through 54–56, 57; in Shire of Harvey 49, 60; vision for future 52–53; Western Australia, as a rural community in 49, 54
Yellow Bird, M. 4, 25
Yindjibarndi Aboriginal Corporation (YAC) 68
Yindjibarndi Ngurra Aboriginal Corporation (YNAC) 66
Yindjibarndi People: Australia, as Indigenous to 17; sovereign land battles 61, 63, 158, 167; *see also* Aboriginal People

Zhang, A. 9, 23, 102, 109

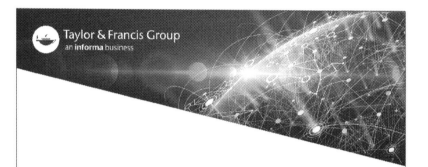

Printed in the United States
by Baker & Taylor Publisher Services